S0-EKC-928

MERCEDES MCCAMBRIDGE

ALSO BY RON LACKMAN

*Women of the Western Frontier in
Fact, Fiction and Film*
(McFarland, 1997)

MERCEDES McCAMBRIDGE

A Biography and Career Record

Ron Lackmann

McFarland & Company, Inc., Publishers
Jefferson, North Carolina, and London

LIBRARY OF CONGRESS ONLINE CATALOG DATA

Lackmann, Ronald W.
Mercedes McCambridge : a biography
and career record / Ron Lackmann.
p.   cm.
Includes bibliographical references and index.

ISBN 0-7864-1979-2 (softcover : 50# alkaline paper)

1. McCambridge, Mercedes [1916–2004].
2. Actors—United States—Biography.
I. Title.
PN2287.M12L34   2005   792.02'8'092 — B22   2004024780

British Library cataloguing data are available

©2005 Ron Lackmann. All rights reserved

*No part of this book may be reproduced or transmitted in any form
or by any means, electronic or mechanical, including photocopying
or recording, or by any information storage and retrieval system,
without permission in writing from the publisher.*

On the cover: background ©2005 Photospin;
photographs of Mercedes McCambridge courtesy Photofest

Manufactured in the United States of America

*McFarland & Company, Inc., Publishers
Box 611, Jefferson, North Carolina 28640
www.mcfarlandpub.com*

Contents

"All the world's a stage and all the men and women merely players. They have their exits and their entrances and each man in his time plays many parts."

William Shakespeare,
As You Like It, Act II, Scene 7

Preface

This biography of the talented Academy Award–winning actress Mercedes McCambridge, major star of radio, television, film, and the stage, covers the life and career of a woman whom no less an authority than Orson Welles once called "the world's greatest living radio actress." Born in 1916, Mercedes McCambridge was active in all four entertainment mediums between 1936 and 1991. Her personal life and her career not only provides wonderful insights into the period of show business history when radio was America's favorite home entertainment medium, but also of the time when the big Hollywood studio system of producing films was beginning to lose audiences to the new darling of the entertainment industry, television, and of the years when it began to dominate show business.

As a long-time admirer of Mercedes McCambridge's work, I became increasingly convinced that she would be an excellent subject for a biography, because her life spanned a fifty-five year period of show business history. I was able to draw from over one hundred reference sources, including books, periodicals and photographs from my own personal collection, as well as material I could obtain from public libraries and the Internet. I also personally interviewed many people who knew and worked with Miss McCambridge over the years. These interviews were primarily conducted over a twenty-five year period, while I was attending annual Friends of Old Time Radio Conventions. The actors and directors I interviewed for this project, either in person, on the telephone or by mail, included producer-directors Sam Levene, Carlton E. Morse, Norman Corwin, William N. Robson and William Spier, and performers Miriam Wolfe, Robert Dryden, Rosemary Rice, Ralph Bell, Grace Matthews, Court Benson, Raymond Edward Johnson, Ian Martin, Elspeth Eric, Gertrude Warner, Alice Rineheart, Les Tremayne, Karl Weber, Blair Walister, Rosa Rio, Earl George, Bret Morrison, Fran Carlon, Parley Baer, Bob Hastings, Larry Robinson, Frank Nelson, Hans Conried, Howard Duff, Burgess Meredith, Arthur Anderson, Bob Guilbert, Eileen Farrell, Arlene Francis, Teri Keane, Anne Burr, George Ansbro, Vivian Smollen, Laurette Fillbrandt, Betty Winkler, Florence Freeman, Mary Jane Higby, Ezra Stone, Betty Lou Gerson, Fletcher Markle, Arch Oboler, Himan

Brown, Peg Lynch, Win Elliot, Joe DeSantis, Jan Miner, Peter Roberts, Jackson Beck, Lon Clark, Charlotte Manson, Sybil Trent, Alan Reed, Joseph Kearns, Elliott Reid, Lurene Tuttle, Jeanette Nolan, Adele Ronson, John Archer, Vanessa Brown, Abby Lewis, Beverly Garland, Pat Hosley, Sam Edwards, Ray Erlenborn (sound technician), Margaret Draper, Anne Elstner, Virginia Payne, Ruth Roman, and George Hamilton. My thanks goes out to each and every one.

I am also indebted to Jay Hickerson and the Friends of Old Time Radio; the Society to Preserve and Encourage Radio Drama, Variety and Comedy (S.P.E.R.D.V.A.C.); Barbara Gelman; Barbara and David Davies; and James C. English, Sam Levene, and Nathan Berman for their help, encouragement, guidance and assistance in the preparation of this book. Special thanks to the Clancy Funeral Home of Kanakee, Illinois; Valerie Browne and the Gannon Center for Women's Leadership; the Joliet, Illinois, Chamber of Commerce; and Howard Mandelbaum of Photofest, New York, for their contributions to this book.

Introduction

Few public figures have experienced the personal and professional highlights and hardships actress Mercedes McCambridge endured during her eighty-plus years on this earth. More than fifty-five of those years were spent in the bright, often blinding glow of a show-business limelight. More like the life of a character in a play than that of an actual person, Mercedes McCambridge's life included unbelievably dramatic highs and lows. Many of the events in her life could certainly have been scenes from a film, TV series, or stage play. Miss McCambridge worked regularly as a professional actress, from the tender age of nineteen in 1936 (when she was heard on such classic radio programs as the eerie *Lights Out!* and one of radio's earliest soap operas, *The Guiding Light*), until 1991 (when she was in her seventies and starred in Neil Simon's play *Lost in Yonkers* on Broadway and during a national tour). During the years in between, Miss McCambridge won a Best Supporting Actress Academy Award in 1950 for her performance in the film *All the King's Men*, played Joan Crawford's antagonist in the cinema classic *Johnny Guitar* in 1954, and received a second Academy Award nomination for her work in the film *Giant* in 1956.

Throughout the 1940s and 1950s, Miss McCambridge also continued to work steadily on radio, as well as on television and in films. She was regularly heard on such legendary radio programs as *Abie's Irish Rose*, *Inner Sanctum Mysteries*, *The Adventures of the Thin Man*, *I Love a Mystery*, *Grand Central Station*, *Big Sister*, *The Romance of Helen Trent*, and many other popular programs; and over the years was featured on such memorable television series as *Dr. Kildare*, *Rawhide*, *Gunsmoke*, *Bonanza*, *Bewitched*, and countless others. In addition to the above mentioned film classics, she was featured in *Lightning Strikes Twice*, *Inside Straight*, *The Scarf*, *A Farewell to Arms*, and *Suddenly Last Summer*, to name just a few. As if this were not enough to keep her busy over the years, Miss McCambridge also starred in two regular radio series, *Defense Attorney* and *Family Skeleton*, as well as in her own television series, *Wire Service*. She appeared on the stage in such celebrated plays as Edward Albee's *Who's Afraid of Virginia Woolf?* on Broadway, and *Cages* Off Broadway, as well as in national touring productions of *The Miracle Worker*, *The Glass Menagerie*, *The*

Little Foxes, The Madwoman of Chaillot, 'Night, Mother, and *Agnes of God.* She earned a Tony award nomination for her performance in the play *Love Suicide at the Schofield Barracks.* In 1972, McCambridge gave a much publicized "vocal" performance as the voice of the Devil in the film *The Exorcist,* and firmly established a place for herself in motion picture history for that effort.

In addition to her remarkable acting career, the actress was an artist-in-residence and lecturer at several colleges and universities, a tireless crusader and campaigner for liberal political candidates and causes, and received countless awards for her many philanthropic endeavors on behalf of alcoholics. One can almost say of Mercedes McCambridge that she had "been there" and "done that," as far as just about every public event in and out of show business is concerned, for a good part of the twentieth century. Unfortunately Mercedes McCambridge also endured a trouble-filled private life that included a serious bout with alcoholism (from which she made a triumphant recovery), two divorces, two miscarriages, two suicide attempts, and the tragic death of her beloved only child, John. Over the years, Miss McCambridge was the intimate friend and confidante of such celebrated twentieth century personalities as 1950s film legend James Dean, who gained fame as the *Rebel Without a Cause* and died in his twenties; the liberal and intellectual Democrat who was twice a candidate for the presidency of the United States of America, Adlai Stevenson; the larger-than-life director-actors John Huston and Orson Welles; the glamorous film stars Marlene Dietrich and Rita Hayworth; the multi-talented singer-actress Judy Garland; and the film and stage impresario Billy Rose. The mercurial, sharp-tongued, outspoken, and often uncompromising Mercedes McCambridge was twice married and twice divorced, first to writer William Fifield, and then to producer-director Fletcher Markle.

The stage has now been set and the curtain is about to rise on the poignant, often melodramatic, story of actress Mercedes McCambridge — an incredible survivor and a true artist whose turbulent personal life and remarkable career in a demanding, often unforgiving profession this author has diligently followed for the past sixty years. As Mercedes' ex-husband Fletcher Markle used to say at the beginning of each of his *Studio One* radio programs, many of which starred Miss McCambridge, "Please to begin!"

PART I

Her Life and Times

1. The Early Years

John Patrick McCambridge and his wife Marie, née Mahaffry, were certainly a less-than-affluent young couple when their soon-to-be-famous daughter, Carlotta Mercedes, was born in 1916. Although John and Marie were the offspring of frugal, comfortably middle class Illinois farmers, the young couple could only rely on their families for limited financial support as newlyweds, and they certainly enjoyed fewer comforts than they had become accustomed to before marriage. As an adult, Carlotta Mercedes recalled that when she was a child, "There were times when we were very, very poor." Not that her childhood was anything like that of the Little Match Girl (the heroine of a late Victorian tale about life among the poorest members of society). The Little Match Girl was, however, a character the imaginative young Carlotta would probably have loved to have enacted when she was a child, because it was a creation of pure melodrama — just the kind of thing everyone in the John Patrick McCambridge household seems to have thrived on.

Carlotta Mercedes McCambridge was born in Joliet, Illinois, a day before St. Patrick's Day, on March 16, 1916, which seems appropriate considering her Irish background. When she became a well known actress, Mercedes claimed that she had been born on St. Patrick's Day in 1918, which she thought made her sound more interesting and shaved a couple of years off her age (not an uncommon thing for people in show business to do). She was given the rather exotic, Spanish-sounding names of "Carlotta Mercedes" by her mother, who had a definite flair for the dramatic, even though she was unquestionably Irish on both sides of her family. In her 1981 autobiography, *The Quality of Mercy* ("Mercy" being her lifelong nickname), Carlotta Mercedes admitted that, because of her name, she actually invented a story about having a Spanish grandmother. Even well into adulthood she continued to refer to her "Hispanic background," because, as she said in her autobiography, she always thought the name "Carlotta Mercedes McCambridge" sounded "a bit improbable … sort of like Tondalayo Rappaport," and she wanted to have a name that gave her more "credibility." Her parents stopped calling her "Carlotta" when she was a toddler, and thereafter she became known as "Mercedes," which they felt gave her name a more alliterative and interesting quality. She later said that she believed even the Spanish-sounding name of "Mercedes" required some sort of a logical explanation, so she concocted an elaborate story about a Spanish grandmother born "in the Calestro district of Andolucia in Spain." Mercedes even fabricated a fantastic tale about how her handsome Irish-American grandfather had been touring Spain on horseback when he met her grandmother, the beautiful "Senorita Herrero," married her, and brought her back to the United States with him. In truth, her real grandmother's name was Kate Weir, and she, like everyone else in Mercedes' family, was one-hundred-percent Irish. Mercedes' ancestry can actually be traced back to the fourteenth century and Coshenall, County Antrim, in Northern Ireland (and definitely *not* to Andolucia in Spain, nor to any Latin American country). True, the Spanish Armada had been defeated off the coast of Ireland during the reign of Queen Elizabeth the First in the sixteenth century, and thousands of Spanish sailors had indeed swam to the Irish shores when their ships sank (resulting in cohabitation with the local Irish lasses). Many contemporary Irishmen, therefore, can indeed claim a "drop or two" of Spanish blood, but that would hardly qualify them as being "part Spanish," as Mercedes said she was.

Mercedes' paternal grandfather died shortly before she was born, and her father received an inheritance that allowed him to live, although modestly, without the burden of having to work very hard. People who knew the McCambridge family in Joliet, Illinois, and then in South Chicago (where Mercedes spent most of her childhood), said that they believed she was probably destined to become an actress. All of the older members of the McCambridge and Mahaffry families, they said, were known to have been given to "unusually histrionic behavior," though it was of the domestic, and not of the professional, kind. Grandly animated arguments, sweepingly dramatic exits and entrances, extreme brooding, and shuddering cold-shoulder treatments, as well as an abundance of boisterous laughter and frequent outbursts of song, were everyday occurrences in the McCambridge household. Both John and Marie McCambridge thrived on attention, and people who lived in Joliet when the McCambridges were in residence there remembered that John Patrick, as a young swain, usually sported fancy Borsolino hats and well-tailored clothes, which was unusual in Joliet. Friends of the couple recalled that both John and Marie could often be seen riding through town on horseback at different times, because John's family only owned one horse. Both were always dressed in fancy riding clothes that they purchased at Marshall Field's department store in Chicago, and looked "as proud as peacocks" as they trotted through town.

John Patrick McCambridge, who was born in 1894, was, according to everyone who knew him, an intelligent, good looking, and well read young man. His parents were determined that he should have a college education, and when he was eighteen years old they encouraged him to enroll at St. Bede's College in Chicago. In a book, *The Two of Us*, which Mercedes had published in England in 1960 (but was never released in the United States), the actress wrote, "My father was a noble young Irishman. My grandparents sent him to St. Bede's school and before he left home for college, my grandmother got him to a priest and made him sign a pledge that he would not touch alcoholic beverages for an entire year. My father went along with the idea but he insisted that a rider be put into the contract saying, 'excepting wakes, weddings, and funerals. Grandmother and the priest agreed. So my father went to his place of higher learning and promptly subscribed to every newspaper within a hundred miles of the school. Each morning, he would read the obituary notices and the Society page. Then away he would go in his sporty touring car with a barrel of beer in the back seat. He didn't have to know the people. The important thing was not breaking his pledge. The important thing was to have a good time. My father wanted everybody to have a good time." This did not mean, however, that John Patrick was not a serious student who was curious about all manner of things. Throughout his life he would tell anyone who would listen that his favorite pastime had always been reading, and that the *Old and New Testaments* and *The New York Times* were his preferred reading materials. Unfortunately, when John Patrick graduated from St. Bede's, he found it difficult to find employment he felt was suitable to his "unique" talents, whatever they might have been. In spite of his apparent lack of industry, John Patrick McCambridge was "an absolutely charming man who was very popular, especially with the ladies," and was nicknamed "Happy" by his numerous male friends and acquaintances. Shortly after graduating from college, John Patrick married the spirited and attractive Marie Mahaffry, who had "lovely auburn hair and a slim, shapely figure," according to people who knew her as a young woman.

In 1914, World War I began in Europe, though the United States did not join the French and English and their allies in the fight against Germany until 1917. John Patrick became increasingly incensed by the reports of Germany's ever-increasing brutality during the war in Europe, and was furious when a German submarine's torpedo sank the passenger ship *Lusitania*. Traveling from New York to Liverpool, England, the *Lusitania* went down on May 17, 1917, off the Irish coast near Kinsale Head, drowning 1,198 innocent civilians, including 124 Americans. Post haste, John Patrick decided to join the fray, and enlisted in the Army. Several people who knew John Patrick at the time said they remembered that when he enlisted in the Army he traveled into Chicago to have his photograph taken wearing full Cavalry regalia, which he rented from a costumer located on Lake Street in the Windy City. "Gloriously wounded" (as the newspapers of the time rhapsodized) at the Battle of Chateau Thierry in France in May, 1918, shortly after he arrived in Europe, the twenty-two-year-old John Patrick was sent home to the United States and his wife and two-year-old baby daughter to recuperate. To the young couple's relief, John Patrick received a small veteran's pension due to his wartime injuries, which, when added to the inheritance he had received from his father, provided the young couple and their daughter, Carlotta Mercedes, with an adequate, if not bountiful, income. Marie had been living on the family farm, located near Joliet, while John was away fighting "the Huns" (as the Germans were called by the U.S. and their Allies during World War I).

Upon John Patrick's return to the U.S., the young couple and their daughter moved into an apartment at 319 Collins Street in Joliet, Illinois, where Mercedes spent the next three years of her life. Before they moved to South Chicago in 1922, John and his wife and baby daughter lived for a short time on the family farm in Kinsman (population 169), where Marie and Mercedes had spent John's Army service days. The farm was located on the outskirts of Joliet. As Mercedes related in her 1981 autobiography, the family home was adjacent to the Santa Fe Railroad tracks, and one of her most vivid childhood memories was of watching trains passing by the family farm when she visited her grandmother at various times. She remembered catching glimpses of the train's dining car as it passed by the farm, and she clearly remembered seeing beautifully groomed people eating meals as they sat at dining car tables that had bright, white linen tablecloths, fancy China plates, and silver eating utensils. It was a world that even as a child she knew was far different than her own, and she daydreamed about the time when she would be a part of that beautiful and more genteel-looking world.

When John Patrick and his family lived there, Joliet, Illinois, was a small city located about forty miles southwest of Chicago, and not a part of the Greater Chicago urban sprawl as it is today. Named after Louis de Joliet, a French-Canadian explorer who discovered the area in 1673, Joliet was a relatively prosperous small city that had benefited from the many manufacturing factories situated in the area at the time. Many Joliet residents also worked at the Statesville Penitentiary, constructed in 1916 and located five miles north and west of the original Joliet State Prison. Others farmed the surrounding areas, as the McCambridge family had for several generations, or they commuted into Chicago to work. In the years following "the War to End All Wars" (World War I), Joliet was, therefore, a typical Midwestern community. Like every other major city and small town in America, Joliet was the scene of jubilant celebrations when the war came to an end in 1918. Fifty thousand people from all over the area gathered in Joliet to cheer the returning troops, who proudly marched down the city's main thoroughfare in a grand victory parade. When the big parade ended, everyone in town gathered in Joliet's Dellwood Park for entertainment and a picnic supper. Returned and newly returning veterans of the war, including John Patrick, were presented with bronze souvenir badges and coupon booklets entitling them to free refreshments and other amusements in the park. There were bands, vaudeville shows, boxing and wrestling matches, and baseball games. A character named "Fearless" Howard was scheduled to perform a daring parachute jump, but, as Joliet's local newspaper of the time reported, "the event was canceled because of high winds." The day ended with a community sing-along, dancing in the park's pavilion, and a large fireworks display.

World War I had created new employment opportunities for many of Joliet's smokestack industries, and during the war salaries had greatly improved in the steel industry, while union organizers had begun to make inroads in the steel and wire plants located in and around Joliet. Labor leaders in the area claimed that the "war to make the world safe for democracy" had secured "economic democracy in the workplace." They were proven wrong. Soon after the war ended, post-war labor problems, due to the dismantling of defense plants, unsettled Joliet, as it did many other places in the nation. More than 3,500 strikes had occurred in the United States by 1919, and four million workers joined picket lines all across America, from New York to Los Angeles. Like many Southern and Midwestern areas of the U.S., Joliet had a sizable number of malcontents who joined local chapters of the Ku Klux Klan, a hate organization actively prejudiced against people they felt threatened their livelihoods and therefore the dominance of their White Protestant majority. The Klan was not only prejudiced against Blacks, but Jews and Catholics, simply because they were *not* Protestants. Its well publicized motto, printed in numerous, well-distributed leaflets and newspaper ads, insensitively stated: "Kill the Kikes, Koons, and Katholics." This undoubtedly made the McCambridge clan, who were devout Roman Catholics, feel less than comfortable in their Joliet surroundings.

By 1920, as post-war employment opportunities improved, the citizens of Joliet began to take an interest in more commonplace things, such as the purchase of the town's first automotive fire engine. By 1924, because of ever-improving employment opportunities, people were more concerned with the opening of the newly constructed and elaborate *Rialto Square Theater*, located in the center of town, than they were with protests and rallies. The theater replicated the grandeur of the eighteenth century Versailles Palace in France. Like Versailles, it featured an impressive Hall of Mirrors, a "Grand Staircase," and a spacious Rotunda with a beautiful eight-arm chandelier. When John Patrick McCambridge, who had by that time moved his family to South Chicago, heard about the impressive new motion picture palace, he took his wife and children back to Joliet to inspect the magnificent new rococo structure. In her autobiography, Mercedes, who was eight years old when the theater opened its doors to the public, recalled standing in the grand lobby of Joliet's *Rialto Square Theater* and feeling like a storybook princess. Thereafter, she always thought of theaters as places where she could easily spend the rest of her life. Of course she didn't know at the time just how prophetic that feeling was.

Until Mercedes gained national attention as a radio actress in the late 1930s, and then received world-wide recognition as an Academy Award winner in 1950, the most celebrated woman born in Joliet had been a sixteen-year-old girl named Lois Delander, who had been crowned Miss America in 1927. A painting of the local beauty hung in the rotunda of *The Rialto Square Theater*, for many years. When Miss Delander won her title, Mercedes McCambridge was nine years old, and one can only imagine the world of possibilities that must have seemed open to the imaginative child when she read in the Chicago newspapers about a girl from her home town being crowned "Miss America" by comedian Bob Hope in Atlantic City. (Two other actors, Audrey Totter and Larry Parks, were also born in Joliet and became relatively well known to the American public, but neither one approached Mercedes McCambridge's—or, for that matter, Lois Delander's—celebrity, as far as the citizenry of Joliet were concerned.)

At a 1979 banquet, the people of Joliet honored their most famous "native born" former inhabitant, Mercedes McCambridge, who by that time had become an internationally known actress. At the banquet, Mercedes recalled her earliest memories of living in Joliet. She remembered the Joliet apartment her family had lived in when she was a child, and recalled that it was "small with a large wooden porch outside." She remembered that the couple who lived upstairs often gave her pineapple, leading to her "lifelong love affair with fruit." "Downstairs," she recalled, "I remember there was a man named 'Bull' who used to give me rides on his shoulders." One vivid memory was of a time she watched a circus parade marching through town while sitting on Bull's shoulders.

At the same 1979 Joliet tribute, people who knew her father (who died in 1966) characterized him as "an amazing storyteller." "He seemed to actually become all of the characters in the many stories he told," one woman attending the event reported. That was something Mercedes was certainly well aware of, since her father often told her wonderful bedtime stories when she was a child. His tales often revolved around his Army experiences in France when he was "fighting the Huns," and he also told passionate stories about "the struggles" back in Ireland and the "repressive occupation" of the birthplace of his ancestors by the British. Several people who attended the 1979 tribute fondly recalled the time John Patrick rented a hall in Joliet where he planned to read poetry to a crowd of invited guests. Shortly after he began his reading, cries of "Fire" and clouds of dark black smoke led to everyone hastily evacuating the building, leaving John Patrick standing alone on the stage. That, it seems, was the end of his career as a public speaker. Highly indignant that providence had dared interrupt what would have been one of his grandest performances, he determined that he would never again subject himself to such an undignified mass embarrassment, saying he was "finished with show business forever!" John Patrick did, however, continue to "hold forth" (as he put it) on certain occasions, and enjoyed taking center stage at small gatherings of friends at various watering holes or saloons, or whenever the opportunity arose. He spent many happy hours in one local saloon or another, having a pint (or two) of "Ireland's mother's milk" (Guinness stout), or a glass (or more) of good Irish whiskey, with a few of his cronies. John Patrick's favorite "watering hole" was a saloon called Paddy Flynn's, which in later life he always rhapsodized over with obvious fondness. At the close of the 1979 Joliet tribute to Mercedes, two very old men came up to the actress after she finished speaking, and stated, with great feeling, "John Patrick McCambridge was a young prince. There never was another like him." They then told her of a night her father and several men were drinking at Paddy Flynn's when he announced that he was going to take "the whole lot" of them "up to Canada" that same evening. The group traveled all the way to Union Station in Chicago, only to discover that there were no trains to Canada until the next day. They reluctantly returned to Joliet, since the effects of the liquor they had consumed had subsided. The two old gentlemen said that they never forgot John Patrick's good-hearted and generous intentions.

Mercedes' mother, Marie Mahaffry McCambridge, was, like her husband, a memorable character to those who knew her, but, apparently was not as generous of spirit as her easygoing, fun-loving husband John. She was of a more "practical" bent, though well remembered in Joliet and South Chicago for spontaneously bursting into song whenever she felt there was an audience worthy of listening to her sing. She was also noted for making spectacular entrances at various family and social occasions. In spite of her somewhat "grand," often bizarre behavior, Marie McCambridge was a seriously devout Roman Catholic woman. "A dramatically pious presence," as Mercedes called her, Marie would often talk of "the harsh treatment" God had in store for the wicked of this world, and of the "hell, fire and brimstone" that awaited people who strayed from the righteous path. She made numerous references to "the blessed bleeding heart of Jesus," regularly fingered her Rosary beads, faithfully said her "Hail Mary's," and made numerous novenas to pray for the souls of those she felt were surely lost. She was especially harsh when it came to the rakish behavior of her spirited husband, and the impishly improper actions of her lively and imaginative daughter, Mercedes. Like her parents, Mercedes loved being in the spotlight, and she would often invent elaborate stories (such as the one about having a Spanish grandmother) simply to attract attention. When her falsehoods were discovered, appropriate punishment (which usually consisted of a resounding slap and exile to her bed to pray and "think about" her "wicked ways") resulted.

In her 1981 autobiography, Mercedes admitted that she had once been "an accomplished enough fabricator to lie to the Pope himself." She was an adult at the time, and was in Rome filming a remake of an adaptation of Ernest Hemingway's novel *A Farewell to Arms*. While visiting the Vatican on one of her afternoons off, she waited in a long line to see Pope Pius XII, shortly before he died, and have him bless an armful of religious objects she was carrying that she wanted to present to her friends and family members back home. When the Pope paused in front of her and asked her in broken English, recognizing that she was probably an American, why she was in Rome, she simply could not tell "Christ's representative on Earth" that she was a "wicked film actress who was remaking *A Farewell to Arms* in Rome," so she demurely told him that she was "just a tourist." All she could think of after she told the Pope that lie was the absolute horror and subsequent wrath her passionately papist mother would express when she heard that her daughter had told a fib to the Holy Father himself. She didn't tell her mother — or anyone else in her family — the truth about that incident until many years later. She simply handed her delighted mother the "blessed by the Pope" crucifix she had bought for her in the Vatican's souvenir shop in Rome. "It was lucky for me," Mercedes later said, "that, even as an adult I was able to fool my mother … sometimes, because I surely would not be standing here today if my mother ever knew I lied to the Pope himself." In her book *The Two of Us*, Mercedes admitted, "I am by nature a liar and some of the things I remember didn't happen that way at all, but I keep thinking that out of these embellished ruminations will come emotional stability and then I will be able to cope with any situation on a natural level."

Mercedes' relationship with her mother had always been somewhat strained, and Marie's disapproving attitude regarding her daughter's often outrageous behavior certainly seems to have impacted what Mercedes thought about herself while growing up, and even later in life as an adult. Nothing her daughter ever did seemed quite good enough for Marie Mahaffry McCambridge. In her autobiography, however, Mercedes understandingly described her mother as being "one of the best actresses I have ever known. I have seen my mother play everything from Rosalind [a character in Shakespeare's comedy *As You Like It*] to Lady Macbeth." "Iambic pentameter was not her meter. Shakespeare was not her source. Mother was never much for dialogue. She played in soliloquy, monologue, uninterrupted, inexhaustible, and mad as a hornet. Very impressive — cunning, pitiable, dangerous, and despairing — this woman ran the gamut from A to Z and back again, stooping to pick up a stray cat, lashing out at all who differed with her, giving everybody the shirt off her back, banishing all Protestants to hell, and praying all Catholics out of purgatory." All of this was apparently accomplished by Marie McCambridge without ever leaving the sanctity of South Chicago.

When she was thirteen and being confirmed in the Roman Catholic Church, Mercedes took the name of "Agnes," which pleased her father, who had never been particularly happy with his wife's decision to name his daughter "Carlotta Mercedes." He often stated that he would have preferred a more down-to-earth Christian name for his offspring. "I took the name of Agnes as my confirmation name," Mercedes later said in a typically melodramatic McCambridge manner, "because Saint Agnes was burned at the stake when she was twelve for her religious beliefs. I thought that would be the ideal way to go ... very dramatic."

Several of Mercedes' more bizarre and unconventional childhood memories remained as vivid to her in later life as the day they happened to her as a child. When she was very young, Mercedes remembered being awakened in the middle of the night by the sound of her mother's and her Aunt Noonie's wailing, moaning, and screaming. Aunt Noonie, like Mercedes' mother, was a very emotional woman who could even outdo her sister, as far as extreme, dramatic behavior was concerned. Mercedes' father was out of town in St. Louis at the time, and Aunt Noonie was staying with her sister because Marie was pregnant and not feeling very well. Mercedes' mother, the young girl discovered, was bleeding heavily and having a miscarriage. The ten-year-old girl followed her Aunt Noonie and her weak and groaning mother as she was being helped down the stairs by a taxi driver called to take her to the hospital. Mercedes was left standing barefoot in the snow as the taxi carrying her mother and Aunt Noonie sped away. Mercedes went back upstairs to the family's apartment with her Uncle Alf, Aunt Noonie's husband, who had been instructed to "look after her." For the rest of the night, Mercedes sleeplessly waited to find out if her mother was alive or dead. Marie McCambridge lost the baby girl she had been carrying, but she survived. The next morning, Mercedes' father was summoned home from St. Louis, and arrangements were made to hold a wake for the tiny, two-pound premature infant. Because the body of the dead baby was so small, Mercedes' doll clothes were used to dress the infant corpse for the public viewing. At Aunt Noonie's urging, Mercedes gazed at the tiny, graying body as it lay in its wee coffin before the lid of the casket was closed. The event could have been a scene from Dante's hellish *Inferno*, as far as Mercedes was concerned, and it remained indelibly stamped on her memory.

Another early childhood event that Mercedes recalled with equal clarity was a visit to Marshall Field's department store at Christmas time when she was about seven years old. Once again, Aunt Noonie was in attendance at this event, as was Noonie's mild-mannered husband, Uncle Alf. Mercedes had been taken to Marshall Field's department store by her aunt and uncle to see Santa Claus, and had waited in a long line for over an hour before she was finally placed on Santa's lap. Santa told her that he would be coming down her chimney soon to leave her presents under the Christmas tree, and asked her what she wanted for Christmas. When Mercedes told him that she didn't have a chimney in her apartment, Santa glared at her reproachfully. She then nervously shouted in his ear, "Anything will be okay," because it was very noisy in the store, which was filled to capacity with hundreds of yelping children. Santa scowled at her and firmly insisted that she tell him what she wanted for Christmas. Frustrated and frightened, Mercedes remembered that she began to cry. When she glanced over at her Aunt Noonie and Uncle Alf, hoping for some sort of sympathy, she saw that they were laughing at her, and she felt like a horse's ass. She hated that feeling. "I am nobody's horse's ass," she always insisted after that, "and don't let anyone ever forget it." She vowed, at the tender age of seven, that for the rest of her life she would never allow anything or anyone to make her feel like a horse's ass again. Unfortunately, many similar embarrassments surfaced during the years that followed, leaving her feeling as frustrated and angry as the incident with Santa Claus did when she was a child.

John and Marie McCambridge were the parents of two other children, both boys and both younger than Mercedes. They apparently did not share their parents', or sister's, penchant for being in the spotlight. One of her brothers, John Valerian, born in 1920, was named "Valerian" after a monk who had treated his father's war injuries in an abbey in France. Mercedes' youngest brother's name remains a mystery, as far as this author could determine, since it was never mentioned in any of the published accounts of Mercedes' life. Like his older brother, he seems to have succeeded in keeping a relatively low profile. The most dramatic thing that appears to have happened to either of Mercedes' brothers was that John Valerian was injured in a plane crash while being transported from one base to another during World War II. His father took great pride in his oldest son's wartime injuries. It is known that one of Mercedes' brothers became a marriage counselor in Los Angeles, valiantly attempting to straighten out the lives of married couples in trouble (as he probably wished he could have done for his own oft-battling parents and his twice-divorced sister).

By 1922, the McCambridge family had, as previously stated, already left Joliet and moved to South Chicago, home to the largest concentration of Irish-Americans in the Chicago area. Mercedes' father believed employment opportunities might be more promising in the inner city. Hard times, however, continued to plague the McCambridge family throughout "the Roaring Twenties," which for most people in the United States were relatively prosperous years. Everyone contacted by this author, and all the sources consulted in the preparation of this book, failed to reveal exactly what John Patrick McCambridge did to earn a living for himself and his family. Some people who knew the McCambridges when they lived in South Chicago said that they believed John was "somehow connected with a school of some kind." Others said they believed he sold insurance, and still others that he and a partner owned a saloon. Whatever he did to provide for his family during the 1920s and into the 1930s, they managed to survive, although Marie McCambridge's constant complaining would seem to indicate that John's financial condition was probably less than optimal. In 1929 the crash of the stock market led the country into the desperate years of the Great Depression, which lasted throughout most of the 1930s. "I think," Mercedes said of those times, "that Franklin D. Roosevelt, the president who eventually led the country out of the Great Depression, was the reason my parents' spirit didn't break." The McCambridge family, including Mercedes, remained staunch Democrats and committed liberals for the remainder of their lives.

In her autobiography, Mercedes stated that although her home life might have been rather unconventional, her grade school and high school experiences were decidedly commonplace, if not exactly ideal. Mercedes attended several different Catholic grade schools in the South Chicago area, depending upon where her family was living at the time, and she was taught exclusively by nuns. Classmates remember Mercedes as a smarter-than-average and spirited girl who frequently got into trouble with the nuns due to her attention-seeking ways. Mercedes' favorite subjects in grade school were literature and history, no doubt prompted by her father's interest in those topics. In her autobiography, Mercedes recalled an incident involving her third grade teacher, an austere nun named Sister Rita, which seems to have affected her more than any other single event that occurred during her grade school tenure. Sister Rita objected to Mercedes being placed in her third grade class when she should have been in the second grade, according to her age. Mercedes' father had taught his daughter how to read and write before she entered grade school, and the Mother Superior, who was the principal of the school, overruled Sister Rita's objections to having the younger child placed in her class. To complicate matters even more, Sister Rita had an aversion to left-handedness, and since Mercedes was left-handed, she became the object of Sister Rita's unsuccessful campaign to eliminate what the nun considered a serious defect that would certainly lead to a severe stuttering problem for the child if left uncorrected. The nun tied Mercedes' left hand to her side, forcing her to use her right hand only, and directed two girls in the class to report to her immediately if Mercedes attempted to use her left hand. Sister Rita's actions led to Mercedes being truant from school for over a week. When Sister Rita inquired about her whereabouts, Mercedes' truancy was uncovered and she was appropriately punished. The strong willed, stubborn Mercedes eventually won her battle with Sister Rita, however, when her father and the Mother Superior in charge of the school agreed that they saw no reason why the girl should not continue to write with her left hand if she wished, since there was no proof, Sister Rita's assertion aside, that "left handedness led to stuttering." The somewhat deflated and unquestionably defeated Sister Rita was forced to abandon her plan to make Mercedes "one of the crowd," but for the remainder of the school year Mercedes became the subject of frequent vengeful and cruel remarks made by the nun, which caused the other students in the class to laugh and greatly upset Mercedes, who, as noted before, did not like being made anyone's fool.

After she graduated from grade school, Mercedes entered St. Thomas Apostle High School, a Catholic secondary school for girls in South Chicago run by the Dominican Sisters. At St. Thomas Apostle, Mercedes enjoyed more freedom to express herself than she did in grade school, and she was a good secondary school student who excelled in speech and drama, as well as in history and literature. In her junior year she earned praise from her speech teacher, and the admiration of her fellow classmates, when she won an elocution contest by reciting Joyce Kilmer's religious poem "A Blue Valentine" in her speech class. She recited the poem with impressive authority and moving emotion.

When she was sixteen years old and in high school, Mercedes fell in love for the first time in her life. The object of her affection was a boy named Lefty Callahan, but shortly after they began dating, Lefty began noticing a tall, red-headed girl who worked in the Blackstone Library, and Mercedes was crushed by his diminishing interest in her. In her 1960 book *The Two of Us*, Mercedes wrote, "Lefty wasn't just any old boy friend. He was a football player and president of his class and a lifeguard in the summer. All I wanted was to grow a little bit older and marry Lefty and live happily ever after. And then this stupid red-haired long drink of water two timing female was going to change everything. She wasn't the girl for Lefty. Something had to be done to save him. It would have to be dramatic and soon!" One evening when Lefty came to her apartment building to pick her up for a date, Mercedes answered his ring in her apartment and told him that she would be right down to join him in the vestibule. Quite deliberately, Mercedes "dramatically"—and that is the key word here—threw herself down a whole flight of stairs, knowing it would certainly get Lefty's attention and probably win him back from the clutches of the library red head. Mercedes screamed all the way as she plunged down the stairs, and her parents, all the neighbors in the apartment building, and Lefty came running to her rescue as she lay at the bottom of the stairs in the building's vestibule. Lefty accompanied the bruised and battered but, miraculously, not seriously injured, Mercedes and her parents as they raced through the streets of Chicago in the family car to Mercy Hospital. Lefty was deeply concerned about the moaning Mercedes, and through her pain she thought to herself, "That's it, he's mine forever!" A few weeks after Mercedes suffered her less-than-fatal fall, and had fully recovered from her minor injuries, she began to lose interest in Lefty, whose behavior had become a bit too "smothering" for her liking, and she told him their love affair was over. Lefty went back to the red head from the library, and Mercedes began to date another teen swain, albeit with less enthusiasm, whom she had met in the local ice cream parlor the day after returning to school.

In her senior year at St. Thomas Apostle, Mercedes was appearing in a school play when Cardinal George Mundelein of Chicago paid a visit to the school. Mercedes' life, although she didn't know it at the time, was about to change forever.

After numerous appeals by three dedicated Sisters of Mercy nuns, who were determined to establish a college for Catholic women in Chicago, Cardinal Mundelein decided to support their cause and set about raising the funds needed to build a women's college in North Chicago. Mundelein College, as the institution was named in his honor, was formally dedicated on June 3, 1931, with much fanfare. Building one large skyscraper with fourteen floors to house the college, it had been decided, would be a much less expensive proposition than trying to find suitable land in the center of the city of Chicago for a college campus. The skyscraper, costing two million dollars to build and designed by architect Joseph W. McCarthy, was heavily mortgaged by the time it opened its doors in 1931. The college's dedication ceremony was a memorable event, and complete with considerable pomp and circumstance. Cardinal Mundelein, all of the 384 registered young female students, the 54-member faculty (all Sisters of Mercy nuns), and the college's president, Sister Mary Justitia, B.V.M (Blessed Virgin Mary), stood at the entrance to the new college as an all-girl band played appropriately dignified music, and guests arrived for the opening day ceremony. On either side of the main door of the building a colorful contingent of uniformed Catholic laymen, all Knights of St. Gregory, stood guard as various dignitaries and distinguished guests, as well as the families of the students, entered the building. Everyone was duly impressed with the imposing Art Deco structure which was later placed on the National Registry of Historic Places as indeed they were with the colorful opening day dedication ceremony.

Three years after the college named after him opened its doors to students, Cardinal Mundelein, who was always on the lookout for promising and intelligent young women he could recruit for the college, attended a performance of a school play at St. Thomas Apostle high school and took note of the slim, dark-haired and talented young student actress named Mercedes McCambridge playing the leading role. Cardinal Mundelein requested that the girl be presented to him when the curtain came down. At the requested audience, Cardinal Mundelein asked Mercedes what her plans were when she graduated from high school, and she told him that she was probably going to look for a job and go to work to help support her family. Cardinal Mundelein suggested that she should think about competing for a full tuition drama scholarship to attend Mundelein College that was currently available. After discussing the possibility with her parents, who were both very enthusiastic about the idea, Mercedes decided to use the same Joyce Kilmer poem, "A Blue Valentine," for her audition piece at the competition, since she had received so much praise for reciting the poem earlier that year in her speech class at St. Thomas Apostle. The poem was very melodramatic and rich with colorful language and poetic images, and, very wisely, it was appropriately religious. Mercedes' well rehearsed recitation of the poem was favorably received by Cardinal Mundelein, but it especially impressed a nun named Sister Mary Leola Oliver, who was in charge of Mundelein College's drama department.

Mercedes' choice of material for her audition piece is very revealing about the young woman's obvious religious orientation and her flair for the dramatic.

> Monsignore,
>   Right Reverend Bishop Valentinus.
> Sometime of Interamna, which is called Ferni,
> Now of the delightful Court of Heaven,
> I respectfully salute you.
> I genuflect
> And kiss your Episcopal ring.
> It is not, Monsignore,
> The fragrant memory of your holy life,
> Nor that of your shining and joyous martyrdom,
> Which causes me now to address you.
> But since this is your august festival, Monsignore,
> It seems appropriate to me to state
> According to a venerable and agreeable custom,
> That I love a beautiful lady.
> Her eyes, Monsignore,
> Are so blue that they put lovely little blue reflections
> On everything that she looks at,
> Such as a wall
> Or the moon
> Or my heart.
> It is like the light coming through blue stained glass,
> Yet not quite like it,
> For the bluest is not transparent,
> Only translucent.
> Her soul's light shines through,
> But her soul cannot be seen.
> It is something elusive, whimsical, tender, wanton,
> Infantile, wise
> And noble.
> She wears, Monsignore, a blue garment,
> Made in the manner of the Japanese.
> It is very blue —
> I think that her eyes have made it more blue,
> Sweetly staining it
> As the pressure of her body has graciously given it form.
> Loving her, Monsignore,
> I love all her attributes;
> But I believe
> That even if I did not love her
> I would love the blueness of her eyes,
> And her blue garment, made in the manner of the
> Japanese.

The poem's poignant ending is deeply moving, and the listeners nodded their heads in approval as Mercedes completed her audition piece.

Monsignore,
I have never before troubled you with a request.
The saints whose ears I chiefly worry with my pleas
   are the most exquisite and maternal Brigid,
Gallant Saint Stephen, who puts fire in my blood,
And your brother bishop, my patron,
The generous and jovial Saint Nicholas of Bari.
But, of your courtesy, Monsignor,
Do me this favor:
When you this morning make your way
To the ivory Throne that bursts into bloom with roses
   because of her who sits upon it,
When you come to pay your devoir to Our Lady,
I beg you say to her:
"Madame, a poor poet, one of your singing servants on earth,
Has asked me to say that at this moment he is especially
   grateful to you
For wearing a blue gown."

To her disappointment, in spite of the eloquence of the poem and her moving interpretation of the material at the audition, Mercedes failed to win the scholarship, and only earned a second place prize. She was indeed offered admission to the college, but it was not on a scholarship. Unable to raise the needed tuition money to attend Mundelein, which was $75 a year (high for a poor girl, but inexpensive for most colleges), Mercedes determined that she would indeed go to college anyway. She enrolled as a student at the Dominican Sister's Rosary College, which was a much less expensive school than Mundelein but still had a good reputation. That September, Sister Mary Leola, the head of the drama department at Mundelein, could not get the talented young woman out of her mind, and the following term she convinced Mercedes to transfer to Mundelein College, after pressing Mundelein's board of directors to offer the talented young woman a full tuition scholarship, which they did.

Jane Malkemus Goodnow, who attended Mundelein College from September 1933 until June 1937, while Mercedes was also a student there, recalled the first time she met Mercedes. In an essay written in 1991 and appearing in the book *Mundelein Voices*, published by the Loyola University Press in Chicago, Goodnow remembered meeting Mercedes at the first rehearsal of Shakespeare's play *Twelfth Night*, which was to be the college drama department's initial production of the 1934–1935 academic year. Mercedes had been assigned the part of Viola, a girl who masquerades as a boy, in order to keep her real identity a secret. "After all these years [almost sixty years had gone by when Ms. Goodnow wrote her recollection], I can still hear Mercedes reading Viola's reply to Olivia's question, 'Why, what would you?' at that first rehearsal of the play. Mercedes, as Viola, answered:

Make me a willow cabin at your gate,
And call upon my soul within the house;

Write loyal cantons of condemned love
And sing them loud even in the dead of night;
Halloo your name to the reverberate hills,
And make the babbling gossip of the air
Cry out "Olivia"!!

"A thrill ran up my spine on hearing that violin voice interpret those lines so movingly, with perfect timing and enunciation," Ms. Goodnow said in her essay. "Having heard good readers at the Jack and Jill Theater and at radio auditions, I could recognize the exceptional quality of the voice and the reading. She became the undisputed star of our drama department. She was perfect in the role of Viola … witty, lithe, and spontaneous."

College was indeed a mind-expanding experience for the intelligent, imaginative eighteen-year-old Mercedes. For one thing, she was relatively free from the constant criticism of her judgmental mother, and she actually received praise for her work in the college's drama department, an unusual experience as far as she was concerned. The key to opening the door to her promising future as an actress was in the hands of the very creative Mundelein drama teacher, Sister Mary Leola Oliver of order of the Sisters of Mercy. Sister Mary Leola was diminutive in size but energetic, and a gifted teacher and drama coach. According to Mercedes, "She had the face of an angel with just a bit of mischief on it." The nun had immediately recognized the theatrical potential of the talented young woman at her audition for the drama scholarship the year before. There was absolutely no question in the nun's mind that this girl, who had the unmistakable stamp of something "special" about her, could become a professional actress. She was vibrant, unafraid to express emotion, poised, graceful, and totally in control of herself vocally. Mercedes, in return, was able to recognize and appreciate a gifted teacher when she came across one, and she took in each and every word of instruction, and all of the wise guidance that Sister Mary Leola Oliver had to offer.

Mercedes' performance in *Twelfth Night* impressed a visiting theater critic from *The Chicago Tribune*, and he extolled the young student's acting talents in his weekly newspaper column. "Student actress Mercedes McCambridge's performance," he stated, "was the finest intellectual reading of Shakespeare I have heard by any amateur player."

Mercedes always claimed that any success she ever obtained as an actress was entirely due to Sister Mary Leola's masterful direction and fine instruction as a drama coach. "She is everything I know about my work," Mercedes later insisted, after she had become a successful professional actress. Mercedes also frequently said that Sister Mary Leola "was a brilliant actress herself and was a wonderful directress, a hard task master and disciplinarian, and she had a widely inventive mind and a dedication to the theater. She was a great lady."

In her autobiography, Mercedes described how Sister Mary Leola used to "love to act, design sets and costumes, to coach a dance group, and to light the stage, and live in her theater … with her God." She also described how Sister Mary Leola would

Mundelein College's Verse Speaking Choir was the creation of drama teacher Sister Mary Leola Oliver. A nineteen-year-old Mercedes McCambridge, center, was the choir's soloist, and Sister Mary Leola's star drama student.

gather the outer skirts of her nun's habit and secure them with the rosary beads that hung at her side to free her legs so that she could move about freely. With her veil pinned back to clear her face, she would show her student actresses how every role in the play they were rehearsing should be acted. Only her students, however, ever saw just how good an actress the nun really was.

Many years later, in the book *Mundelein Voices*, Mercedes wrote of Sister Mary

This was Mercedes' first professional photograph as an actress, taken in 1936 by a staff photographer at the NBC Merchandise Mart studios in Chicago. Mercedes had just been signed by that network to a five-year contract as a staff actress. Still a college student at Mundelein College, Mercedes was just beginning what was to be a long and distinguished career as a professional actress, first on radio and then in films, on television, and on the stage.

Leola, "Sister was, for me, a very hard teacher, a taskmaster. But I think my best teachers have always been the ones who have been hardest on me … the ones who kept insisting that I had more to give than I wanted to give … the ones who really believed that it wasn't so important that I would make a fool of myself by overdoing something. They would insist that the important thing was to go ahead … do it! 'Show me what you can do, not what you are afraid to do because you don't want to have anybody notice your lacks. If you lack something, let's see what we can do to overcome it.' This is Sister talking."

In the autumn of 1936, the first drama department production of the new term was Henri Gheon's play *The Comedian*, about an actor in ancient Rome who was an early convert to Christianity and became the patron saint of actors. Mercedes played the actor's patrician lover in the play. "Usually," Mercedes said of this production, "Sister Mary Leola had her eyes set on one of the roles in the play that might have gone to her, had she been a student instead of a teacher. Heaven help the girl who was enacting the role that Sister might have wanted for herself. I remember most vividly in Gheon's play *The Comedian*, in which I played Paupier, that Sister would have liked that part. One day in rehearsal, she got it. And I don't know if I ever came up to her performance. Oh, boy, some of us used to say, 'Don't bring your father to meet Sister Mary Leola because he'll never go home to your mother.' We didn't mean it irreverently. It was really an appreciation of a very charming and determined little person."

Also in 1936, Sister Mary Leola presented one of her most innovative productions. It was a performance by her newly formed Verse Speaking Choir. The choir featured sixteen female voices—eight light voices and eight deeper ones. The group read poetry in unison, and when a solo voice was needed, it usually fell to Mercedes, who had become Sister Mary Leola's star pupil. It was at a performance of the verse choir towards the end of Mercedes' sophomore year at Mundelein College that fate changed the young woman's life forever and set her on a course that would eventually lead to world-wide, award-winning acclaim as an actress. As luck would have it, Sid Strotz, a vice president at the National Broadcasting Company (NBC) in Chicago, attended a performance of the verse choir, becoming totally captivated by it. He was especially impressed with the choir's soloist, Mercedes, in whom he saw great potential as a radio actress because of her amazing vocal versatility. Strotz invited Sister Mary Leola and her choir to the NBC Merchandise Mart studios to audition for a spot on one of the network's radio variety shows. None of the girls had ever been in a professional radio studio before, and only a few of them had ever been in the downtown area of Chicago. The group spoke their verse into the radio microphone with the authority of seasoned professionals, and the result was a one-year contract with the National Broadcasting Company for Sister Mary Leola's choir, and a five-year contract to perform in a minimum of ten radio shows a week as a staff actress at NBC for the group's talented soloist, Mercedes McCambridge. The verse choir's first radio performance was on an NBC variety show in 1936.

Immediately upon reporting to work at NBC, Mercedes, in addition to her appearances with Mundelein's Verse Speaking Choir, was assigned parts on two of the company's daytime drama serials that were making their debuts in 1936: *Dan Harding's Wife* and *Timothy Makepeace*. *Dan Harding's Wife* was about a middle class wife and mother and her domestic concerns. *Timothy Makepeace*, which proved less successful than *Dan Harding's Wife* and remained on the air for less than two months, was a 1930s Dickensian daytime drama series about a young man growing up in Middle America. NBC's makeup, wardrobe and hairdressing departments set about glamorizing their fledgling young college student/actress, and the network's publicity department photographed their new discovery to introduce her to the public. McCambridge's first NBC publicity release, printed on October 5, 1936, stated: "Mercedes McCambridge, a 20-year-old Mundelein College senior, was signed to an NBC contract the first time she tried out for radio, and now plays important roles on two network dramatic programs. The pretty, five foot, two inch brunette, is keeping up with her classes and maintaining a B average in her college work, while performing in radio."

With two years remaining to complete her college education, Mercedes was about to enter her junior year at Mundelein, and begin what was to be the busiest and most physically and emotionally demanding time of her young life.

2. The Thirties and Forties

During her final semesters at Mundelein College, Mercedes McCambridge hardly had time to sleep, what with trying to keep up with her studies, remaining active in college drama department activities, and working as an increasingly busy professional radio actress on several programs broadcast on the National Broadcasting Company's Red network. (NBC had two radio networks at that time, called the Red and the Blue.) "Radio," Mercedes said in an interview several years after her debut as a professional actress, "was the first place I earned an honest dollar. It also became like a home to me." The time it took for the young actress to commute between her parents' home in South Chicago to Mundelein College in north Chicago, and then from Mundelein to the NBC studios, which were located at the Merchandise Mart in downtown Chicago (sometimes back and forth several times), occupied as many as eighteen hours of Mercedes' day. "It meant fifty miles of commuting each and every day by train and bus," Mercedes said in a radio interview conducted by Arlene Francis on WOR radio in 1981.

During that same interview, Arlene Francis asked Mercedes if she remembered her first role as a professional radio actress. Mercedes answered that some people at NBC recalled that it was a part on the *Pretty Kitty Kelly* soap opera series (which was actually a series on the Columbia Broadcasting System and never featured on NBC), but she thought it was the leading ingénue role on *The Guiding Light*. She had undoubtedly forgotten that her "first" actual professional radio acting performance was as a soloist with Sister Mary Leola's Verse Speaking Choir on an NBC variety show, and that her first professional radio acting roles had been on the *Dan Harding's Wife* and *Timothy Makepeace* daytime serial drama programs.

When she first began working as a professional radio actress, Mercedes admitted that she didn't take the work very seriously. "I didn't know that I was supposed to be constantly at their disposal," she said of her first few months at NBC. "I'd go off on weekends and they wouldn't know how to get in touch with me. Since they weren't paying me unless I worked, I didn't see why I had to tell them where I was every minute." She was soon convinced by NBC executives, who threatened to release

Mercedes was one of NBC's busiest radio actresses in Chicago in the late 1930s, and was heard on countless daytime drama serials, such as *Dan Harding's Wife*, *The Guiding Light* and *Girl Alone*, as well as on such primetime programs as Arch Oboler's *Lights Out* and *The Arch Oboler Theater* series, and the popular dramatic anthology program *First Nighter*.

her from her contract, that being a professional actress was serious business, and that she should either "shape up or ship out." Mercedes did indeed settle down and conscientiously began fulfilling her professional obligations to the network. It didn't take long before she began enjoying a variety of roles on NBC's various programs, and her short-lived casual attitude towards her work, which was no doubt due to her youth and lack of experience, came to an abrupt end.

In addition to playing continuing major roles on daytime radio serials such as *Dan Harding's Wife*, *The Guiding Light* and *Girl Alone*, Mercedes was also kept busy working on several prime time shows such as Arch Oboler's *Lights Out!* and *The Arch Oboler Theater*, as well as playing occasional supporting roles on NBC's popular *The First Nighter* and *Modern Romances* programs. Mercedes participated in many original radio plays written and directed by Arch Oboler during her first few years at NBC in Chicago. Oboler was one of NBC's most successful young writing and directing talents in the late 1930s. *Lights Out!*, which first aired on April 17, 1935, had been the brainchild of NBC writer and producer Wyllis Cooper. Oboler assumed responsibility for the series when Cooper left for Hollywood to become a screenwriter. *Lights Out!* epitomized a new type of radio drama emerging in Chicago. The series offered some of the goriest plots and most macabre sounds effects heard on radio. These weird sounds included heads being crushed, human flesh being eaten, and the cutting off of limbs, which had never been heard on the air up until that time. By 1936, when Mercedes first began performing on the series, *Lights Out!* was one of the most talked-about radio programs in the United States. It was billed as "the ultimate horror show" by *Radio Mirror* magazine, and at the beginning of the program the listening audience was warned, "If you frighten easily, turn off your radio now!" The show aired at midnight because NBC thought it too violent for young children. The midnight broadcasts certainly added to the series' fright factor. After becoming a world-famous novelist, author Stephen King said that as a little boy he had been "scared out of his wits" when he turned on the program late one night when unable to sleep, and heard one of the many re-runs of the *Lights Out!* program that were rebroadcast in the 1940s.

Arch Oboler later said of those years at NBC in the late 1930s: "Chicago was the fountainhead of drama and the best actors and actresses were there. They were just outstanding. They ranged from Mercedes McCambridge (and she was in her late teens at the time) to Howard Duff and Raymond Edward Johnson. NBC had so many affiliates at that time, some in the same cities, that there were two complete competing networks, the Red and the Blue (which kept everyone employed by NBC very busy)." One night in the late thirties, Mercedes was working on Oboler's *Lights Out!* program with horror-film star Boris Karloff, who was guest starring on the program and playing a vampire. The show was broadcast from NBC's Studio D in the Merchandise Mart. In keeping with the series' eerie, frightening story lines, and in order to provide the actors with the proper atmosphere, Oboler insisted that Studio D be kept dark, except for a single overhead light for the actors to read their scripts by. Mercedes later recalled that the story they were performing the night Karloff was on the show called for the vampire to bite into her neck at one point. During the show's rehearsal, the sound man, Tommy Horan, did everything he could to try and come up with an acceptable sound effect for the action. He experimented with everything from snapping chicken bones to cracking his knuckles to approximate the sound of Mercedes' neck being bitten, but he remained unsatisfied. Just when the task seemed hopeless, Horan pulled out a package of Life Savers from his pocket, put two of them in his mouth, and bit down hard. The sound effect was perfect — just like a neck being bitten. It suddenly dawned on the young actress that the secret of good radio was simply ... *sound*! She gained a new respect for her craft that night, and her vocal performances ever after were greatly enhanced by the realization that radio audiences only heard, and did not see, what was supposed to be happening — whether it was physical or vocal. The sheer magic of sound alone had to make the listener believe. This was a simple but essential fact for any radio performer to understand.

Mercedes' most notable continuing role on a soap opera in those early years at NBC was as the leading actress on *The Guiding Light*. One of the broadcasting industry's longest-running soap operas, the series still airs on television as of 2004, meaning, since its debut on radio on January 25, 1937, it has been on the air continuously for well over sixty years. On *The Guiding Light*, directed on radio by Joe Ainsley, Gil Gibbons, Harry Bubeck, and others, Mercedes played "Mary Rutledge," the daughter of a widowed minister, Reverend John Rutledge. Also heard on the program was Arthur Peterson (an actor who was in his twenties and not much older than Mercedes at the time, but who played her father) and Ruth Bailey (who played a popular character named "Rose Kransky" on the program). John Hodiak, Ed Prentiss, Theodore Goetz, Lyle Sudrow, Laurette Fillbrandt, Raymond Edward Johnson, and Sam Wanamaker, among many others, featured in the regular cast at various times as well.

Mercedes often had to play several different roles on one program — sisters, mothers, even whole families of both sexes. Looking back on these times, Mercedes said that working on radio gave her a great deal of freedom, since directors let her do "just anything she wanted to do on the shows."

Another soap opera on which Mercedes had a continuing role in her early years at NBC was *Girl Alone*. *Girl Alone* introduced a new breed of courageous heroine to radio audiences. Without the benefit of a male partner, the main character on this program faced the many adversities of life. When Mercedes joined the cast of *Girl Alone*, also heard on the program were Betty Winkler, Arthur Peterson, Kay Campbell, Fran Carlon, and Donald Briggs.

In an article published in the July 1951 edition of *Theater Arts* magazine, Arch Oboler summed up what it was like working in Chicago radio in the late 1930s: "Radio drama (as distinguished from theater plays boiled down to kilocycle size) began at midnight, in the middle of the thirties, on one of the upper floors of Chicago's Merchandise Mart." The 'pappy' was a rotund writer by the name of Willis Cooper, and the godfathers were an ex-instructor for a small Indiana University by the name of Strotz, and an ex-salesman by the name of Trammell. Chicago radio gestated other entertainment forms indigenous only to radio. Among them were the soap opera, that endless serialization of feminine woes [that] dipped *True Story* type literature and Procter and Gamble soap commercials into the American kitchen."

"But it was in the play especially written for radio," Oboler continued in the article, "that Chicago had its greatest national influence…. [T]here was created, by trial and many errors, a new art form that began with Don Ameche and the frothy *First Nighter*, and went through the horrific *Lights Out!* until it had matured to the point where, as a radio playwright, I was given the precious network time to produce, write, and direct this new type of play written for the ear and the listener's imagination alone."

"Chicago radio," Oboler went on to say, "became the focal point of a new breed of actors-for-radio; the mushrooming soap opera needed a large supply of voices. They came from all areas and sectors of show business; from stock company character veterans to morning-glory-eyed college play hopefuls, they were attracted to this honey-pot of actors needed daily, all week, pickup-your-experience-as-you-go-along, short rehearsal hours, no make-up, bring along your facile tongue, an equal facility for quick characterizations, and the ability to hold a script and read on sight with never a flub, a fluff, or a fumble. I remember the cold winds that blew down Michigan Avenue around CBS's Wrigley Building, and Mutual's [the now defunct Mutual network] Tribune Tower, then whistled upriver toward NBC's Merchandise Mart. It was a wind that brought a new approach and execution."

In addition to acting assignments on most of NBC's Chicago-based radio programs, Mercedes was also required by the network to answer the ever-increasing number of fan letters sent to her care of NBC. Many of the letters she received were addressed to "Mary Rutledge," the character she played on the popular daytime soap opera series *The Guiding Light*. Ever-increasing numbers of women were tuning in to hear *The Guiding Light* regularly five days a week. Apparently Mercedes played the role so convincingly that listeners had begun to think of Mary Rutledge as an actual person. Mercedes' busy work and school schedules would have been a full plate for any young woman, much less a girl still in her teens with all the normal social interests of any pubescent teenager. The fledgling actress had little time for dating, though she did occasionally go out with a good looking young radio announcer, actor, or junior executive she met at NBC.

By the time she graduated with honors from Mundelein College in June 1937, Mercedes had managed to put $1,150 in the bank, a princely sum for that time which would be the equivalent of about $10,000 in 2004. The young actress was so totally exhausted from the strain of working and being a full-time student that she decided to take a three week vacation in Guatemala after graduation in order to regain her strength before returning to work full time. After her vacation, she spent the next few years in Chicago working as a contract player with the National Broadcasting Company. Her voice became so familiar to listeners of the many soap opera series produced at NBC that a radio show commentator labeled her as "a sort of latter day Pearl White of the air lanes." Pearl White was a Silent Screen star from the early days of cinema, and had starred in numerous cliff-hanging serialized adventure films of the early twentieth century.

Freed from the exhausting rigor of trying to balance an acting career with a full-time student schedule, Mercedes finally found time to enjoy a more active social life. She moved into her own apartment in downtown Chicago, in spite of her mother's objections, and began to feel, for the first time in her life, that she was finally in control of her own destiny.

The program director who guided Mercedes' career during her early years at NBC was Sid Strotz, the man who had discovered her when she was performing with the verse choir at Mundelein College. Strotz became Mercedes' mentor. He was, according to everyone who knew him, a very good looking man. "The handsomest man I had ever met," Mercedes later said of the forty-something Strotz. "He was always bronzed from the sun, had wonderful black hair that was beginning to turn gray, a neat mustache that made him look a bit like film actor Clark Gable, graceful hands, and the kind of swagger any convent bred girl could see had *sin* written all over it." She was a young woman in her late teens, and then early twenties, and this handsome, mature man told her he would teach her all she needed to know. Apparently, this is exactly what he did, both in regards to her radio career and her private life. "He taught me the ABCs and the XYZs of radio technique and I ate it up," Mercedes admitted. The last time Mercedes saw her handsome mentor was several years later, when both were working in New York City. They briefly resumed the personal relationship they had enjoyed in Chicago several years before, but both decided it would probably be best to terminate their friendship and parted company once and for all after a few months together in New York.

When she was twenty-five years old in 1941, Mercedes met a young man closer to her own age who became the center of her personal life for the next several years. His name was William Fifield, and, at the time, he was an announcer-in-training at

NBC who wanted to become a writer. Fifield was good looking, boyishly enthusiastic, romantically idealistic, extremely intelligent and, like her father, a charmingly self-assured man and a master raconteur. "A great Tolstoyan terror" is what Mercedes called him in her 1981 autobiography, but by that time she did not mean it as a compliment. Fifield was, much to Mercedes' mother's horror, the son of a Congregationalist minister. A Protestant! When Mercedes and Bill decided to marry in a civil ceremony, after a whirlwind three-week affair, Marie McCambridge declared her daughter "dead," and told everyone that she had just "held [Mercedes'] funeral." The forgiving, but never forgetting, Marie McCambridge, however, eventually "resurrected" her daughter, and the two made a sort of a cautious "peace" that lasted until Marie died many years later.

The name "Mercedes Fifield" did not sound quite right to the young thespian, and since she had already established herself as an actress of some note as "Mercedes McCambridge," she decided to retain that name for professional purposes. The very attributes that had attracted Mercedes to Bill Fifield when she first met him in the drug store at the Merchandise Mart in 1939 became the very things that eventually disenchanted her just a few short years later.

Even though she was acting on practically every soap opera series broadcast from Chicago in the late 1930s and early 1940s (and there were many), and was heard regularly on several of NBC's prime time programs as well, Mercedes did everything she could to try to be as good a wife to her new husband as was possible. The young couple decided that Bill would stay at home and write the novel they hoped would make him famous, and she would continue to work as a radio actress at NBC. Mercedes tried to cook the couple's meals whenever she had a night off, and attempted to keep their apartment as clean as she possibly could, but soon realized that she was a miserable failure as a housewife, resulting in the Fifields hiring a housekeeper to cook for them and keep their home clean. In 1941, Mercedes and Bill decided to leave Chicago and go to Mexico on a vacation. Soon after the couple arrived in Mexico, Mercedes discovered that she was pregnant. Although the young couple continued to daydream about his writing plays in which she would star on Broadway, their money situation soon became a problem, and, after much deliberation (and several months South of the Border), they decided it was time for Mercedes to return to work. Instead of going back to Chicago, however, the couple chose to go to Hollywood, where Mercedes hoped she would be able to obtain work in "the Movies," as well as continuing as an NBC staff actress on radio.

Never a woman to stand on ceremony, as soon as she arrived in Hollywood she lost no time getting down to the business of establishing herself as a ready and able, willing-to-work radio actress. Before long she was acting on many radio shows broadcast from the West Coast.

Mercedes was pregnant and working on *The Rudy Vallee Sealtest Hour* on Christmas Eve in 1941. Only a few weeks earlier the United States had declared war on Japan after that country attacked the U.S. fleet at Pearl Harbor in Hawaii on December 7, 1941. The special guest on Rudy Vallee's program that Christmas Eve

When she was an NBC staff actress in Hollywood in 1941, Mercedes posed for a publicity photograph that demonstrated different leg wear that could be substituted for nylon stockings, since nylon was needed for the war effort in Europe, even though the United States did not enter the war until after December 7, 1941, when the Japanese bombed Pearl Harbor. She is seen here with three other actresses under contract to NBC in the early 1940s. Left to right: Mercedes (wearing cotton stockings), Sybil Chism (sporting lisle socks), and Martha Tilton and Gloria Blondell (applying pancake makeup to their legs) (Photofest).

was the prominent stage and film actor John Barrymore. Mercedes was very obviously "heavy with child" at the time, and members of the show's orchestra placed bets as to whether she would give birth to her expected baby while the program was still on the air. The always-inebriated Barrymore was fascinated that the pregnant young woman about to have a baby at any minute would risk working at a time that was so close to the "blessed event," and told her he admired her for her courage. That evening Mercedes was performing in a sketch that spoofed Charles Dickens' *A Christmas Carol*. Barrymore was playing Scrooge, Vallee was narrating the sketch, and Mercedes was playing, of all things considering her girth, the part of "Tiny Tim." During the broadcast, the audience giggled at the sight of the obviously pregnant actress playing someone called "Tiny." She made it through the performance, and at the end of the broadcast went home to help her husband decorate a small Christmas tree he had bought that afternoon.

While reaching up to hang an ornament on the tree, Mercedes' labor pains began. Four-and-a-half hours after having been heard by millions of listeners on the Rudy Vallee show, she gave birth to her first child at the Cedars of Lebanon Hospital in Los Angeles. It was seventeen minutes before midnight, and Mercedes' thoughts turned to the "Blessed Virgin" and the celebrated birth of the Christ child as she drifted off into unconsciousness after having been given a sedative. The next morning she awoke to learn that she had given birth to a healthy, seven-pound baby boy the Fifields named "John Lawrence." Among the many telegrams she received at the hospital on Christmas Day congratulating her on the birth of her son was one that particularly delighted her. The telegram read: "Congratulations to you and all the other Wise Men. Imagine their surprise when they found that the star they came to see ... was you." It was from John Barrymore. Every year on his birthday, Mercedes told her son, that story about the night he was born, and she did so until John was well into his adolescence.

After she recuperated from the ordeal of giving birth, Mercedes had little difficulty resuming her radio career, since she had already firmly established herself as a major radio acting talent in both Chicago and Hollywood. At the time, *Radio Mirror* magazine previewed a new program that would air the week after Mercedes gave birth to her son. It was called *Arch Oboler's Everyman's Theater*, and it was being broadcast from Hollywood, where Oboler had relocated and begun working for NBC. "*Everyman's Theater*," the announcement read, "will star Mercedes McCambridge and Howard Duff in 'Papa Johnson,' on January 1, 1941." The article continued, "According to NBC, two outstanding radio actor *discoveries* are in this comedy, which is about babies. We are not acquainted with the work of Howard Duff; perhaps he is indeed an 'actor discovery,' and if such is the case his appearance in this play is interesting news. We are inclined to take with a grain of Hollywood salt the reference to Mercedes McCambridge as a 'discovery.' Mercedes went to Hollywood chiefly because her writer-husband had business there. The dark-eyed, vivacious colleen may well turn out to be a motion picture discovery, but she is certainly no newcomer to radio listeners. She was a popular ingénue, comedienne, tragedienne and all-around actress in Chicago several years before going to the West Coast: she even played quite frequently in the *Lights Out!* horror shows of Arch Oboler."

Soon after she arrived in Hollywood in 1939, Mercedes had been hired by producer-writer Carlton E. Morse to appear on his popular *I Love a Mystery* radio program. On Morse's series, McCambridge was often the only woman heard on the program, except for fellow NBC contract actress Gloria Blondell, who was occasionally heard in the role of the main characters' secretary, "Gerry Booker." Mercedes played all of the major female featured roles in several of the program's episodic adventures. To devotees of what has been dubbed "Old Time Radio," the *I Love a Mystery* series is legendary, and remains almost as popular with fans of the show today as it was when the program first aired in the late 1930s, and then again during its revival in the late '40s. Today, fans of this radio series listen to each and every cassette, record and CD they can uncover, and do so with as much enthusiasm and

Listeners were curious to see what their favorite radio performers looked like in the late 1930s and early 1940s, and NBC obligingly released glamour photographs of their young contract players to radio fan magazines. Mercedes is pictured above in one such photograph taken in 1941 when she worked for the NBC Blue network in Hollywood (Photofest).

excitement as those who initially listened to the programs when first broadcast over sixty years ago. To advocates of the *I Love a Mystery* series, Mercedes, who was heard on both the original and the later revival of the program, is a legendary figure, as are her *I Love a Mystery* fellow performers Michael Raffetto, Barton Yarborough and Walter Paterson, who starred on the 1939–1941 series, and Russell Thorson, Jim Boles and Tony Randall, who took on the roles of A-1 Detective Agency private eyes Jack Packard, Doc Long and Reggie Yorke during the 1949–1953 revival. Years after she worked on *I Love a Mystery*, Mercedes said that of all the hundreds of radio shows she worked on in the 1930s, '40s and '50s, this is the series most talked about by those who recognized her in public.

I Love a Mystery's creator, writer and director, Carlton E. Morse, recalled (in Martin Grams' book *The I Love a Mystery Companion*) McCambridge's early years on the series: "Mercedes McCambridge came out to Hollywood from Chicago, and the first thing she did was drop in and say, 'I want to work on your show.' As a result of that she became an almost permanent member of the cast doing various characters in each show. A heroine or a character or whatever her [part] was. It got to the point when we were getting to the end of one show, she'd drop in at the office and we'd talk and she'd ask, 'Do you have any idea for a new character? Any idea of what you'd like me to do?' And she'd give me some of her little dialects. One time she was a thirteen-year-old girl and did a beautiful job of it. She gave me the idea [for] a character and I wrote [a part] for that character. One of the best characterizations she gave me was of a drunken woman and so I did 'The Widow with the Amputation' based on this woman in the South Pacific when the Japanese were invading the [islands] over there. It fit in with the war [that] was going on at the same time. We had this little problem on an island in which this British woman was trying to save something. It turned out to be one of the best shows we ever did ... I think."

Mercedes remembered her early appearances on *I Love a Mystery* in the 1930s and early '40s as chaotic but always great fun. "Terrible things happened on *Mystery*," she related in Grams' *I Love a Mystery* book. "Honestly, Barton Yarborough, who played Doc, was an imp! A delightful imp ... but maddening sometimes. And [once] right in the middle of a very dramatic speech, he [came] by and set fire to my script. [He] just [lit] the bottom of my page and walked away and left me there. And I'm trying to emote and I'm trying to get the flame to go out [with] my bare hands and he'd [be] over in the corner laughing. Carlton [Morse] was in the control room laughing and he loved it. We had fun!"

While in Hollywood, Mercedes, in addition to Arch Oboler's and Carlton E. Morse's programs, was also featured on other popular NBC radio comedy-variety shows that starred singer Bing Crosby, comedians Bob Hope and Jack Benny, and radio personality and film actor Don Ameche. She also regularly appeared on the children's adventure series *The Adventures of Red Ryder*, playing various female roles. She once even played cowboy Red Ryder's young Indian boy companion, Little Beaver, when the young actor (Tommy Cook) playing the part had to leave the studio to relieve himself just before the live broadcast was to begin. Mercedes saved the day by stepping up to the microphone and reading his part, as well as her own.

In Hollywood, Bill Fifield grew a beard, began looking and acting appropriately poetic, and continued to cloister himself in his office writing his "great American novel." He was gradually becoming the Bohemian artist Mercedes had unadvisedly believed she wanted to be married to. Mercedes continued to work steadily on radio in Hollywood until the autumn of 1942, when she was offered an acting job on a hit NBC show that originated from New York City. The program was called *Abie's Irish Rose*, and Mercedes was asked to replace actress Betty Winkler, who had a conflict with another radio show in which she starred. The timing seemed right for Mercedes and Bill, who were experiencing increasing difficulties in their marriage, to pull up stakes and leave Hollywood, with perhaps a chance to eventually work together on Broadway, the mecca of the American Theater. They also thought they might be able to patch up their faltering marriage if they were in new surroundings and presented with new challenges that they could face together.

When Mercedes worked as a contract actress for the National Broadcasting Company's Blue Network in Hollywood in 1941, she featured on radio programs that starred some of the biggest names in show business: Jack Benny, Rudy Vallee, Bing Crosby and Bob Hope, to name just a few (Photofest).

Before Mercedes left Hollywood to go to New York, she appeared on two more Arch Oboler series, *Everyman's Theater* and *Plays for America*. The *Everyman's Theater* production, a play called "Chicago, New York," starred movie queen Joan Blondell. Along with Mercedes, the cast included Hans Conried and Joseph Kearns, two often-featured Oboler cast members whom the actress had worked with many times in Chicago, and who had also relocated to Hollywood. "Chicago, New York" was about a stenographer who had to get into a typing pool in order to obtain the wartime food cards necessary for her survival in a war-ravaged city. The girl had to degrade herself more and more to provide for her family, and especially her nagging mother. The play must have given the young Mercedes McCambridge some food for thought, since she was the major breadwinner for herself, her husband, and her son, and was a major contributor to her parents' income at the time as well.

Shortly before Mercedes departed for New York City in April 1942 to star on NBC's *Abie's Irish Rose*, the network arranged for her to pose for a full-page publicity photo spread that appeared in the *Movie-Radio Guide* magazine. The article showed Mercedes taking a tour of a merchant marine ship at the U.S. Maritime Training School in Southern California in a publicity layout to promote Arch Oboler's radio play "The S. S. Ugly Duck," one of the programs on his new *Plays for America*

By 1942, World War II was raging in Europe and the Pacific, and Hollywood actors did what they could to help with the war effort by appearing on patriotic radio programs. Film star James Stewart, who had enlisted in the United States Army Air Force, was heard in a wartime drama, "A Letter at Midnight," presented on *Arch Oboler's Plays for America* series. The drama featured NBC conract actress Mercedes McCambridge, a frequent leading lady on many Oboler radio programs, as Stewart's co-star (Photofest).

series. The major characters in Oboler's play were merchant marines and their families. The Merchant Marines were the "little glamorized heroes who carry consignments of oil through submarine infested waters," the article stated. Photos in the layout showed Mercedes taken through a porthole, standing on the deck of a battle ship with Oboler, two merchant marines and Lt. Commander A. C. Richmond, inspecting equipment with a seaman, and looking at engine room valves on the ship. The article was called "Research for 'S. S. Ugly Duck.'"

Before Mercedes, her baby, and the Fifield's African-American housekeeper left Hollywood and traveled to New York, Bill went ahead to find the family a proper place to live in the city. Mercedes daydreamed about dwelling high in the sky in a lofty and lovely apartment with a breathtaking view of the Manhattan skyline. When she arrived in New York, after a long and difficult train trip from the West to the East coast with a crying baby and a maid who spent the entire trip regurgitating because she suffered from motion sickness, she discovered that Bill had rented a small row house in the Bronx, a borough of the city well north of the glamorous Manhattan's city center. Bill had felt that the house would be a more suitable, quiet place for him to work on his novel. The house, according to Mercedes in her autobiography, could have been the place Archie and Edith Bunker inhabited in the 1970s TV situation comedy series *All in the Family*. In addition to its not being particularly pleasing aesthetically, the row house was a considerable distance from Studio 6A at 30 Rockefeller Plaza in Manhattan, where NBC's *Abie's Irish Rose* was being broadcast from each week. The subway trip from Manhattan to the Bronx, followed by a short bus ride to the neighborhood where her house was located, took an hour. Since the second program for the West Coast ended at ten o'clock in the evening, and the director spent time critiquing the actors' performances after the show, it was often well after one a.m. before the exhausted Mercedes finally fell into bed next to her already soundly sleeping "Tolstoy." She was the star of a successful prime-time radio program, and she was living in an atmosphere she felt befitted a struggling neophyte.

Abie's Irish Rose had been a long-running hit comedy play on Broadway before becoming a popular radio situation comedy series. The radio show was directed by Axel Gruenberg. In *The Golden Years of Radio Directors*, edited by Ira Skutch, Gruenberg said of *Abie's Irish Rose*: "It was an interesting experience. Ann Nichols, who had written the original Broadway play, also wrote the weekly radio show scripts. We'd rehearse on Wednesday afternoon and do a run through with a full studio audience, just to see where the laughs came. Then on Thursday, I would meet with Ann [Nichols] and we would go through what changes ought to be made. We also had an audience on Saturday, when we broadcast the show, because we needed the laughs. We'd have a different audience for the West Coast repeat, and do it all over again. Because *Abie's Irish Rose* was well known as a successful play on Broadway, people would flock to it to be in the audiences at the broadcasts." It was a very busy Saturday schedule for the show's female lead, especially since she lived so far uptown in the Bronx. Mercedes starred in the show (only one of the many radio programs she contributed to at the time), for almost a year. By the time she left the series, she had become one of New York's busiest and most sought after radio actresses.

Over the next several years, Mercedes McCambridge was heard on many of the most memorable shows of radio's so-called "Golden Age," the 1930s, 1940s and 1950s. She won the title role (over hundreds of other actresses who auditioned for the part) on the popular daytime serial drama *Big Sister*, which continued for the next several years. She was also regularly heard on such soap operas as *The Second Mrs. Burton*, *Betty and Bob*, *The Romance of Helen Trent*, *Stella Dallas*, *John's Other Wife*, *Hilda Hope MD*, *Joyce Jordan Girl Intern*, *David Harum*, and *This Is Nora Drake*, as well as on the *Dick Tracy* children's adventure serial, playing several different female characters on the program. In addition, she regularly appeared on such popular prime-time programs broadcast from New York as *Grand Central Station*, *The Adventures of Philo Vance*, *The Adventures of the Thin Man*, *Gangbusters*, *Nero Wolfe*, *The Adventures of Bulldog Drummond*, *Carrington Playhouse*, *Quick as a Flash*, *Inner Sanctum*

Mercedes was flushed with excitement in 1942 when she reported to NBC's Rockefeller Center studios in New York City to take over the leading role of Rose on NBC's hit situation comedy series *Abie's Irish Rose.* She is seen here (left) with NBC receptionist Patricia O'Hara (Photofest).

Mysteries, The Philip Morris Playhouse, and many others throughout the 1940s, securing her place in show business as one of the most successful and well-known radio actresses in America.

The two soap opera series that Mercedes became most identified with during these years were *Big Sister* and *This Is Nora Drake,* which featured her in major, long-

In 1942 and 1943, *Abie's Irish Rose* was one of the most popular prime-time radio programs on the air. The stars of the show, Mercedes, who played Rose, and Richard Coogan, who played her young husband Abie, are seen here in a November 10, 1942, photograph, reading the hundreds of letters from fans that arrived at NBC daily. They personally answered as many of the letters as they could, with the help of the NBC office staff (Photofest).

running roles. On *Big Sister*, Mercedes played "Ruth Evans," the eldest sibling of two young ladies who apparently needed her wise and moral guidance in order to merely get through their everyday lives. Also heard on this series (directed by Mitchell Grayson, Theodore T. Huston, and Thomas Vieter, Jr., at various times) were Peggy Conklin, Dorothy McGuire, Arnold Moss, Ian Martin, Arlene Francis, Berry Kroeger, Ralph Bell, Anne Burr, Richard Widmark, Richard Kollmar, and others. *Big Sister's* announcers, either Hugh Marlowe or Nelson Case, always began each show by saying, "Ninety-nine and forty-four one-hundredths percent pure ... enjoyment! That's *Big Sister*" and the series' theme music, "Valse Bluette" by Dirgo, played on an organ, would swell before the daily drama began.

It was while appearing on *Big Sister* in the early 1940s that Mercedes first became friendly with fellow radio actress Elspeth Eric, with whom she developed a life-long friendship. Eric, who, like Mercedes, was one of radio's busiest actresses throughout the 1940s, had made her Broadway debut in the play *Small Miracle* in 1934 and had

In New York in the 1940s, Mercedes played the title role on one of radio's most popular soap opera series, CBS's *Big Sister*. During World War II, stars of successful radio shows often were asked to pose for "cheesecake" photographs that members of the Armed Forces could pin up in their barracks to remind them of what they were fighting for back home. Mercedes was happy to oblige, and the "leggy" picture above appeared in the ***Radio Mirror*** fan magazine (Photofest).

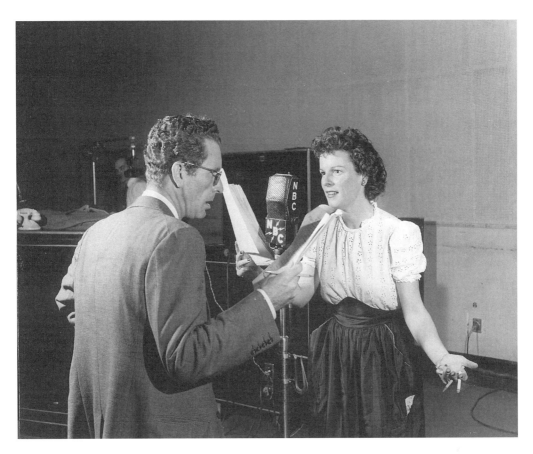

Above: Throughout the 1940s, Mercedes McCambridge was one of the busiest radio actresses in America. Heard on hundreds of programs each month, she frequently featured on such prime-time mystery series as *Inner Sanctum Mysteries, Gang Busters, The Adventures of Bulldog Drummond, The Adventures of the Thin Man* and, in the photograph above, *Philo Vance.* She is seen here during a July 30, 1945, broadcast of the *Philo Vance* program with actor Maurice Mells (Photofest).

Right: In the mid 1940s, Mercedes developed a close friendship with fellow radio actress Elspeth Eric (pictured at right), who, in addition to her sccessful radio career, also appeared in several Broadway plays. Eric frequently played gun molls, shop girls, ladies with criminal intent, and whining wives on various radio programs, such as *Gang Busters* and *The Mollee Mystery Theater.* She also played the title role on the *Joyce Jordan, Girl Intern* soap opera series for several seasons (Photofest).

subsequently appeared on Broadway in *Dead End* and *Too Many Heroes* in 1937, and *Margin for Error* in 1939. Mercedes was duly impressed with Eric's ability to balance her radio and stage acting careers, which was one of McCambridge's ultimate ambitions, and it was Eric's guidance and advice that eventually led to Mercedes fulfilling that goal.

On *This Is Nora Drake* (directed by Dee Engelbach, Art Hanna, and then Charles Irving), Mercedes played a popular character named "Peg Martinson." Also heard on the series were Elspeth Eric, Alan Hewitt, Everett Sloane, Ralph Bell, Leon Janney, Lucille Wall, Roger DeKoven, and Charlotte Holland (as the title character). The "sudsy" opening of *This Is Nora Drake*, which was announced by either Bill Cullen or Peter Roberts, stated, "*This Is Nora Drake*, a modern story seen through the window of a woman's heart."

Many of the prime-time programs Mercedes worked on regularly in the 1940s, featured openings that were equally as memorable as those of her soap opera series. *The Adventures of Bulldog Drummond*, a mystery/detective series, for example, began, "Out of the London fog and into his American adventures comes Bulldog Drummond!" while the sound of a fog horn bleated in the background. Himan Brown's *Inner Sanctum Mysteries*, on which Mercedes frequently performed, offered one of radio's most famous openings. First came the sound of a squeaking door (the program has earned the nicknames "*The Squeaking Door*" and "*The Creaking Door*"), and then the program's host, Raymond Edward Johnson (later Paul McGrath), said in a chillingly sinister, sly voice, "Good evening, friends, this is your host [Raymond] welcoming you into the Inner Sanctum!" In Martin Grams' book *Inner Sanctum Mysteries: Behind the Creaking Door*, producer-director Himan Brown says of Mercedes' appearances on *Inner Sanctum* in the 1940s: "Mercedes McCambridge was wonderful. She wanted to appear in every show, because in those days it paid the rent for a lot of people and McCambridge was not very rich. One show I didn't call her. She called me and said, 'What happened? I didn't get a call for *Inner Sanctum*.' And I said, 'Well, we don't have any women on this week. It's an all male cast.' And she said, 'What difference does that make? I'm coming and I'm playing an elevator operator.'" Brown said that he could not recall if she ever played an elevator operator, but he remembered that she did show up to play a small role in that week's show.

In 1944, actor Walter Huston, the father of director John Huston and a great admirer of Mercedes' work on radio, suggested that McCambridge would be a perfect choice to play the tomboy Jo in a remake of Louisa Mae Alcott's classic novel *Little Women*, which Metro Goldwyn Mayer Studios was planning to film in Hollywood. Huston arranged for Mercedes to take a screen test for the role at MGM. The test proved to be a great disappointment to Mercedes and to MGM. Not pleased with what they called her "flaring nostrils," the MGM makeup department decided to try to restrict her nostril movement with some sort of metal clips, and subsequently made a plaster cast of her face. Apparently no one at MGM was impressed with the actresses' "new" nostrils either, and Mercedes never heard from MGM again. Five years later, Metro Goldwyn Mayer did indeed film their remake of *Little Women*, with

June Allyson playing Jo, and Elizabeth Taylor, Janet Lee and Margaret O'Brien playing Jo's sisters (all four actresses were contract players at MGM).

Mercedes hadn't realized it at the time, but a film actor's career was all about what they looked like and who sold the most tickets, facts that were driven home to her when *Little Women* was released in 1949, with its cast of pretty, young and very popular contract actresses. Fortunately, another chance to prove herself as a film actress had, by that time, already been set in motion … but more on this later in this book. The greatest advantage Mercedes enjoyed as a result of the *Little Women* debacle was that the actress became a friend and oft-time associate of the gifted actor-director Orson Welles, with whom she had worked before on radio but now became better acquainted with through his friendship with the Huston family.

Orson Welles, a child prodigy, was born in 1915 in Kinosha, Wisconsin. At his mother's insistence, Orson, who was a gifted writer, painter and actor, attended the prestigious Todd School at Woodstock, which catered to artistically talented youngsters. At the Todd School, Welles directed and starred in classic works of the theater, including many of the plays of William Shakespeare. When he was sixteen years old, Welles traveled to Ireland, where he made his professional acting debut at the Gate Theater in Dublin. Before he was twenty years old, Welles, who returned to the United States after making a name for himself as an actor in Ireland, was appearing on Broadway and starring on radio's popular *The Shadow* mystery program. With producer and friend John Houseman, Orson formed "The Mercury Theater," a repertory theatrical company in New York City. The Mercury Theater won praise from theater critics for its creatively inventive productions, and in 1939 the Columbia Broadcasting System brought Welles' Mercury Theater to radio as *The Mercury Theater of the Air* in a weekly hour-long dramatic anthology series. The program enjoyed enormous success and led to Welles being signed by the RKO motion picture studio to produce, direct and star in his first film, *Citizen Kane*, which ultimately became a film classic and established Welles' reputation as one of show businesses most creative geniuses. It was not until many years later, however, that Mercedes and Orson worked together in films. She did, though, enjoy a close friendship with Welles, and acted on several radio programs with the man the Hollywood Press labeled "a boy genius."

By 1945, Mercedes' marriage to Bill Fifield had disintegrated into a contentious, bickering affair, and the couple, for all intents and purposes, had almost totally lost touch with each other. "My marriage to Bill," Mercedes wrote in her book *The Two of Us*, "had fallen apart and nobody thought it was a tragedy. Except me. I hated the failure." Bill was totally absorbed in his writing, and Mercedes had to admit that she had little time, because of her busy radio acting career, to be much of a wife to him, or even much of a proper mother to her young son John, who was being raised by the Fifield's housekeeper. "The only good part about the bad times," Mercedes said, "is that I know they couldn't go on forever. But that means the good times aren't about to last very long either. I believe we pay for everything, and there have been periods when I seem to have piled up a sizable backlog of credit."

When she returned to New York in 1947, after touring Europe and her unsuccessful attempt to establish herself as an actress in London, Mercedes went right back to work on radio. One of the first programs she appeared on upon her return to the U.S. was her old friend Orson Welles' *Mercury Summer Theater of the Air* series. Welles, who had become world-famous as the director and star of the much-publicized *Mercury Theater of the Air* 1939 Halloween broadcast of "War of the Worlds," had frightened many people into believing that the United States was actually being attacked by alien invaders. The broadcast led to his directing, and starring in, his first motion picture, the classic *Citizen Kane.*

It was at this time, however, during World War II and in spite of her troubled personal life, that Mercedes finally realized her dream of being cast in a Broadway-bound stageplay. The play was not, however, as the Fifields had hoped, one written by Bill. Mercedes made her professional stage acting debut playing a nurse, Sister Margaret, in a wartime drama called *The Hasty Heart,* by John Patrick. Mercedes must have felt the author's name was some sort of good omen since her father's name was also John Patrick, but, unfortunately, she never got to play the role of the nurse on Broadway. She was fired during the play's out-of-town tryouts after only nine performances, and replaced by an actress named Anne Burr, who went on to essay the role on Broadway. The director, Bretaigne Windust (nicknamed "Windy" by people in the Theatre), knew that Mercedes had been struggling with the role because it was the first time she had been in a play since her college days. He called her performance "pregnant with warmth," and sadistically added that until she gave birth to that quality, she was "as ugly to watch onstage as a woman large with child." In *The Two of Us*, Mercedes wrote, "During rehearsals for *The Hasty Heart* I never doubted for a minute that I was good in the part. I worked very hard. And on the ninth day, I was fired. The Mssrs Lindsay and Crouse [the producers] were disappointed in me. I was green and inexperienced. It was indeed my first part on the stage since college and I knew they were right. Years later I asked the director what he had meant about my being 'pregnant with warmth but ugly to watch.' He didn't remember having said it. The play had gone on without me to become a smash hit."

Undaunted, Mercedes, who continued to work constantly in radio, auditioned for Broadway stage plays whenever a suitable role appeared. The same year she was fired from *The Hasty Heart*, 1944, she won a part in another Broadway-bound play called *Hope for the Best*, which starred film actor Franchot Tone. Mercedes was having lunch at the Stork Club in New York with writer Sidney Sheldon when playwright Marc Connolly saw her and sent a message to her table asking that she pay him a visit at the Ambassador Hotel the next day to read for a part in a new play he had written which was headed for Broadway. She auditioned for Connelly and got the part in *Hope for the Best*. During a pre–Broadway tryout in Washington, D.C., on New Year's Eve, 1944, Mercedes received excellent reviews for her work, but once again was fired before the play ever reached "the Great White Way." The producers were concerned that the play, which was not doing particularly well at the box office, needed a "name" actress in the major female role. They felt that a female film star would give the play a better chance of paying off its investors and making a profit. Mercedes was disappointed when she was replaced by the well known film actress Jane Wyatt, whom the producers had originally wanted for the role, and who had suddenly found herself free to accept the part when a film deal fell through. About her firing, Mercedes wrote, "When *Hope for the Best* was playing its last pre–Broadway tryout in Washington, D.C., two leading drama critics in that city, Jay Carmody and John Maynard, wrote entire articles about my being given the heave-ho. I bought a dozen copies of their papers and when I left the theatre after my last performance, there were people at the stage door who cheered when I came out into the alley and one lady gave me an orchid. I caught the late train back to New York."

Disappointed, but not defeated, Mercedes had better luck the following year when she was cast in a play called *A Place of Her Own*, by Elliott Nugent. The play did indeed make it to Broadway — with Mercedes still in the cast. It opened on April 2, 1945, but closed after just a few performances due to poor box-office receipts. Of this experience Mercedes wrote in her book *The Two of Us*, "The morning after the opening in New York the *New York Times* review was headed 'Eviction Notice.' We closed after only five performances.

This was followed by another stage role in Arthur Koestler's play *Twilight Bar*, but this play directed by the esteemed Broadway director George Abbott failed to make it as far as Broadway and closed out of town. In *The Two of Us*, Mercedes wrote, "Abbott said he thought there were about seventy-five laughs in the piece that we weren't getting out of it. I never thought it was meant to be a funny play. We closed in Philadelphia without ever seeing New York."

The next year Mercedes was cast in yet another Broadway-bound play, Sam and Bella Spewack's *Woman Bites Dog*. Also featured in the cast were Frank Lovejoy, E. G. Marshall and Kirk Douglas. When the play did indeed open on Broadway, it was not very well received by the critics, and it closed four days after reaching New York in April 1946. Fortunately, Mercedes was spared the disappointment of appearing in another unsuccessful production that closed after only a few performances on Broadway, or never even made it to Broadway at all. She withdrew from the *Woman Bites Dog* cast, and was replaced by actress Elaine Stritch.

McCambridge had been having difficulty commuting between Philadelphia and New York, where she continued to work on her high-paying radio soap opera series *Big Sister*, and decided either the play or her active radio acting career would have to go. It was either big money for *Big Sister*, or the chance to appear on Broadway in what she felt was going to be yet another flop play. *Big Sister*, and the many other well paying acting jobs Mercedes had on radio, finally won out over Broadway.

Apart from her stage acting disappointments, Mercedes was riding high as a

In 1946, Mercedes was cast in Sam and Bella Spewack's less-than-successful Broadway-bound comedy *Woman Bites Dog*. Mercedes, sitting, is pictured above in a scene from the play with fellow actors (from the left) Dudley Sadler, Kirk Douglas, Ida Heineman, and Taylor Holmes. Mercedes withdrew from *Woman Bites Dog* when it reached Broadway and was replaced by actress Elaine Stritch. The play closed after only four performances (April 17 through April 20, 1946) at the Belasco Theater in New York City (Photofest).

radio actress during World War II. "Radio paid the bills during the interim of my stabs at artistic achievement," Mercedes said. "Radio saved the lives of many actors who were 'between shows.'"

In 1946, less than one year after the war ended, an article about her successful career as a radio actress appeared in the September 24 issue of *Life* magazine. Many articles written about Mercedes and the various radio shows she was acting on had been published in various radio fan magazines, such as *Radio Mirror* and *Radio Guide*, throughout the 1940s, but this was the first time she — or any other radio actress— had ever had an article written about them that appeared in a national, popular and well circulated general news magazine like *Life. Life* magazine usually featured articles about prominent political and literary figures, as well as successful film and stage performers, or offered photo stories about people and events that were currently

Pictured standing in front of an ABC microphone in 1946, Mercedes was one of the busiest radio actresses in America. Now a freelance actress, she appeared on hundreds of programs that were heard on all of the major radio networks — CBS, NBC and Mutual, as well as on the new network, ABC, which had formerly been NBC's Red network (Photofest).

"in the news." The article, an impressive three-page photo layout, showed Mercedes, in a black leotard, posed dramatically in an imagined scene from the radio play "Specter of the Rose," on which she had been heard the previous season. In addition, a series of eight small photographs depicted the many moods and emotions she had conveyed when heard on the radio play "Portrait of a Girl" on *The Carrington Playhouse* program. There also appeared two photographs of Mercedes and her young son John frolicking in a stream and jumping into a pile of hay at a farm she had rented in Brewster, New York, the summer before the article was published. The article, titled "Mercedes McCambridge, Radio Star Shows Her Versatility," said, "Miss McCambridge, wife of a writer and mother of a four-year-old son, is currently appearing in a staggering number of radio programs— among them the *Big Sister* soap opera series, *Gangbusters, Inner Sanctum, Dick Tracy, Bulldog Drummond*, and *The Adventures of the Thin Man*."

William Fifield's name was not mentioned in the article, nor was he pictured. The Fifields had, in truth, already separated long before 1946, and were in the process of filing for a divorce. "At the beginning of the war I married a boy I had known for three weeks," Mercedes said. "When he came home after it was over, we were strangers. The marriage spattered and died." In spite of the Fifields' marital difficulties, little John Lawrence had matured into a good-natured and sensitive little boy. In her book *The Two of Us*, Mercedes said, "When he was in nursery school, John's teacher wrote me a note saying that she had particularly noticed John's gentle concern for people. It bothered him to see beggars and very old ladies. I wondered about the hurt he would know in his life."

In 1944, Bill, who declared himself a conscientious objector during World War II, had been obliged by the government to work with the American Friends Committee as an attendant at a municipal hospital for the insane in Philadelphia, or risk being sent to prison for draft evasion. The separation had proven to be, as previously stated, a permanent one, and by the mid–1940s Mercedes had already moved into a lovely, sublet midtown apartment on East 57th Street, where she lived with her son and loyal African-American maid.

In the summer of 1946, Mercedes was hired to appear on Orson Welles' *Mercury Summer Theater* series, which was a revival of his previously successful *Mercury Theater of the Air*, a program that had been one of radio's sensational successes from the late 1930s. The original series had introduced many listeners to such classic works of literature as Stevenson's *Treasure Island*, Stoker's *Dracula*, and Dickens' *A Tale of Two Cities* (not to mention H.G. Wells' *War of the Worlds*, featured in the famous *Mercury Theater* broadcast of 1938). Welles was a great admirer of Mercedes' work on radio, and at one point labeled her "the world's greatest living radio actress." Welles hired Mercedes to act in a new radio play titled "Life with Adam," to be aired for the new summer series on July 19, 1946. "Life with Adam" had previously been broadcast in Canada, and was to be directed by and star a young Canadian named Fletcher Markle, who had written the play and to whom Welles had turned over his directorial reins for the week's broadcast. Markle arrived at the rehearsal for his play with a Canadian actor named John Drainie, and a Canadian leading lady, Grace Matthews (who a year later replaced Mercedes on the *Big Sister* series). Markle had previously worked with them in the Canadian production of his radio play. During the first reading of the script, Mercedes realized that the part she had been assigned was being drastically cut by Markle. By the end of the rehearsal she was left with a mere two lines to say. Although she found Markle physically attractive, and was certainly impressed by his directorial skills, she was furious at his arrogance; and when the broadcast ended, she stormed out of the studio without saying a word to him. When Markle, who had been partying all night after the broadcast called her at four a.m. to thank her for her contribution to the program, Mercedes angrily slammed her phone down on its receiver without even answering him.

By the autumn of 1946, Mercedes had become disenchanted with her personal and professional life in New York, despite the fact that she was one of the most successful actresses in radio at the time. Armed with the *Life* magazine article, she decided to pull up stakes. After spending some time in the Caribbean Islands, and touring the European continent with her son, she intended to resettle in Great Britain, where

Canadian Fletcher Markle was the producer, director and sometimes leading male player of CBS's *Studio One* and *Ford Theater* dramatic anthology radio series from 1947 through 1949. Markle and McCambridge became romantically involved while she was appearing on these programs, and were later married (Photofest).

she hoped to find work on the British stage. In a *Films in Review* article about the actress that was published years later in May 1965, McCambridge said of this time in her life: "I didn't like what was happening around me. Analysts couches, nose-bob jobs and pills…. I thought there must be more than that." The article continued: "She sold her fur coat and took off, with her son, on a year-and-a-half trip around

Europe." The actress eventually wrote a book about her European travels with her son that was called *The Two of Us*, which was published in Great Britain in 1960.

On a radio interview conducted many years later by actress and TV personality Arlene Francis, Mercedes rather pompously said of her temporary departure from radio in the mid–1940s: "I resigned from *Big Sister* to go find my artistic life in the British Theater. I told everybody in radio what fools they were for wasting their lives in this ridiculous business. Why weren't they out accomplishing something the way I was about to do in England."

After spending several months relaxing in the Caribbean, Mercedes and her son John went to London, England, where she rented two rooms in a "nice little hotel" on Upper St. Martin's Lane, near the West End's Theater District, and set about trying to establish an acting career in that city. Most of the people living in the hotel were theater people and slept during the early daylight hours. Since Mercedes' young son was most active in the morning, he was constantly being told to "be as quiet as possible." Mercedes decided that it would be best, therefore, to move to another place that might be more advantageous to her son, and took up residence in the Pembridge Carlton located on Pembridge Square. Pembridge Square sounded like a much better address than it actually was. The "PC," as it was affectionately called by the people who roomed there, was a boarding house in the Bayswater section of London. It was indeed situated on a square (or small park), where little John could play with other children who lived on or around the square (whenever the weather would allow, which was not often). John and Mercedes' living quarters at the PC consisted of one large room with two beds, two dressers, one sink, and two large easy chairs with popping springs that would pinch their bottoms whenever they sat down. The other residents in the boarding house were mostly elderly people, but they were certainly more child-tolerant than the theater people who lived at the West End hotel had been.

Mercedes had always been enormously impressed with the British theatrical tradition. She was an admirer of the eighteenth-century English stage actress Sarah Siddons, of whom she had learned while a drama student of Sister Mary Leola's at Mundelein College. Siddons was born in 1755 and died in 1831. The actress, who was called "one of the greatest English actresses of tragedy in her time," came from a theatrical background. Her brothers, John Philip and Charles Kemble, and her niece, Fanny Kemble, were also famous actors in their day. Mercedes, who retained fond memories of the college lectures on the great English actress, hoped that while she might finally become the accomplished stage actress, that she had always wished she could have been in America. Well aware that she was no great beauty (the "flaring nostrils" incident still being very fresh in her memory), Mercedes was encouraged by the fact that her idol, Sarah Siddons, had not been a looker either. While painting a portrait of the actress, the famous artist Gainsborough had said to Siddons, "Damn it, Madame, there is no end to your nose." And yet Siddons, Mercedes knew, was the most celebrated actress of her time — in spite of her looks.

Late one afternoon, Mercedes said in her 1981 autobiography, she lingered a bit longer than any of the other tourists in the St. Andrew chapel in London's West-minster Abbey to "pay homage" to the woman she believed was the greatest actress who had ever lived (and whom she hoped to emulate). Mercedes sat in front of a statue of Siddons located in an alcove in the chapel and read a pamphlet she had picked up in the church's souvenir shop. "Sarah Siddons," the pamphlet stated, "was the most intellectual actress who ever interpreted Shakespeare. She has never had an equal, nor will she ever have a superior." Siddons, in spite of that sort of praise, had modestly said of herself after her retirement from the stage: "I was an honest actress." Mercedes cried that evening. In her heart she knew that she would probably never become as revered an actress as Sarah Siddons, but she vowed to keep striving to become as good an actress as her idol until the day she died. She desperately wanted to have the epitaph "She was an honest actress" engraved on her tomb as well, when her time on this earth ended.

She had not been in England long, and had made "the rounds" of practically every theatrical agent and producer in London, when she came to the realization that it was not going to be as easy to obtain employment on the English stage as she had hoped it would be. Mercedes had been given three letters of introduction to people who might be able to help her get acting jobs. One of the letters was to a producer for the J. Arthur Rank organization, which made films in England. Another letter was addressed to an important producer-manager who turned out to be very difficult to make an appointment with. The third letter was to an agent who had an office in Picadilly Circus. It was that agent who told Mercedes, quite directly, that it would be "next to impossible for an actor from America to obtain work on the stage in London, because of England's strict labor-permit laws. No American," the agent stated with absolutely certainty, "can fill a part if there is any possibility of a British actor's doing it." That was that! Mercedes' dream of a career on the English stage had apparently been an impossible quest.

One positive thing that happened to Mercedes during her sojourn in Great Britain was that for the first time since he was an infant, the actress and her son, John Lawrence, developed a bond between them. For much of the time Mercedes and John were in Great Britain, John kept complaining that he was hungry. It was, after all, only one year after World War II had ended, and much of London was still a bombed-out shell; food was hardly plentiful. There were still wartime shortages of eggs, milk, butter, meat, and practically everything else edible. Because they were foreigners, Mercedes and John were, however, allowed a more generous amount of sweets than the average Englishman—a quarter of a pound per week. Mercedes always bought sourballs, because hard candy lasted longer than chocolate, caramels, or peanut brittle. It was a decision that Mercedes and John mutually agreed upon.

Since little seemed to be happening that would push her career as a stage actress toward the heights of the remarkable Sarah Siddons, and because her cash reserve was fast dwindling to just enough money for a few more months abroad, Mercedes decided it was time to leave Great Britain and see some more of Europe before returning to the United States.

In 1946, McCambridge decided to abandon radio temporarily and travel around the world with her son, John Patrick. While in London, she tried to establish a career on the British stage, which she failed to do. This was one of the photographs she used to introduce herself to British theatrical agents and producers.

Ireland was just "a stone's throw" across a channel from England, and Mercedes thought it would be a good thing for John and herself to see a bit of the ancestral homeland. John was excited about going to Ireland, but he was also sad because he was going to have to say "goodbye" to a dear, ninety-year-old lady who lived in their London boarding house on Pembridge Square, and with whom he had shared many happy hours playing cards and good-naturedly arguing about such trivial things as him leaving his shoes in the middle of the floor, and her leaving her false teeth in a glass on the sink (scolding each other, "How can you be so careless!"). The little boy and the frail old lady also liked to take long, slow walks together in the park as they held hands and commented on the trees and flowers, or the birds, or "the naughty behavior of the other children in the park." The dear old lady had been John's constant companion during their stay in London, and she had been his frequent babysitter whenever Mercedes was off trying to conquer the British stage. Goodbyes were, however, sadly said, and mother and son set off for their visit to "the Old Sod."

The ferry ride across St. George's Channel was a stormy one, unsettling the mother and son's fortuitously less-than-full stomachs. The moment they docked at Rosslare in Ireland, Mercedes felt at home. She knew these people well! She knew their looks, their friendly chatting, their colorful way of telling a story, and their sometimes disapproving glances. But most familiar to her was their Irish laughter, which seemed to spring forth at the slightest provocation. It was as if she were at home in South Chicago again with her mother and father and Aunt Noonie and Uncle Alf, and all of the many, many Irish nuns and priests who had been her teachers and preachers. It was comfortable being in Ireland, and what Mercedes needed most at that time, because of her rejection by the British Theater, was to be in a comfortable place. Everything about Ireland also interested her inquisitive and sensitive young son. He easily talked to everyone he met, frequently striking up conversations with people in St. Stephen's Green in Dublin, which became Mercedes and John's favorite, special city. Even the food in Ireland was, compared to the food in England, delicious and plentiful. Ireland had remained neutral during World War II, rather than come to the assistance of their long-time enemy, England, even if it was to fight the dreaded Adolph Hitler and his wicked band of Nazis. As much as they were enjoying their visit to Ireland, by late summer in 1947, Mercedes knew that if she was to see any more of the world before she returned to the United States, it was time for John and her to leave the Emerald Isle. After touring France and Italy, Mercedes booked passage home to the United States to pick up the pieces of whatever was left of the acting career she had abandoned six months before. Acting on the stage in England had been, after all, merely a dream, and it was time to "wake up and smell the coffee," as she so bluntly put it, and settle down to the reality of going back to work.

Back in New York, Mercedes resumed her radio acting career as if she had never been away. Radio directors and producers, whose shows she had worked on for so many years, welcomed her back with open arms. Immediately upon arriving in New York she let people know that she was back in town and ready to work. Within a matter of weeks she was on the air, acting on most of the same shows she had worked on before she left New York. She even returned to the *Big Sister* series, although not in the title role, but in a long-running part of a *bad girl* on the program, which she thoroughly enjoyed.

Mercedes' return to New York radio even warranted a cover story in *Radio Mirror* magazine. "If you are anxious to locate Mercedes McCambridge, it's easy," the article began. "Just look around New York City for a convertible station wagon with a brunette behind the wheel ... who's obviously reading a part. While she speeds, she shouts in anger ... murmurs in sorrow ... and both hands gesture in tempo. That's Mercedes all right. The same Mercedes you hear on *Big Sister, Inner Sanctum, Grand Central Station* and *The Thin Man.* Presently she has no home thanks to the housing shortage. For a while she lived in the New York home of her friends, Mr. and Mrs. Sam Wanamaker. But they finally sold their house [and moved to England], thus sending Mercedes scurrying into Connecticut to co-rent a house with her friend, radio actress Elspeth Eric. This haven lasted only a few months, though. So now Mercedes and her *five* [sic] year old son, John, are hotel-hopping, whenever they aren't hopping into friend's guest rooms. Mercedes' husband and John's father? Oh, he has a home ... he's a writer, busily at work on a book ... in Haiti!" Mercedes had not yet received her final divorce papers from Bill Fifield, and was apparently not quite ready to forgive him for being such a failure as a husband and father.

The *Radio Mirror* piece also provided some interesting insights into Mercedes' chameleon-like personality. In the article, the actress admitted that she "flatly despised gossips, gin rummy, bridge, indifference, and people who wasted time." She also "loathed harsh voices, corsages, and books wrapped in stores," and felt that "gold fish [were] hard luck." Her "likes" were equally as well defined as her "dislikes," and included "the late President Roosevelt and such writers as Dostoyevsky, Thomas Wolfe, Eugene O'Neill, Ibsen and Shakespeare [Tolstoy was not mentioned], and all [unwrapped] books." "That," the article concluded, "gives you a very neat idea of Mercedes, the girl who rehearses while she drives, who doesn't have a home ... but who nevertheless manages to be one of the best actresses on the airwaves."

In 1947 there was one program that every radio actor and actress in New York wanted to work on — CBS's hour-long dramatic anthology series *Studio One.* Mercedes was no exception. The series was produced and directed by none other than Fletcher Markle, the same Fletcher Markle who had temporarily taken over Orson Welles' directorial duties on the *Mercury Summer Theater* series shortly before Mercedes left on her European odyssey. Emulating Welles' *Mercury Theater* practice of presenting well written adaptations of classic works of literature and the stage, as well as showcasing new works by current writers, Markle produced and directed a first rate program that proved popular with radio listeners from the moment it made its on-the-air debut on April 22, 1947, with an adaptation of a recently published story, "Under the Volcano." *Studio One* always began with an announcer saying, "From Studio One at CBS" (hence the title). Subsequent productions, over the following six months, included adaptations of *Wuthering Heights, The Hunted, Ah, Wilderness, Holiday, Pride and Prejudice,* and *The Barretts of Wimpole Street,* to name just a few.

In 1947, CBS *Studio One* radio series was one of the most prestigious dramatic anthology programs on the air. The director, and sometimes star, of the series was Fletcher Markle (pictured far right), who had temporarily taken over for Orson Welles on his *Mercury Summer Theater* series in 1946. Every radio actor in New York wanted to work on the *Studio One* series, including Mercedes. Pictured above, from left to right, are actors Hedley Rennie, Anne Burr, and Everett Sloane, all regular performers on the program. Mercedes did indeed become one of the series' regulars, replacing Anne Burr as the show's frequent leading lady shortly after this photograph was taken.

Further emulating Welles, Markle employed a talented cast of outstanding radio actors as regulars on his series. Leading lady roles were usually played by the sophisticated, Boston-born-and-bred actress Anne Burr, who had a wonderfully distinctive, throaty vocal quality, and could effectively play classic as well as contemporary roles. Burr, it will be remembered, was the actress who had replaced Mercedes McCambridge as the nurse for the Broadway run of the play *The Hasty Heart* in 1944. Leading male roles on *Studio One* were usually essayed by the gifted actor Everett Sloane, who Mercedes believed was one of the finest thespians on radio. Sloane had been a regular performer on Orson Welles' *Mercury Theater of the Air* program, played a major role in Welles' film *Citizen Kane*, and was heard on hundreds of other radio shows over the years, including many of the programs Mercedes had worked on. He was, according to Mercedes (and anyone else who knew anything about acting), "a gifted actor, by anyone's standards, both in films and on the stage." "Everett," Mercedes stated, "was usually restricted to offbeat, even weird parts, because no one who ever saw him would say that he was a handsome man. But in radio nobody was more enchantingly romantic than Everett. I have looked into his eyes, behind their thick glasses, and swooned for the beauty there, and that, combined with his voice and characterization, would put Gable to shame." Markle himself occasionally took leading roles on the program, and was a good, if not great, actor. But he was an excellent director. Important, and sometimes small, supporting parts on the *Studio One* programs were regularly played by Miriam Wolfe and Robert Dryden. Miss Wolfe could effectively play anything from a downtrodden Scottish housewife to a giddy young scatterbrain, as well as any imperious lady or mother called for in the script. Her voice was well known to radio listeners for her work on the *Let's Pretend* children's fairy tale show, on which she usually played wicked witches and evil queens. Actor Robert Dryden was equally adept at playing all manner of character roles, and, like Miss Wolfe, could effectively produce any accent of any age that the script might require. Also heard as regulars on the series were Hedley Rennie, an actor Markle had worked with in Canada and had summoned to New York when hired by CBS; Hester Sondergaard, who played the more mature leading lady roles on the series; Rosemary Rice, who occasionally played young ingénue leads on the program, and featured in *Studio One*'s radio adaptations of *A Tree Grows in Brooklyn* and *The Constant Nymph*; and Ronald Liss, who was the resident teenage male on the program. Gregory Morton, Ian Martin, and Alan Devitt "actively assisted," as Markle used to say at the end of each program when he read the cast credits. Mercedes' old fiend, actress Elspeth Eric, who specialized in playing gun molls, ladies with criminal intent, shop girls, and whining wives on radio, also occasionally appeared on the series as well.

Mercedes desperately wanted to become a member of Markle's *Studio One* repertory company of actors, in spite of her rather unpleasant earlier encounter with the

director in the summer of 1946. Fletcher Markle, who was five years younger than the thirty-one-year-old Mercedes, had been born in Winnipeg, Canada, on March 27, 1921. "Winnipeg," he said in the book *The Golden Age of Radio Directors*, was "a place that was colder than anything south of the North Pole." His Pennsylvania Dutch grandfather had emigrated to Ontario, Canada, as a young man, where

Radio character actress Miriam Wolfe, well known for playing witches and wicked queens on the CBS children's program **Let's Pretend,** was a regular supporting player on the **Studio One** series, and she became a long-standing friend of Mercedes McCambridge. Wolfe, who appeared in all of the dramas heard on the **Studio One** series, convincingly played characters of every age, every nationality and every social class.

both of Fletcher's parents were born. After he met and married Fletcher's mother, the senior Mr. Markle moved his family to Winnipeg, where, with a partner, he established a jewelry business called "Porter and Markle." The Markles later moved to Vancouver, which everyone in the family agreed offered a much more pleasant climate than Winnipeg. As a teenager, Fletcher, who had a stuttering problem, was encouraged by his speech teacher–therapist, Ruth Lynn, to listen to *The March of Time* radio program, and was instructed to pay particular attention to the narration of a man named Westbrook Van Vorhees, who she said "had great projection and enormous assurance." Although Markle followed Miss Lynn's advice, he became much more interested in the voice of another performer on the program. He later learned that the voice belonged to a young man named Orson Welles, and Fletcher became an avid fan of the impressive sounding actor. Totally fascinated with everything about radio, Markle began to write scripts for the local Vancouver radio station, which eventually led to his being given the chance to direct his first national Canadian radio show, *Baker's Dozen*, in 1941. In 1942, when Canada entered World War II, Markle, who was a loyal subject of the British Crown, enlisted in the Royal Canadian Air Force and was stationed in England with the Air Force's Press and Communications Department. When the war ended and he was discharged from the Royal Air Force, Markle briefly returned to Canada, where he produced several radio dramas before deciding to go to New York and seriously try to "break into" big-time American radio. It was his well received direction of his play "Life with Adam," presented on Orson Welles' *Mercury Summer Theater*, that led to Markle's being asked to produce and direct a new dramatic anthology series at CBS similar to Welles' *Mercury Theater* program. The result was the *Studio One* series. Markle's and McCambridge's recollections of their first meeting differ considerably. Fletcher recalled the time he met Mercedes as "a fairly extraordinary day," because he "met an actress who later worked on my *Studio One* and *Ford Theater* programs, and whom I subsequently married and was married to for eleven years." Before Fletcher came to America and directed *Studio One*, and certainly before Mercedes and Markle met, he was married to a young writer–script editor named Blanche in Canada, who had given birth to his son, Stephen Markle. Stephen eventually became an actor, and, after graduating from Canada's National Theater School, he made his professional acting debut at Canada's Stratford Shakespeare Festival. He subsequently appeared in such popular films as *The Manhattan Project* (1986), and on such television series as *The Edge of Night* (1982), *JAG* (2000; as "Kevin Lee"), and *Crossing Jordan* (2001). Because they had little contact with one another as Stephen was growing up, the young actor reportedly remained rather bitter about his father's early departure from his life in the late 1940s, and the father and son never really got to know each other very well.

In 1952 an article titled "When My Love Came Along" appeared in an issue of *Radio and TV Mirror* magazine. The article chronicled Mercedes' and Fletcher's second, more significant, encounter with one another. Reading the article, it becomes apparent that Mercedes and Markle were, at that time, immediately attracted to one another. For the magazine, Mercedes recalled that although she had been initially less-than-impressed with the young Mr. Markle, she had an entirely different reaction when she auditioned for his *Studio One* program in 1947. "All the anger was blurred with time, when next she saw him," the 1952 article gushed. "This time he wasn't just a Canadian actor playing a role, but the director of a big CBS series, *Studio One*. In 1947, this was the top prestige show in radio. A show Mercedes coveted and would love to act in. Seeing him, she thought back to the 4 a.m. telephone call and she held out her hand, smiling in recognition. The young man looked blankly at her. His assistant stepped forward and introduced the two. Anger blazed through Mercedes again. The insulting so-and-so ... he didn't even remember her! As the anger burned hot and heavy, however, Mercedes looked into his face, and thought, with the complete illogic of a woman, that ... he was so handsome. Mercedes read her audition script, which was a radio play called "An Act of Faith," with all of the intensity and control the script called for. She had to get this part, if for no other reason than to show this young man that she was *good*. For one breathless moment, after her reading, she waited and then ... casually, without fuss or bother, he said, 'You'll do.' Mercedes became a regular on his *Studio One* program. As they began working together in the weeks that followed, Mercy looked at this young man through new eyes. His acting and directing ability had a touch of genius. Coming home from rehearsals at night, Mercy would recall each hour of the rehearsal with delight. For two years, Mercy and the young actor-director worked together, occasionally flirting, and then one May night she played opposite him in F. Scott Fitzgerald's 'The Last Tycoon.' It was an ordinary work night like any other. Listening to the program that night, as she had been for months before, was the young man's mother. Shortly after broadcast time, as the pros and cons of how the show went were being mulled over, the telephone rang and the young man went to hear his mother's reaction to the show. To his sur-

prise, she didn't say he was good, didn't tell him the production was special, but instead said, 'I think you and that young lady who played opposite you are in love.' Later that night, a young dark-haired actress and a tall, dark and handsome actor-director were asking each other, 'Is mother always right?'"

It was soon after Mercedes' first appearance on the *Studio One* presentation of "An Act of Faith," which aired on September 23, 1947, that she began playing leading roles on the series. Her first was in an adaptation of the best-selling novel *Anthony Adverse*. She subsequently

This portrait of actress Mercedes McCambridge, taken while the actress was appearing on Fletcher Markle's *Studio One* and *Ford Theater* programs (and was just about to make her screen acting debut), was one of her favorite publicity photographs.

played the title role of "Kitty Foyle" on *Studio One* on November 4, 1947, with Markle as the male lead. This was followed by a major role in the radio play "Let Me Do the Talking," which was heard on November 11, 1947, and starred motion picture actor John Garfield. As the popularity of *Studio One* increased, the public had begun to request that well-known Hollywood film stars be featured on the program, as they were on CBS's very popular dramatic anthology program *The Lux Radio Theatre*. "Young Man of Manhattan" was heard on November 17, 1947, and starred film star Robert Mitchum. Actress Anne Burr once again played the leading female role (in what was to be her last *Studio One* performance), while Mercedes played a major supporting part in "Young Man of Manhattan." There followed "Earth and High Heaven," which starred film and stage actress Geraldine Fitzgerald (and featured Mercedes in another major supporting role) on December 1, 1947; "To Mary with Love," heard on December 8, 1947, starring Gene Kelly, with Mercedes playing the title role of "Mary"; "Painted Veils," broadcast on December 22, 1947, starring James Mason and opera singer Eileen Farrell, with Mercedes enacting Farrell's speaking voice in what was actually the major female role on the show; "King's Row," heard on February 24, 1948, featuring film star Robert Young and co-starring Mercedes as the female lead; and many other shows. The last *Studio One* broadcast, *The Constant Nymph*, starred ingénue Rosemary Rice in the title role, and was presented on July 27, 1948. The memorable "Last Tycoon" broadcast, which convinced Fletcher's mother that her son and Mercedes were in love, aired on May 19, 1948. In fact, the two had become lovers long before "The Last Tycoon" was presented on the *Studio One* series.

Actresses Miriam Wolfe and Rosemary Rice, who both worked regularly on *Studio One*, characterized Fletcher Markle as "quite a ladies man," and claimed he often made sexual advances toward the young actresses appearing on his show. Miriam said that she had been offered leading roles on *Studio One* on the condition she agree to Markle's request for a more-than-merely-professional relationship. She claimed that she discouraged his advances, telling him she was happy working as a supporting actress on his series (and knowing very well that several of Markle's leading ladies had disappeared from the cast once their personal relationship with Mr. Markle had cooled down). To his credit, Markle, who appreciated Miss Wolfe's superior and versatile talents as a character actress, kept her working on his programs for the next two years, in spite of her rebuff.

In the autumn of 1948, Markle's series began its second season on the air, but the show was no longer called *Studio One*. *Studio One* had been a "sustained" program on CBS, which means that it was a show without a sponsor, and was produced by the radio network on which it aired. Because of the popularity of the series, the Ford Motor Company took over the show's sponsorship during the 1948–1949 season. *Studio One* became *The Ford Theater*, faking the name of a program that had already aired for a year, with an entirely different staff and cast of radio actors each week. The premiere broadcast of the new series took place on October 24, 1948. It was a "live" broadcast that became a major theatrical event. All of the actors in the cast wore formal clothes for the broadcast, which was presented on a stage, in a theater, in front of a large, enthusiastic audience. The first show of the season was Gustav Flaubert's "Madame Bovary," and it starred film actress Marlene Dietrich, who had previously been heard on Markle's *Studio One* series the season before. Film stars Van Heflin and Claude Rains also starred on the program. In the supporting cast were Mercedes, Miriam Wolfe, Robert Dryden, Ronald Liss, Hedley Rennie, Ivor Francis, Alan Devitt, Gregory Morton, John Stanley, Abby Lewis, John Merlin and Neil Fitzgerald. The drama was narrated by Mr. Markle. Supporting cast member Miriam Wolfe recalled that the opening night performance of the new and revised *Ford Theater* series became a front page photo item in *The New York Daily News* the next morning. Miriam's parents, who lived in Brooklyn, were photographed smiling broadly as they stood behind actress Marlene Dietrich, looking stunningly glamorous as she arrived at the theater for the broadcast. The event was, Wolfe said, "one of the most exciting evenings any of us mere radio actors had ever experienced." At the premiere broadcast of *The Ford Theater* series, members of the audience even received formal printed programs, with the names of the cast and the roles they played, as well as the production staff, prominently listed.

Subsequent *Ford Theater* broadcasts included "Double Indemnity" on October 15, 1948, which starred Burt Lancaster and Joan Bennett in the leading roles, and featured Mercedes, Myron McCormack, Miriam Wolfe, Hedley Rennie, Robert Dryden, Joe DeSantis and Ivor Francis in the supporting cast; "Of Human Bondage," heard on October 29, 1948, with Ray Milland and Joan Lorring playing the leads; and, from Hollywood, "The Horn Blows at Midnight," which aired on March 4, 1949, and starred comedian Jack Benny in the same role of a somewhat inept angel that he originally played in a much maligned film several years before. Markle's radio production of "The Horn Blows at Midnight," broadcast from Hollywood, was well received by the radio audience, as well as favorably reviewed by the newspaper and magazine critics. Mercedes was Benny's leading lady on this program, which also starred film actor Claude Rains. The supporting cast included Jane Morgan, Robert Dryden, Hedley Rennie, Hans Conried, Miriam Wolfe, and Jeanette Nolan. Helen Hayes was heard in a new radio adaptation of Ernest Hemingway's "A Farewell to Arms," a production broadcast from New York that co-starred Markle, and featured Hester Sondergaard, Everett Sloane, and Robert Dryden in the supporting cast; Montgomery Clift starred as Heathcliff in an adaptation of *Wuthering Heights*, which had previously been heard on Markle's *Studio One* series. *The Ford Theater*'s final program was an adaptation of the novel *Cluny Brown*, broadcast from New York on July 1, 1949, and starring Leueen MacGrath and Walter Pidgeon.

By the time the new *Ford Theater* series was launched, Mercedes and Fletcher Markle were deeply involved in their serious love affair. They had moved into an apartment together in New York City, and when *The Ford Theater* temporarily transferred its productions to Hollywood later in the season, and Mercedes was in Los Angeles filming interior scenes for *All the King's Men*, Mercedes and Markle shared a home on the West Coast. By that time, obviously, Mercedes' career had already taken a decidedly different path, one which will be covered later in this book.

While the couple were still living in New York City, Mercedes, in addition to her very busy radio acting schedule, signed a contract to appear in yet another Broadway-bound play, *The Young and the Fair*. The play, set in a girl's junior college in Boston, was written by a new, young playwright, N. Richard Nash, and it opened on Broadway on November 22, 1948. *The Young and the Fair* featured a large, all-female cast, which, in addition to Mercedes, included actresses Julie Harris, Rita Gam and Doe Avedon, among many others. In *The Young and the Fair*'s "Who's Who Among the Cast," which appeared in the *Playbill* program, Mercedes' brief biography (in addition to continuing to perpetuate the myth that she had a "Spanish grandmother") stated that "as a child" she had lived in Mexico City, which must have come as a surprise to her parents when they read about it. She had indeed visited Mexico on a short vacation after she graduated from Mundelein, and then again went south of the border when married to her first husband, Bill Fifield, in the early 1940s, but by that time she was hardly "a child." Mercedes included the plays *Hope for the Best* and *A Place of Our Own* in her list of Broadway credits, and said that she had "lived for a year and a half in Martinique, the South of France, and in Italy," never mentioning that she had also spent considerable time in England and Ireland in 1946–1947, or her failure to storm the British stage. The short biography in the back of the program also claimed she had several short stories published, although none could be found by this author, and that a novel she penned was "now making the rounds." Her run in *The Young and the Fair* proved to be a short-lived one, but when it ended, it was Mercedes, and not the producers of the show, who decided to break her contract. She had found a bigger and better project than yet another play that seemed destined for a less-than-successful Broadway run.

In the spring of 1948, Mercedes' friend, actress Elspeth Eric, read in *Variety* about an open audition for a role in a film that Columbia Pictures was casting in New York City. The film was an adaptation of Robert Penn Warren's best-selling novel *All the King's Men*, and the role that was being cast was a character named "Sadie Burke," who was the hard-boiled assistant, then lover, and finally rejected paramour of a one-time poor, but-later-corrupt, married Southern politician named Willie Stark. Elspeth was convinced that either Mercedes or she would be perfect for the part of Sadie Burke, and urged her friend to go with her to the "open call" interviews held in Manhattan. Although Mercedes was reluctant to attend an open casting call, and would have preferred to have had her name submitted by her agent, Elspeth insisted they attend the audition. After finishing their lunch at Sardi's restaurant, the two actresses joined the long line of hundreds of hopefuls gathered at the audition site, waiting to be interviewed and (hopefully) to read for the available film role. As the line dwindled down to a precious few, and the number of hours Mercedes and Elspeth waited to be called into the office for their interview increased, Mercedes' Irish temper approached the boiling point. The receptionist finally called out the name "Mercedeees MacComber," without ever looking up from the magazine she was listlessly thumbing through. As she wrote in her autobiography, Mercedes was sure that no one else in the room could possibly have a name as close as that to hers, so she rose, stiff-backed from the uncomfortable chair she had been sitting in, and proudly — and angrily — walked to the door of the office behind which the people who were to judge her were gathered. The "judges" were seated at a long table when she entered the room. They did not ask her to sit down, did not speak to her, and did not introduce themselves to her. One of the judges, who was shorter than the others, finally spoke. "Miss McComber, you are..." Mercedes stopped him the middle of his sentence and imperiously stated, "No, sir, I am not Miss McComber," her eyes narrowing to slits.

"I beg your pardon," the man who had addressed her said, a puzzled look on his face.

"Thank you for the apology," Mercedes sneered contemptuously. "And personally, I don't care if you ever find out *who* I am. I don't care if *I* ever find out who *you* are. I think it will be just dandy if we maintain our anonymity all the way around."

By then, the panel of judges were staring at the actress with open mouths.

"I don't know what you are here for," she continued, because she had apparently caught their attention, "but I want to tell you that if you were planning to film the Last Supper with the original cast, and if you offered me a million dollars to play a part in it, I wouldn't be interested, thank you very much! I have been sitting out there in that stagnant room, jam packed with people who live by their wits, and I have watched you shoot them down, some in two minutes' time. In, out, in, out! Who the hell do you think you are, gentlemen?" Now she had really caught their attention. "Why did you make this foolish trip? If you want pretty faces, go back to Schwab's drugstore on Sunset Boulevard! If you want cowboys, go back and talk to John Wayne, but don't come riding your palomino ponies into New York City and mow down a whole room full of live actors in the space of one afternoon!" She had finished her tirade and turned toward the door, but looked back at them to deliver one final parting shot over her shoulder. "Thank you for the use of the hall, gentlemen," she hissed, and turned towards the door.

"Wait," someone said and she whirled around to face whoever it was who spoke. "That was great," said one of the larger men sitting at the table, "Really great," and then he applauded. "Please, sit down."

Mercedes declined his offer to sit and continued to assume her attitude of total indignation. She later admitted in her autobiography that she was relieved they didn't tell her to "Get the hell out of the room!"

"Oh, for Christ's sake, sit down!" the big man said, and Mercedes relaxed a bit and sat down in a large leather chair placed in front of the judges.

Mercedes later discovered that the big man's name was Max Arnow, and he was the head of talent for Columbia Pictures. The smaller man, she learned, was the film's director, Robert Rossen. Rossen asked her if she had read the book *All the King's Men*, and she told him that indeed she had. "You could play the pants off the part of Sadie Burke," the part they were casting, he said, smiling. "You just did!"

After a few tests were made, Mercedes received the role that would change her life forever and make her an internationally known film actress. With little regret, she left the cast of *The Young and the Fair* (which she suspected was doomed to failure on Broadway anyway), and, after winding up the continuing radio roles she had been playing on various programs (including a few more of her boyfriend Fletcher Markle's *Ford Theater* broadcasts), she headed for Hollywood to begin filming *All the King's Men.*

Not long after Mercedes left New York for Hollywood, a love-sick Markle convinced his sponsors, the Ford Motor Company, that he would have a far greater choice of well-known actors to feature on *The Ford Theater* program if they temporarily moved the broadcasts to Hollywood on the West Coast. The Ford Motor Company saw the business logic behind Markle's request, and the director and several of the regular actors on his series, including Miriam Wolfe, Robert Dryden and Hedley Rennie, left for Hollywood, where for several weeks of the 1948–1949 season *The Ford Theater* broadcasts were produced. *The Ford Theater* brought down its final curtain in New York in June 1949. Markle decided to leave New York to join Mercedes in Hollywood, and accepted a contract with Metro Goldwyn Mayer to produce and direct films and television shows. Wolfe and Dryden remained in New York, where they continued their active radio acting careers, and Hedley Rennie returned to the CBC in Canada.

Acting in films was different than anything Mercedes had done on radio or on the stage. Film acting, she felt, was closer to radio acting than performing on the stage, because it required a more intimate, less broad approach. A fast learner, she easily adjusted to acting in front of a camera. She became especially interested in the technical aspects of filmmaking and spent many of her off-camera hours observing how

the movie was being made. She sought out the company of the behind-the-camera technicians—cameramen, props people, makeup artists, "grips" (as film stagehands were called), electricians, script supervisors, and all the other behind-the-scenes workers, whom she admired for being "down to earth" and "hardworking" crafts-

Mercedes McCambridge as Sadie Burke, the hard-boiled secretary (and later mistress) of politician Willie Stark, who becomes the ambitious and ruthless governor of an unnamed Southern state in the 1949 film *All the King's Men.* The role, which marked her film debut, garnered praise from film critics and won the actress numerous awards, including a coveted "Best Supporting Actress" Academy Award in 1950.

While making her first motion picture, *All the King's Men* in 1948, everything about filmmaking fascinated the 30-year-old Mercedes McCambridge. She spent most of her off-camera time watching the production crew going through their paces. Here she joins the film's still photographers and cameraman preparing to shoot a scene.

men and total professionals. Since most of her time was spent waiting for a particular scene to be filmed, there was plenty of opportunities to socialize with the other actors. She found the film's star, Broderick Crawford (playing the role of her politician boss and lover), "down to earth and easy to talk to," and she also thought him a wonderful actor who was comfortable to work with on camera. Mercedes was happy to be working once again with fellow New York radio actress Anne Seymour, who played Willie's wife in the film, although they shared only a few scenes. She also got along well with the picture's young female lead, Joanne Dru, and also John Ireland, with whom she became especially friendly. The number of different locations actors had to deal with while making a film proved especially interesting and exciting to Mercedes. She had become accustomed to performing in a solitary radio studio, or on a stage, and so working at diverse locations was a new challenge. Mercedes enjoyed working in the medium and was only bothered by the fact that so much of her time was spent waiting to appear in front of the cameras, as various shots were being set up by the technicians. Fletcher used to visit her as often as his schedule permitted

Mercedes (sitting left), during the filming of *All the King's Men*, waits to shoot a scene with actress Joanne Dru (sitting right).

during the filming of *All the King's Men*. And Mercedes occasionally managed to find the time to work with him on his *Ford Theater* radio program when she was in Hollywood filming interior scenes for *All the King's Men*. The few instances in which she could steal time to spend with the handsome Mr. Markle became much-anticipated events over the course of her busy filmmaking schedule.

From *All the King's Men*: McCambridge, seated, appears with actor John Ireland (playing a political hatchet man in the film), in the lobby of a small hotel in a small Southern town near New Orleans.

When *All the King's Men* premiered in 1949, the film critics were unanimous in their praise. Everything about it was labeled "first rate," from the direction of Robert Rossen to the production values and performances of the various cast members. Special plaudits were given to Broderick Crawford, who appeared in practically every scene in the film, and to newcomer Mercedes McCambridge. Kate Cameron of *The New York Daily News* named *All the King's Men* "One of the best films of 1949, an outstanding motion picture." In her review, Cameron posited that writer-director Robert Rossen had "made a powerfully dramatic political film," and called it "one of the most vital and honest films to come out of Hollywood in a long time." She added, "Mercedes McCambridge, as Willie Stark's secretary in her first screen role, gives such an effective performance that she will be sought after by every Hollywood producer." *Life* magazine, in a featured article about the film, said it was made "with a frankness rare in Hollywood and has outstanding acting by Broderick Crawford as Willie Stark and Mercedes McCambridge as a tough hanger-on. The film rips into the mechanics and morals of politics." *Motion Picture* magazine named *All the King's Men* "The Movie of the Week," and said of McCambridge's performance, "Newcomer Mercedes McCambridge is excellent as the secretary." *The New York Mirror*'s Justin Gilbert called the film "a forceful, penetrating study of the life of Huey Long"

Shooting "on location" was new to Mercedes, who was used to working within the confines of a radio studio or on a stage. Many scenes in *All the King's Men* were filmed at various city and rural outdoor locations throughout the South. Left to right: actors John Ireland, Broderick Crawford and Mercedes during a scene filmed in New Orleans.

the corrupt real-life governor of Louisiana whose name had been fictionalized as "Willie Stark" by author Robert Penn Warren. *Time* magazine praised *All the King's Men* as "the best Hollywood attempt to fuse studio and documentary styles" and "a slam bang indictment of grass roots demagoguery." One of Mercedes' best personal reviews for her work in *All the King's Men* appeared in *The New York World Telegram and Sun*, which said of her performance: "She is the cynical, imperious guide for the politician's early steps, seething with impotent and suppressed rage, as she watches him grow out of her control. She has a clipped, dynamic style that is tremendously effective."

When the Academy Award nominations for 1950 were announced, no one was surprised when *All the King's Men* earned a nomination for "Best Film of the Year," along with *Battleground*, *The Heiress*, *Twelve O'Clock High*, and *A Letter to Three Wives*. Broderick Crawford was nominated for the "Best Actor" award for his performance as Willie Stark in *All the King's Men*, as were John Wayne for *Sands of Iwo Jima*, Gregory Peck for *Twelve O'Clock High*, Kirk Douglas for *Champion* and Richard Todd for *The Hasty Heart*, the film version of the play Mercedes had been fired from in 1944. Members of the filmmaking community and movie fans alike were delighted when Mercedes McCambridge was nominated for the "Best Supporting Actress"

When *All the King's Men* was released in 1949, Columbia Pictures launched a major publicity campaign to promote the film. (An original newspaper and magazine ad that first introduced the film to the public.)

This photograph of an attractive, youthful looking, and smiling Mercedes McCambridge was used by Columbia Pictures, who produced the film *All the King's Men*, after the film's release to try and make the actress look more appealing to filmgoers, who had seen her as an embittered, hard-boiled woman in the film.

award for her work in *All the King's Men*. Also nominated in that category were Ethel Barrymore for *Pinky*, Elsa Lanchester for *Come to the Stable*, Ethel Waters for *Pinky*, and Celeste Holm for *Come to the Stable*.

Due to Mercedes' newfound celebrity as an Academy Award nominee, newspapers and magazines printed numerous photos of Mercedes and Fletcher Markle when they married

In this scene from *All the King's Men*, a candidate for governor, Willie Stark (played by Broderick Crawford, left) and his assistant, Sadie (Mercedes McCambridge), call room service in a sleazy hotel during Stark's campaign for governor; they need black coffee delivered to the room of a drunken Jack Burden (John Ireland), who has become disillusioned with Stark's ruthless campaign tactics.

An obviously excited Mercedes McCambridge and her brand new husband, Fletcher Markle, whom she had just married days before the photograph was taken, are seen arriving at the Pantages Theater in Hollywood on March 23, 1950. That evening she gracefully accepted the award for "Best Supporting Actress" for her work in the film "All the King's Men" (Photofest).

on February 19, 1950, in Las Vegas in a civil ceremony. The headlines and captions announced: "Oscar Nominated Star Married to Producer," "Mercedes Markle now!" "Romance in the Air," and "Start of Their Aerial Bridal Jaunt." Pictures showed the happy couple smiling broadly, gazing into each other's eyes, and touching foreheads as they snuggled in Ciro's night club. Fletcher was obviously enjoying the attention and being in the spotlight as much as his wife, who was the reason for all the press coverage. An item printed in *Photoplay* magazine at the time stated: "You'd better save a lot of space in your scrapbooks for this gal. She's that good."

When it was announced that Mercedes McCambridge was the winner of the "Best Supporting Actress" award at the March 23, 1950, Academy Awards ceremony (presented at the Pantages Theater on Hollywood Boulevard), there was a loud burst of applause, as there was later in the evening when Broderick Crawford's name was read as "Best Actor," and again when *All the King's Men* was awarded the "Best Film of the Year" Oscar. An obviously thrilled McCambridge rushed up on the stage and was handed her award by actor Ray Milland, who had won the "Best Actor" Oscar the year before. In her short-but-sweet acceptance speech, she stated breathlessly, "I would like to say to every waiting actor, hang on. Look what can happen."

The next day, every major newspaper in the world had pictures of the evening's winning actors on their covers, or in their center spread photo sections. Photographs of Broderick Crawford, Olivia deHavilland (who had won the "Best Actress" award

Broderick Crawford as Willie Stark, and Mercedes McCambridge as his assistant and lover Sadie, both won Academy Awards for their work in the film *All the King's Men*. The role was Crawford's first major part in a motion picture and McCambridge's first role in any film.

for her work in *The Heiress*), Dean Jagger (the "Best Supporting Actor" recipient for *Twelve O'Clock High*), and Mercedes showed them smiling broadly and clutching their treasured Oscars.

In addition to winning the Academy of Motion Picture Arts and Sciences "Best Supporting Actress" Award for her performance as Sadie Burke in *All the King's Men*,

Mercedes also won two Hollywood Foreign Press Association Golden Globe Awards—"Best Newcomer to Films" and "Best Supporting Actress of the Year"—and received the Associated Press Poll and the *Look* and *Photoplay* magazine awards as the "Best Newcomer to Films."

Mercedes had been a professional actress for fourteen years when she made her film debut in *All the King's Men*, and was certainly no "newcomer" to the business of acting. After she won her Oscar, her old friend, radio director-producer Arch Oboler, said of her acting in general: "Mercedes is able to keep her integrity no matter what kind of material she is working with. The fire's there, whether she's reading a soap ad, or giving an Academy Award performance."

Of all of the letters, telegrams and phone calls congratulating her on her Academy Award victory, none meant more to her than a cable she received from her beloved teacher and mentor, Sister Mary Leola Oliver of Mundelein College. The nun wired Mercedes that she had "been with her in spirit" at the Academy Awards and had "never faltered" in her belief in the actress' talents. Mercedes had received her divorce from Bill Fifield shortly before she married Markle and won her Oscar, and the actress, knowing her Church's position on divorce, was concerned about what her former teacher might think of her actions. When Sister Mary Leola visited New York while Mercedes was in that city promoting *All the King's Men*, the actress and the nun had lunch together at the Hotel Pierre's restaurant one afternoon. After they finished eating, Sister Mary Leola gently took Mercedes' hand in hers and told her former star pupil that she had "been saddened" by the news of her divorce from Bill Fifield. She said that she had prayed so hard that they would be reunited. Mercedes asked the

In 1950, McCambridge, in addition to a "Best Supporting Actress" Oscar, won many other awards for her performance in *All the King's Men*. She is seen here holding two Golden Globe awards (for "Best Newcomer to Films" and "Best Supporting Actress") presented to her by the Foreign Press Association.

Mercedes McCambridge is pictured above with her beloved Mundelein College drama teacher and mentor, Sister Mary Leola Oliver, whom she often said taught her "everything I know about my work." The photograph was taken in the 1950s when Mercedes gave Sister Mary Leola temporary custody of the Oscar she received in 1950 for her performance in *All the King's Men.*

nun if she thought God would forgive her for getting the divorce, and Sister Mary Leola answered that it was not for her to say. She then added that she was sure God did not mean for Mercedes to live alone for the rest of her life, apparently indicating that she accepted Mercedes' decision to marry Markle. "I sent Sister Mary Leola my Oscar when she was living at the Holy Angels Convent in Milwaukee. I told her it wasn't a permanent gift, but I wanted her to enjoy it with me for a while. And what did she do? This humble woman of Christ and a Sister of Charity of the Blessed Virgin Mary took the Academy Award down to the local theater and said, 'Put a display case around this and show it to everybody.'"

3. The Fifties and Sixties

The 1950s were, without question, the most productive years of Mercedes McCambridge's career, and they were certainly among the most active years of her personal life as well. She was not only in great demand as an Academy Award–winning film actress, she also continued to work regularly on radio, as well as on the entertainment industry's new diversion, Television. Mercedes and Fletcher also thoroughly enjoyed their newfound status as prominent members of the Hollywood entertainment community's "in" crowd.

For most of the next decade the couple lived the lives of Hollywood royalty, with ever-increasing fame and fortune, as well as the ever-increasing pressures of maintaining the luxurious lifestyle to which they were becoming accustomed. Hollywood gossip columnist Louella O. Parsons conducted an interview with Mercedes in 1950, soon after she received her Academy Award, and the interview appeared in the Hearst Syndicate's numerous newspapers all around the world. In the interview, Louella wrote: "Mercedes believes that no girl in the world has ever been as lucky as she is. She is married to Fletcher Markell [the misspelling did not please Mr. Markle], who is a wonderful father to her eight-year-old son, a good husband, and so interested in his own job as an M.G.M. producer that he doesn't interfere with her work." Louella ended the interview by saying, "Hollywood is still so new and fascinating to Mercedes and has meant so much happiness to her that she prays every night it will always be her home."

In 1950, the same year she won her prized Academy Award, Mercedes made three feature films, all released in 1951. None of these pictures rivaled *All the King's Men* as far as critical acclaim was concerned, and they were not particularly successful at the box office. They did, however, give her a chance to play three very different kinds of roles.

Inside Straight, set in nineteenth-century San Francisco, co-starred David Brian, Arlene Dahl, and Barry Sullivan, and was directed by Gerald Mayer. It was an interesting film about an ambitious and greedy couple, played by Brian and McCambridge, whose ruthless behavior leads them into corrupt and ultimately less-than-fulfilling lives.

By the mid–1950s, Mercedes McCambridge's career in films and on television was at its peak, and she was thoroughly enjoying the financial rewards that came with her celebrity. Here she stands poolside at the Bel Air mansion she shared with her much-adored (at the time) producer husband, Fletcher Markle (Photofest).

Lightning Strikes Twice starred Mercedes, Ruth Roman, Richard Todd, and Zachary Scott, and was directed by King Vidor. This was a mystery-action film about an ex-convict, wrongfully sent to prison for killing his wife, who eventually discovers the real murderer's identity. Mercedes played a deranged woman in this odd, film noir drama.

The Scarf, directed by Anthony Mann and starring Mercedes and her *All the King's Men* costar John Ireland, was by far the best of the three films she made in 1950. It was certainly McCambridge's most successful screen effort since playing Sadie Burke in *All the King's Men*. The

Inside Straight (1951) was a moderately well received film about a greedy and corrupt couple, played by Mercedes and actor David Brian, who attempt to outdo one another in wickedness.

In the movie *Inside Straight* (one of three pictures starring Mercedes released in 1951) offered the actress her first "period piece" film drama. Set in San Francisco in the late 1800s, Mercedes played Ada Stritch, a financially-oriented female tycoon.

Scarf is about a man accused of murder who is determined to prove his innocence — with the help of a good-hearted, down-to-earth waitress (played by Mercedes). Both the film and Mercedes received favorable critical notices upon *The Scarf*'s release.

Mercedes made her professional singing debut in *The Scarf*, although the film's director, Anthony Mann, had not wanted to use her voice for the scene in which her character sings the sultry "Summer Rain," thinking it would be better to have a professional singer dub the song in the film. Mercedes reminded him that the waitress she was playing would hardly be "slinging hash" if she warbled that well. Mann realized she was absolutely right, and Mercedes sang the song herself on the movie's sound track.

Above: In *Lightning Strikes Twice* (1951), one of Mc-Cambridge's co-stars was actress Ruth Roman (left). McCambridge and Roman were reunited thirty years later when they both appeared in the 1983 film *Echos.*

Right: Numerous films were offered to Mercedes after she won the coveted Academy Award in 1950. She played a major role in *Lightning Strikes Twice*, released in 1951. This first follow-up film, according to Leonard Maltin in his 2003 *Movie and Video Guide*, was "a muddled but engaging yarn of an ex-con returning home to start a new life, who finds the actual killer of his wife."

Mercedes and her former *All the King's Men* co-star, John Ireland, played a couple who become romantically involved in *The Scarf*. Ireland and McCambridge had become good friends during the filming of *All the King's Men*, and, according to critics, they "had good chemistry between them" in this film. In fact, Mercedes and Ireland remained friends for many years after *The Scarf* was released.

In between shooting these three films, Mercedes made her television acting debut, appearing on two dramatic anthology series—*The Chevrolet Tele-Theater* and *The Lux Video Theatre*. By 1953, McCambridge was so much in demand as an actress that she could "pick and choose" what she decided to appear in, a luxury few actors ever attain. She turned down a leading role in the film *The Woman They Almost*

In the film *The Scarf*, Mercedes sang for the first and last time in a film. The song was "Summer Rain."

Lynched, a role ultimately played by the well-established film actress Audrey Totter (who, like Mercedes, was a native of Joliet, Illinois). "The terms were all fine," Mercedes said in an interview with her newly-formed fan club's president, Kevin Corbett, "but it would have meant being separated from my husband [Fletcher Markle] when he launched *Studio One* [the television series] in New York. I felt my place was with him, so I let it go. I have promised myself that I will not make a bad picture just to be in one. And there are few good ones being made. But there will be. And I'll do them!" In the same

Mercedes was very active on television through the 1950s. She appeared in numerous early TV shows, such as *Studio One, Lux Video Theatre, Front Row Center* and *Four Star Playhouse.* Here she appears with actor Louis Hayward in a scene from the teleplay "Crossed and Double Crossed," telecast on December 11, 1952, on the *Ford Television Theater* series.

In 1953, Mercedes was a big enough star to have her own fan club. the club even published a newsletter called *The Mercedes McCambridge Fan Club Journal.* The club's president was Kevin Corbett of New York City, and its vice president was Kay Daly of Los Angeles, California. This candid photograph of Mercedes was taken by Corbett.

interview, which appeared in her fan club's newsletter, she admitted rejecting two stage play scripts that season as well. "One I felt was vulgar and cheap, the other is a revival and I think a little dated. Having done six flops on Broadway, I am very hesitant about jumping into another."

In the early 1950s, Mercedes enjoyed a brief foray into the music industry when orchestra and choral conductor Gordon Jenkins asked her to record a song for Decca Records that he felt required the talents of an experienced actress, rather than a pop singer. The song, entitled "While You Danced, Danced, Danced," was in the tradition of the French chanteuse Edith Piaf, and was rich with pathos. Mercedes sang in a breathless, half talking–half singing style.

Jenkins had become familiar with Mercedes' work on various radio shows he had heard over the years, and felt that capitalizing on her recent film fame as an Academy Award–winning actress certainly wouldn't hurt the recording's commercial possibilities. For a brief time in the early fifties the song was played quite often on several of the disc jockey radio shows heard throughout the United States, but the recording never made *Billboard* magazine's list of best-selling records.

By spring of 1953 Mercedes was a full-fledged movie star; in another interview published in *The Mercedes McCambridge Fan Club Journal* the actress was asked which she preferred — acting in movies, on radio, on TV, or on the stage. Apparently not wanting to say anything that might place herself in professional jeopardy, Mercedes answered diplomatically, "I prefer any of the mediums which offer [me] the best vehicles. A bad stage play runs a poor second to a superior TV script. A run-of-the-mill movie is hardly as satisfying as a good radio program. Therefore, each branch has its own rewards and drawbacks, and it seems to me the average are about equal." When the interviewer asked her which character she most enjoyed playing on the screen thus far, she answered, "Oddly enough, Connie in *The Scarf.* She was a girl who met life on its terms and was false to no one. Her honesty and her loneliness appealed to me greatly. She made no pretense. She was herself and the world could take it or leave it. I wish I had a friend like Connie. It would be good to talk to her." The interviewer ended the article by asking the title of her favorite book, and Mercedes answered, "My favorite book — until this past fall — has always been *A Passage to India.* And *Treasure Island* is a close second. But now, I like best the collection of Governor Stevenson's speeches. This man writes like Lincoln and Mark Twain and Ralph Waldo Emerson, and his speeches are inspiring and full of love of America and what she stands for."

According to critics, the best of Mercedes' trio of films made in 1950 was *The Scarf*. In *The Scarf*, McCambridge played a character named Connie Carter, a good-hearted waitress who helps a man prove that he is innocent of murder. The man was played by Mercedes' *All the Kings Men* co-star, John Ireland.

In addition to her appearances in films and on television in the 1950s, Mercedes continued to work on radio. She was featured on Carlton E. Morse's revised version of his *I Love a Mystery* series, which starred Russell Thorson, Jim Boles, and Tony Randall as private investigators Jack, Doc, and Reggie of the erstwhile A-1 Detective Agency. She also starred in two radio series of her own in the fifties—*Defense Attorney* in 1951, and a CBS soap opera series called *Family Skeleton* in 1954, which was written and produced by Mercedes' old friend and former employer, Carlton E. Morse. Morse created *Family Skeleton* especially for Mercedes. A five-day-a-week domestic drama series, *Family Skeleton* was loosely based on Morse's immensely successful *One Man's Family* program, but unlike that series, which unfolded in "books" and "chapters," *Family Skeleton* was presented in "episodes" and "phases." On this radio drama, the main character, Sarah Ann Spence (played by McCambridge), returns home pregnant and worried, unable to prove her marital status because her marriage license has been obliterated by bloodstains. She thus becomes the "family skeleton." In addition to Mercedes, the series also featured Bill Idelson, Herb Vigran, and Russell Thorson, and ran from June 1953 until March 1954, when Mercedes had to leave the show due to a very busy moviemaking and television show schedule.

McCambridge's 1951 series, *Defense Attorney*, was a half-hour, once-a-week mystery–crime drama radio program on which McCambridge played a sharp lawyer named Martha ("Marty") Ellen Bryant, who spent more time solving crimes with her boyfriend, Jud Barnes (played by Howard Culver) than she did in the courtroom. (An audition recording for a radio series titled *The Defense Rests* had originally been produced by NBC on April 17, 1951, but the half-hour show didn't actually air until August 31, 1951, and on the ABC network of stations.) *Defense Attorney* remained on the air for the remainder of the season, but was canceled from ABC's programming schedule in June 1952. Typical of this series' scripts were "The Man in the Death Cell" and "Sixteen Year Old Hit and Run." The supporting casts on the *Defense Attorney* programs usually featured Tony Barrett, Harry Bartell, Dallas McKennon, Irene Tedrow and Parley Baer. The Martha Ellis Bryant role won McCambridge "Honorary Membership" in the Los Angeles Women's Bar Association, as well as a Phoenix Bar Association award. Betty Mills, of *Radio/TV Mirror* magazine, also named Mercedes "Favorite Dramatic Actress" for her work on *Defense Attorney*.

Throughout the 1950s, Mercedes continued to feature regularly on various television series as well. She appeared on Carlton E. Morse's television version of his long-running and popular radio series *One Man's Family*, playing the character of Beth Holly on the serial drama; and she was also seen on *The Lux Video Theatre* in November 1952, *Tales of Tomorrow* in March 1953, *Studio One* in April and May of 1953 (as well as in January 1956), *Four Star Playhouse* in April 1955, and on the popular TV series *Wagon Train*, *Rawhide*, and *Riverboat* in 1957 and 1959. Two of the 1950s television plays she starred in, were directed by her husband, Fletcher Markle, presented on his *Front Row Center* series. They were an adaptation of F. Scott Fitzgerald's "Tender Is the Night" (in which Mercedes played Nichole Warren), which was telecast on September 7, 1955, and a production of an original television play called "Pretend

You Belong to Me," which aired on April 22, 1956. Of his production of "Tender Is the Night," Markle said, "I did it because Mercedes had always wanted to play Nichole."

In the 1950s, Mercedes also starred on a television series of her own, *Wire Service*, which was first telecast in October 1956. The series was about the newspaper business; and, in addition to Mercedes, it alternately featured film stars George Brent and Dane Clark, each appearing on every third episode. *Wire Service* lasted thirty-nine episodes. Mercedes never received any further money for her work on the series other than her original salary. At the time, she opted for a percentage of the producer's profits instead of asking for residual rights. This proved a poor choice, since her series was canceled after just one season.

As if all this was not enough to keep the actress in the spotlight, Mercedes made two of the most successful films of her motion picture acting career in the 1950s—*Johnny Guitar* (in 1954) and *Giant* (in 1956).

In 1951, even though she had become a major film star, Mercedes continued to work in radio. From August 1951 until December 1952 the actress starred on a weekly radio series called *Defense Attorney*, playing a spirited lady lawyer named Mary Ellen Bryan. McCambridge was honored by several lawyer organizations, including the Los Angeles Women's Bar Association and the Phoenix Bar Association, for her positive portrayal of a lawyer on this weekly radio series.

These films, for a few years at least, made her one of the most popular young character actresses in Hollywood. *Johnny Guitar* has become a cult favorite among film devotees, but it is Mercedes' unpleasant relationship with the film's star, Joan Crawford, that has become the stuff of Hollywood legend. In *Johnny Guitar*, Crawford played "Vienna," owner of a lofty saloon and gambling parlor somewhere out West in the middle of nowhere. The saloon has remained unopened because a group of resentful cattle owners, prompted by McCambridge's character, Emma Small, are trying to drive the stalwart Vienna off their range. McCambridge plays Emma as a nasty, rather dour and intense-looking woman who dresses like the Wicked Witch of the West from *The Wizard of Oz* (albeit *sans* the witch's pointed hat and green makeup, and *avec* a holster and gun at her side). Emma is fiercely jealous of Vienna's "great beauty" and is infatuated with a tough-guy gunslinger (played by Scott Brady), who has his sights set on Vienna, the saloon owner. During the filming of an important scene in *Johnny Guitar*, Crawford became incensed when, as she sat in her trailer–dressing room removing her makeup after a day of filming, she heard Mercedes receiving a loud round of applause from the grips after the actress finished a long monologue in just one take. This meant that the cast and crew could go home early that evening; consequently, everyone on the set was grateful to McCambridge for finishing the scene so promptly. Jealous, because she thought Mercedes must have been far more popular with the company than she was (since Crawford had never earned their applause), Crawford waited for everyone to go home for the evening, and then, it has been speculated, set about tearing Mercedes' costume to shreds. This resulted in a long delay before the next day's filming could begin, and a duplicate costume could be assembled for McCambridge to wear, meaning a late night of filming for everyone involved could be expected. Mercedes'

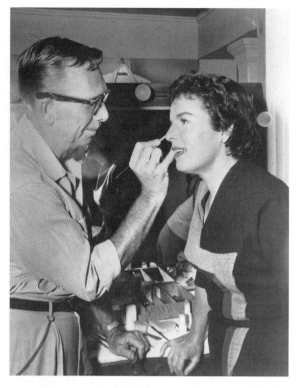

Mercedes enjoyed the glamorous, exciting, and pampered life of a motion picture and television star in the 1950s. Here she receives a makeup touch up before going in front of the camera during the filming of her TV series *Wire Service* in 1956 (Photofest).

boots had mysteriously disappeared altogether, and had to be replaced, which took some doing. The relationship between the two actresses remained "strained," to say the least, for the remainder of the shoot. Actually, the strain seemed to add to the effectiveness and realism of their on-screen feuding. Although she could undoubtedly have said many more negative things about her *Johnny Guitar* co-star's behavior, to her

Pictured here as Emma Small, the character she played in the 1954 Western classic, *Johnny Guitar*, Mercedes became actress/star Joan Crawford's nemesis both on and off the screen. Over the years, the film has gained a cult-like status among motion picture devotees, and today is considered a masterpiece of double entendres and symbolic meanings with supposed hidden lesbian overtones.

Above: Actor Ward Bond and Mercedes, as irate cattle owners, appear in a scene from *Johnny Guitar* (1954). They are hot on the trail of saloon keeper Vienna, played by Joan Crawford, and are determined to "do her in." Mercedes' costume had been mysteriously torn to shreds days before this scene was shot, after she earned a round of applause from the film's cast and crew for successfully completing a "one take" monologue. This had incurred the wrath of the film's star, Miss Crawford.

Right: One of Hollywood's most famous feuds was between Joan Crawford and Mercedes McCambridge. It was apparently put on temporary "hold" when the two actresses greeted each other at a premiere of one of Joan's films in the mid–1950s. Crawford had invited McCambridge to the premiere to squelch rumors about the trouble said to be brewing between the two women. The film they made together, *Johnny Guitar,* was about to open, and Joan felt that stories concerning their conflict on the set might be bad publicity for her and the movie (Photofest).

credit, all Mercedes said in her autobiography about the actress she called "a poor rotten egg of a person" was: "I really can't be bothered thinking about Joan Crawford, or whoever she was. I never wanted to be what she was." According to Robert Osbourne, one of the hosts on the Turner Classic Movies channel, the director of *Johnny Guitar*, Nicholas Ray, was so stressed by the antipathy between Crawford and McCambridge during the filming that he "threw up every morning" before he had to report to work. "There's not enough money in Hollywood," Ray said when shooting had ended, "to make me go through anything like that again."

The film *Giant*, released in 1956, is an epic motion picture that primarily takes place in the Panhandle area of Texas. It starred Elizabeth Taylor as an Eastern girl who marries the rich owner (played by Rock Hudson) of a vast ranch in the Lone Star State. The film chronicles the couple's marriage over a period of about thirty years. Mercedes played the sister of the ranch owner, Luz Benedict, who, until Taylor's character arrived on the scene, had been the woman in charge of the household. Also starring in the film was James Dean, a very popular newcomer to Hollywood, who played a moody and awkward ranch hand named Jett Rink. In the film, Luz Benedict has some sort of undefined relationship with Jett, and when she is killed in a horseback riding accident about a third of the way through the picture, she leaves him some land on which oil is found. Jett eventually becomes a very rich man. Mercedes received a second "Best Supporting Actress" Academy Award nomination for her portrayal of Luz in *Giant*.

During the filming of *Giant* in Texas, Mercedes and Dean developed a close friendship as they spent many long hours together in between shooting their various scenes. Mercedes fondly remembered the actor in her 1981 autobiography as a rebellious, sensitive and unconventional young man who was not at all like any of the other more self-centered, traditional Hollywood juveniles she had met since arriving in Tinseltown. The two enjoyed drinking hard liquor, talking about politics, show business, and the other members of the cast and crew, and occasionally partaking of various other inebriants together, as they wiled away their off-camera time. During their lengthy stay in the Texas Panhandle, they often said something that became a catch phrase between the two of them and was frequently repeated during their conversations. "If you weren't here," Mercedes and Dean said to each other almost daily, "I would kill myself."

James Dean was born in Marion, Indiana, in 1931. According to *Who's Who in the Cinema* (edited by Ann Lloyd and Graham Fuller), Dean had a "disrupted childhood ... the classic grounding for an unhappy adolescence." Like Mercedes, Dean had won a recitation contest while in school, and attended the University of California in Los Angeles (U.C.L.A.), where he became interested in acting. Leaving college before receiving his degree, he appeared in several television commercials, and then won small, but increasingly larger, roles on several "live" dramatic anthology television series, which led to his being signed to a film contract. He earned immediate success in the films *Rebel Without a Cause* and *East of Eden*, becoming — after just two films — one of Hollywood's biggest box office attractions. *Who's Who in the*

In 1956 the film adaptation of Edna Ferber's book *Giant*, Mercedes McCambridge (above) played the role of Luz Benedict, the sister and co-owner of a vast Texas ranch. For her efforts, the actress received a second Academy Award nomination for "Best Supporting Actress in a Film." McCambridge is also shown below with her co-star and friend, actor James Dean, in a scene from *Giant*.

Cinema describes Dean as "a brilliant, natural Method actor who filled the screen with tortured emotion." By the time he signed to play Jett Rink in *Giant*, Dean was one of the most publicized and successful young actors in the film industry, and *Giant* was one of 1955's most anticipated films.

Mercedes was shocked and then depressed when she learned of Dean's untimely death in an automobile accident a few months after she had completed her work in the film. "Such a waste of talent and young life," she later said when asked about the tragedy. The author of the novel the film *Giant* was based upon, Edna Ferber, had also developed a friendship with Mercedes during the filming of *Giant*, and she sent the actress a letter shortly after she heard about Dean's death. She wrote that she remembered how close Mercedes and Dean had become during the shoot, and said, "Perhaps it is strange, my dear Mercedes, but when I learned of Jimmy's death, I thought immediately of you." She ended the letter by saying, "You understood the boy, tried to help him, and did not resent him. Jimmy surprised me by sending me his photograph in costume as Jett Rink. I wrote to him: 'I loved the picture. Your profile is startlingly like John Barrymore, but then I know your motorcycle racing or one thing or another will fix that." Mercedes answered Ferber's letter, telling her exactly where she was when she heard the news about Dean's death, how badly she had felt, that she wished she had done even more to try to help him, and then philosophizing about his talent and the fragile condition of life in general. Mercedes, by this time, was already well into her life as an alcoholic and having some trouble herself finding any solace in what so many people saw as the apparent "perfection" of her own personal and professional life.

At Oscar time, with the memory of Dean's tragic death still fresh in her mind, she found it difficult to take very seriously the concerns everyone else seemed to be having about such trivial things as what she should wear to the annual Academy Awards ceremony. She had been nominated for a second Oscar for her work as Luz Benedict in *Giant*, and she indeed felt honored, but the ghost of James Dean hung over the entire event like a dark cloud. Mercedes' fellow nominees for the "Best Supporting Actress" award were Eileen Heckert (for the film *The Bad Seed*), Mildred Dunnock (for *Baby Doll*), Patty McCormack (for *The Bad Seed*), and Dorothy Malone (for *Written on the Wind*). Drinking seemed to ease the anxiety Mercedes was feeling, and so she drank even more than usual. Actress Marlene Dietrich, with whom Mercedes had became friendly when they both appeared on Fletcher's *Studio One* and *Ford Theater* programs, decided that she would take charge of Mercedes' "glamorization" for the Academy Awards. The day before the Awards ceremony, Marlene had four gorgeous gowns delivered to Mercedes' Bel Air home, and instructed her to select a frock to wear at the Awards. Mercedes, who was used to less "showy" clothes, doubted she could carry off wearing any of the beautiful gowns Marlene had sent to her, but she chose a lovely black chiffon dress designed by Galonas. Even Mercedes

had to admit that she looked every inch the star on the night of the Oscars, and everyone commented that she "had never looked better," and "how absolutely beautiful [she] was." No one looked happier or more adoring of her than her husband, Fletcher Markle, as the two of them entered the auditorium arm-in-arm before the Academy Awards ceremony began. She did not win the "Best Supporting Actress "award that

During the long and drawn-out filming of *Giant* in Texas in 1955, Mercedes became the drinking buddy and good friend and confidante of the young acting sensation of the fifties, James Dean. A tragic automobile accident, which occurred shortly before the film wrapped, cut short his meteoric career (Dean made only three films), but he became a screen legend when he died.

night. Dorothy Malone took home the Oscar, and, in her usual fatalistic way, Mercedes, who always referred to herself as a "cheerful pessimist" (which is what psychoanalyst Sigmund Freud had called himself), began to worry that perhaps this was a sign that her film career might be about to come to an end. Drinking seemed to offer her at least some solace, and so, once again, she drank more than she should at the post–Oscar party. Fletcher and Marlene assured her that her film career was definitely *not* about to end, and Marlene even scolded her like a reproachful parent, reminding her that *she* had never won even one Academy Award and that *she* was still a "Very Big Star!" For the time being, Mercedes' concerns had been placed in their proper perspective.

The next day Mercedes had the gowns that Marlene had sent to her taken back to the star. In a gesture that was so typical of the generous and giving Marlene Dietrich, the black chiffon gown was returned to Mercedes with a note that read, "It never looked that marvelous on me. Please, I want you to have it. Wear it all the time! Don't wear anything else." In her autobiography, Mercedes admitted that she had never known anyone "more giving" than Marlene Dietrich. A short time later, when a recovering Mercedes awoke in the hospital the morning after suffering a miscarriage, Marlene was sitting at her bedside. She had flown all the way from New York to California on a fifteen hour overnight flight to be with her friend — just the way Mercedes' mother had done when Mercedes had lost another baby a few short years before.

The world-famous film star Marlene Dietrich was born in 1901 in a small town outside Berlin in Germany, and was fifty-four years old when she first met Mercedes in 1947. The daughter of a militaristic Prussian police lieutenant and his homemaker wife, Marlene trained in music and began working as a cabaret entertainer soon after she finished her schooling. Eventually, she started making silent films when she was twenty-five years old. In 1930, Marlene appeared in a German picture called *Der Blaue Engel*, playing an immoral young cabaret singer who brings about the destruction of an older man, a college professor, by taking advantage of his sexual interest in her. The film, an enormous success in Europe, was subsequently remade in English and released in the United States and England as *The Blue Angel*. It made Marlene an internationally famous movie star. Press releases for the movie labeled her "the

The glamorous film star Marlene Dietrich, pictured at right, was one of Mercedes McCambridge's closest long-term friends. The two women had met when Marlene was starring on Mercedes' husband Fletcher Markle's *Studio One* and *Ford Theater* radio programs in the late 1940s. They remained good friends until Marlene's death in 1991.

greatest symbol of unfulfilled desire … a
woman safe in the knowledge that the men
always came back for more." Off-screen, Marlene, like her mother, was actually a rather
simple woman who enjoyed nothing more
than cleaning her own house and the houses
of her friends, and cooking meals for people,
which was totally unlike her femme fatale
screen persona. Mercedes, who certainly
benefited from Marlene's kindness and friendship, often said of her, "she is one of the best
friends any woman could ever hope to have."
The two women remained good friends for
the next forty years.

Fletcher Markle, pictured above, was
Mercedes' husband from 1950 until 1961.
Mercedes often referred to Fletcher as
her "Adonis." She adored her talented
and cultured husband, who became a
motion picture and television producer
and director. He first directed Mercedes
in leading roles on his *Studio One* radio
program in 1947–1948, and then later
when he directed several telelvision programs in the 1950s (Photofest).

Fletcher's career throughout the 1950s,
although perhaps not quite as visible as Mercedes', also flourished, and he developed into
a successful Hollywood producer and director.
Markle directed three films in the 1950s—*Jig-
saw* (1950), which he also wrote, *Night into
Morning* and *Man with a Cloak* (both 1951).
He also directed and hosted the *Front Row
Center* television series in 1953, and produced
and directed a TV series based on the long-
running Broadway hit play *Life with Father*, which starred Leon Ames and Lurene
Tuttle.

At one point, Markle also produced and directed the TV version of his *Studio
One* radio program. In a Christmas production of the passion play *The Nativity*,
actress Miriam Wolfe, a regular on the radio series, played the Virgin Mary. Mercedes also appeared on several of the *Studio One* television dramas, including "Shadow
of the Devil" and "Fly with the Hawk" in 1953, and "A Public Figure" in 1956.

Shortly after Mercedes and Fletcher Markle married in 1950, Markle adopted
her son, John, with the blessing of her first husband, Bill Fifield, who had already
settled down into a new life with a new wife. As with Fletcher and his own boy, Stephen, Bill had never been as close to his son as perhaps he should have been. Fifield
arranged for occasional visits with John, but the two never managed to develop a
good father and son relationship, which had always concerned Mercedes.

During this period of their lives in the 1950s, the Markles were more financially
secure than either Mercedes or her "Adonis" (as she called Fletcher) had ever imagined that they could be. The couple owned a large and expensive house in the Bel
Air section of Los Angeles, and lived the life of a very successful young Hollywood
couple. Sandwiched in between their many professional obligations, were numerous
cocktail parties, trips to exotic ports of call (such as Nice, Paris, Buenos Aries, and

the Caribbean Islands), and premieres and nightclubbing. Mercedes had a Ford and Fletcher had a Cadillac parked in their driveway. There were maids and gardeners and handymen to take care of their every need; and, according to Mercedes' autobiography, at this time in her life she enjoyed "Music [Fletcher liked entertaining her by pretending to conduct an orchestra as a phonograph record played, while Mercedes clapped her hands with delight], mums [there were always fresh mums on the table, as per Markle's instructions], Adonis [Markle himself, according to Mercedes], the Pacific Ocean [the view from their house], escargot [the one gourmet dish Mercedes could prepare to the satisfaction of her finicky husband], martinis [a great many martinis], good wine [a good deal of wine], and the top of the world for my oyster." But in addition to her rich and full "ideal" life, Mercedes was gradually becoming a hopeless alcoholic.

These were, however, blindly fun-filled days which the Markles enjoyed as members of the international show biz "jet set." Typical of the madcap, devil-may-care activities the couple enjoyed during this period of their lives was a vacation the couple spent on the French Riviera one summer in the mid–1950s. The glamorous film star of the forties, Rita Hayworth, was also there on the Riviera, trying to escape from the amorous pursuits of the rich potentate Ali Khan, whom she later married. Rita had met Markle several years before when Markle and Orson Welles, to whom she was married at the time, were writing the screenplay for Orson's film *The Lady from Shanghai*, which starred Rita and Orson. When she heard that Fletcher was on the Riviera, she tracked him down at his hotel and insisted that they get together the next evening. Fletcher told Rita that he was on the Riviera with his wife, Mercedes; but, not about to miss an opportunity to go out on the town, Rita asked if they could make the get-together a foursome, providing Fletcher could find her a suitable date for the evening. Fletcher, who adored hobnobbing with the rich and famous, told Rita that he most certainly could get her a date. When he hung up the phone receiver, he began to agonize as to who he could ask to escort Rita around town the following evening. The next morning he still hadn't come up with a name. As Mercedes and Fletcher were having their breakfast in the hotel dining room, their favorite waiter, a young and handsome fellow named Jean Nery whom they had befriended, came up to their table to take their breakfast orders. The minute Fletcher saw Nery, he knew that he had found the perfect escort for Rita. Nery was young, handsome, and charming — all of the things that Rita would require for the evening's activities. As Mercedes, Fletcher and Nery entered the night spot where they had arranged to meet up with Rita, they heard a loud squeal coming from the other side of the room. When they looked towards the origin of said squeal, they saw the beautiful film actress Rita Hayworth, her lovely red-turning-blonde hair piled high upon her head and her gorgeous figure tightly squeezed into a full-skirted white gown, charging toward them. "Fleeetttccchhheeerrr!" she squealed again, as she approached Fletcher, Mercedes and Nery. Rita, although certainly one of Hollywood's loveliest film stars, was not one of its most secure personalities. She had never gotten over the fact that she had been a plump brunette with a low hair line and one thick eyebrow over her eyes.

This was before Columbia Pictures had dyed her hair red, put her on a strict diet, and changed her name from Marguerita Cansino to Rita Hayworth.

Rita and Mercedes got along famously, which surprised Mercedes because she was not particularly impressed with the typical Hollywood glamour girls she had met during her years in show business. The Markles had told Nery that "mum was the word" as far as his being a waiter was concerned. They told Rita that Nery was a young businessman they had met on the beach that week. Rita and the handsome young Monsieur Nery got along very well indeed, and before long they were romantically gazing into each other's eyes as they danced the tango and drank the rest of the evening away. When the two discreetly retired to Rita's hotel room for the remainder of the night, Fletcher and Mercedes knew that the date had been a great success. The Markles, according to Mercedes in her 1981 autobiography, continued to drink the night away until "dawn came up like thunder on the Mediterranean Sea the next morning."

There was, however (much to her credit), a more serious side to Mercedes' celebrity during her most socially active years in the 1950s. One of the actress' closest non–show business relationships in the 1950s was with the Democratic Party's 1952 and 1956 candidate for the Presidency of the United States, Adlai Stevenson, a man Mercedes had admired as the Governor of her home state of Illinois. Mercedes was urged by her father, who was campaigning for Stevenson in Illinois, to lend her support for the liberal candidate's bid for the presidency by using her ever-increasing celebrity to attract voters to him. Mercedes readily agreed to go on the campaign trail for Stevenson, whenever her busy acting schedule permitted. An outspoken, avid Democrat (and she didn't care who knew it), Mercedes traveled 25,000 miles with Adlai Stevenson during his 1952 campaign, and did it again when he ran for the same office in 1956. She was also active on his behalf at the 1960 Democratic convention in Los Angeles when he once again made a bid for the Party's nomination. Mercedes became very impressed with Stevenson's ready wit and charm, his down-to-earth attitude, and his articulate intelligence. He became equally as impressed with her outspokenness and sense of humor, and was genuinely touched by her desire to do whatever she could to help him get elected. The thirty-seven-year-old Mercedes and the fifty-seven-year-old Adlai Stevenson became very close friends during the campaigns. Many people believed that Stevenson was "too intellectual to be president," but Mercedes could not have disagreed more. She was convinced that intellect should be a "plus," and certainly not a "minus," for any President of the United States to have. Since Stevenson was a divorced man, Mercedes became his frequent female companion at various fund-raising activities, as well as at numerous rallies and other public occasions that required his presence.

Adlai Stevenson was born in 1900 in Los Angeles, California, and became one of three members of his family to serve in various government posts. After receiving a law degree from Northwestern University in 1926, he practiced law in Chicago, where he made quite a name for himself as a champion of several liberal causes. He held a number of governmental posts in Washington, D.C., before running for the office of Governor of Illinois. He was elected to that office in 1948 by a large major-ity of votes, and because of his successful tenure in that office, he became his party's candidate for the Presidency of the United States in 1952, running against the pop-ular Republican Party candidate, General Dwight D. Eisenhower. Eisenhower, one of World War II's hero generals, easily won the election. In 1956, Stevenson once again ran for the office against the then-incumbent President Eisenhower, and once again the election ended in Stevenson's defeat. During the 1960 Democratic con-vention, Stevenson once more sought the Democratic Party's nomination, but did not win it. The party nominated a young, good-looking senator from Massachusetts, John F. Kennedy, as their candidate for president. In 1961, Kennedy, after winning the presidency, appointed Adlai Stevenson Ambassador to the United Nations, a posi-tion that earned him wide respect. Stevenson became well known for the eloquent speeches he made at the United Nations.

Mercedes once said of Stevenson, "No person, aside from my son, has ever shown me the gentle concern I knew from Governor Stevenson. He always endeavored to understand, and gave logical reasons, to the dumb things I did. He even carried my cause to others." Stevenson did indeed dote on Mercedes, and she responded to him accordingly. When he was the Ambassador to the United Nations, he would intro-duce Mercedes to foreign dignitaries as "America's finest public speaker ... female!" (Stevenson was America's finest *male* public speaker, of course.) One of the things that Mercedes said she particularly liked about Stevenson was that he could always laugh at himself — never with bitterness, but "with a tolerant acceptance of his own stuffiness." He once said to the actress, "Dear girl, you are going to kill yourself work-ing for me," to which she answered that she couldn't think of "a better way to go." Twice, she added, she almost did die for him — if not literally, then certainly figura-tively — when he lost his two bids for the presidency. To describe her close friend-ship with Stevenson, in her autobiography Mercedes wrote about a time she and a group of his celebrity supporters, including Mercedes, Humphrey Bogart and his wife, Lauren Bacall, and actor Robert Ryan, were returning by airplane to Los Ange-les after he made his final concession speech. The Governor, Mercedes said, patted the seat next to him and said, "Now my Illinois girl, this is where you belong. Right next to an Illinois boy."

"Mr. Stevenson knew," Mercedes said, that she "worshipped the ground on which he walked." She told him so many times. There were a great many women who loved Adlai Stevenson, the actress said, but only she had gotten to read for him when they were alone, and was "sustained by [her] lion's share of his legacy." "He loved me so," she said. "He told me so."

In the late 1950s, Mercedes McCambridge made four more feature films, in addi-tion to her appearances on television, her work on radio, and her active campaign-ing on behalf of Governor Stevenson. In 1957 she played the part of a stern nurse in a lackluster adaptation of Ernest Hemingway's novel *A Farewell to Arms*, which was directed by Charles Vidor and starred Rock Hudson and Jennifer Jones. Elaine Stritch, with whom Mercedes shared most of her scenes, played the less stern of the two

While Mercedes campaigned for Adlai Stevenson during his bid for the presidency of the United States in 1952 and then again in 1956, the actress logged in thousands of air miles as she criss-crossed the country speaking on Stevenson's behalf (Photofest).

nurses in the film. Mercedes also had a cameo role in a film called *A Touch of Evil* in 1958, which she agreed to do as a favor for her long-time friend Orson Welles, the picture's director and star. Several years before, Mercedes and Fletcher had come to Orson's rescue when he needed two people to act as his daughter Beatrice's godparents, having forgotten all about the christening until a few hours before the event

In 1952 and 1956 the Democratic Party's liberal candidate for the presidency of the United States was Governor Adlai Stevenson of Illinois, pictured above during the 1952 campaign. A lifelong liberal, Miss McCambridge, became one of Stevenson's most ardent supporters and campaigners, and the two became very good friends. They remained close until Stevenson's death in 1965.

took place. In the middle of his filming of *A Touch of Evil*, Welles had an inspiration for a new scene he wanted to add to the film, and called Mercedes early one morning, telling her to report to the Universal Studios lot by 1:30 that afternoon wearing a black leather jacket. One did not refuse such a request when it came from Maestro Welles, and so she borrowed her son's leather jacket, put on black slacks, and arrived at Universal Studios as she had been instructed to do. She shot the scene at five o'clock that evening. She later admitted, "I would do anything for Orson." In *A Touch of Evil*, Mercedes played the cameo role of a tough, boyish-looking gang member who terrorizes the film's heroine, Janet Leigh, with a group of fellow thugs in a sleazy motel room on the Mexican-U.S. border.

Another time, Mercedes had been patiently waiting for Orson to shoot a scene in one of the on-going films he was always working on whenever he had gathered up enough money to continue the project. It was late in the afternoon, Mercedes was tired and hungry after a long day spent sitting around waiting to shoot her scene, and she was obviously peeved at all of the delays. Orson berated her for looking so "gloomy," and she shouted at him, "Orson, I am one hundred percent Irish. I was born to be gloomy, intense, and thoughtful. Where would Eugene O'Neill have been if..."

Welles stopped her dead in her tracks when he shot back: "It comes to this, does it? We have Damien the Leper, Jude the Obscure, and now Mercy the Morbid." Everyone in the studio laughed, including "Mercy," and preparations for the scene proceeded.

Later that year, Mercedes was in England filming an adaptation of Tennessee Williams' *Suddenly Last Summer*, directed by Joseph L. Mankiewicz. *Suddenly Last Summer* boasted a stellar cast of Hollywood luminaries that included Katharine Hepburn, Montgomery Clift, and Elizabeth Taylor. In the film, Mercedes played Taylor's weak-willed mother. *Suddenly Last Summer* received mixed reviews from the

critics when released in 1959, but the filming proved memorable for Mercedes because of a relationship she developed with one of the film's stars, Montgomery Clift. During the shoot, Mercedes became friendly with actor Clift when the two of them shared a daily limousine ride from Central London, where the cast was living, to the film studio on the city's outskirts. Like Mercedes "Monty" Clift, who was born in Omaha, Nebraska, in 1920, made his professional acting debut while in his teens. Mercedes had first met Clift years before when he appeared on her husband Fletcher Markle's *Studio One* and *Ford Theater* radio programs in the late 1940s. At that time he was already an established film star.

When fans wrote to film star McCambridge in the mid–1950s asking for a photograph, this is one of the pictures the actress sent to them with her compliments. The photograph is certainly one of the most attractive portraits of the actress ever taken.

A sensitive, moody and introspective actor, Clift (who, it was later revealed, was a homosexual) had already begun to sink into the abyss of alcoholism and pills that eventually took his life at the age of forty-six, less than seven years after he appeared in *Suddenly Last Summer* with Mercedes. The actress later said of her friendship with Clift, "I saw myself in that sensitive, kind wreck of a man that I came to know during the long months of filming in England." She admitted that although she could not help but love the man, she hated what she knew he was doing to himself, and therefore also began to hate herself for her own excesses. Unfortunately, she appears to have been helpless to do anything about either her own, or Monty Clift's, crippling addictions at that time.

Actor Montgomery Clift and Mercedes became good friends when the two of them shared a limousine each morning during the filming of *Suddenly Last Summer* in London in the late 1950s. Clift was in the throws of his various addictions at the time, and his obvious drinking problem and self-destructive nature gave Mercedes, herself a serious alcoholic by that time, pause regarding her own addictive behavior.

At the height of her film fame in the late 1950s, Mercedes was rewarded with a star on the famous "Hollywood Walk of Fame" in Los Angeles. One day Mercedes and her son John were on their way to her dentist's office, which was near Hollywood and Vine, when she stopped at the spot where her newly laid "star" had been set in cement. She had not told John about it, because she wanted to surprise him. Without saying a word, Mercedes knelt down, took out a Kleenex from her pocketbook and began to polish the star, hoping that John would be bowled over with amusement. He wasn't at all impressed with her behavior and merely stood there, looking down imperiously at his mother making a horse's ass of herself, and never said a word. Mercedes, you must remember, did not like to be made anyone's fool, so she simply got up and the two silently continued on their way to the dentist's office.

By the beginning of the 1960s, Mercedes' career and her marriage to Fletcher Markle were in serious trouble because of her heavy drinking. Eleven years after they were married, Fletcher decided that that it would be best for them to come to a final parting of the ways, and he sued Mercedes for divorce. *He* had been able to handle his liquor, *Mercedes* had not. By that time, she was a full-fledged alcoholic, and their home life had become unbearable for the "everything-must-be-perfect" Mr. Markle. Two years after he divorced Mercedes, Fletcher Markle enjoyed one of the most important successes of his film directing career. In 1963, Markle directed the charming film *The Incredible Journey*, which was about a cat and two dogs who, after they become separated from their owners while on vacation, embark upon an incredible journey over thousands of miles to find their way home. Based on a book by Shelia Burnford, the film featured Fletcher's Canadian actor friend John Drainie, whom he had brought to New York with him years before when he first began his radio directing career in the United States. Soon after the film's release, Fletcher moved back to Canada with a new wife, Dorothy, to whom he apparently remained happily married for the remainder of his life. In Canada, Fletcher produced and hosted a successful television series for CBC called *Telescope*, which presented half-hour biographical programs about various well-known Canadian celebrities. Fletcher and Dorothy moved back to the United States in the late 1960s; and although he resumed his producing and directing career in Hollywood, he never enjoyed the acclaim, nor fulfilled the promise, of his earlier career.

When Fletcher left her, Mercedes sank into a deep depression and tried to take her own life, but failed. She continued to drink with ever-increasing intensity, but somehow she managed to continue working. In 1961, Mercedes made one of the best movies of her filmmaking career. The picture was *Angel Baby* directed by Paul Wendkos, and it was one of her favorite films. Her performance as the shrewish wife of a much-younger man (a promoter for a pretty, young female evangelist) was well received by the critics, if not by the public. *Angel Baby* had the misfortune of being

In the film *Angel Baby* Mercedes McCambridge had one of her most challenging roles. As the considerably older, shrewish wife of a female evangelist's promoter, played by George Hamilton (pictured above with McCambridge), the actress received some of the best critical reviews of her career. Over the years, the film has taken on classic status among a cult-like following of movie buffs.

By the time the film *Angel Baby* was released in 1961, Mercedes' alcoholism had become a serious problem for the actress. A scene in *Angel Baby* in which she gets drunk after learning that her much younger husband has become attracted to a younger woman is painfully realistic in its intensity.

released at the same time as another film about evangelists—called *Elmer Gantry*—which possessed a considerably larger advertising budget. "Poor little *Angel Baby* got pushed around because the wonderfully trusting producers mortgaged everything but their wives and children to make it," Mercedes said in a May 1965 *Films in Review* magazine article. "It's an honest and true picture," she continued, "but because there was no money for promotion, nobody will ever know about it." In reality this did not prove to be the case, because, once again, film devotees eventually made *Angel Baby*, like *Johnny Guitar*, a cult film classic.

With her alcoholism at its peak, life almost came to an end for Mercedes when, in desperation, she drank a bottle of wine vinegar because there was nothing else alcoholic in her home. She was alone at the time. Her son was away at boarding school, her husband had left her and there was no liquor in her apartment to offer her "a bit of comfort." She knew as she lay in the hospital suffering from the damage done to her stomach by the vinegar that she was in serious trouble, and that she either had to change her life style and continue to live, or drink and die, like her friend James Dean. She pulled herself together temporarily, recovered from the cider vinegar poisoning, and went back to work.

In addition to *Angel Baby*, in the early 1960s Mercedes also featured in the epic Western saga *Cimarron*. In this film, a remake of the classic motion picture of the same name made in the 1930s, Mercedes played a rough and ready pioneer woman named Sarah Wyatt who, with her crusty old husband (played by Arthur O'Connell) and their passel of kids, heads across the frontier to begin a new life. Mercedes, in spite of her increasingly heavy drinking, also managed during this time to appear on episodes of such popular television series as *Overland Trail*, *Rawhide*, *The Dakotas*, *Bonanza*, *The Nurses*, *The Defenders*, *Dr. Kildare*, *Lost in Space*, and *Bewitched*.

In November 1962, Mercedes' personal life suffered another serious setback when her son John was beaten by muggers in Santa Monica. His skull was crushed and he was not expected to live, but John survived the attack and made a full recovery. The following February, however, while Mercedes was on the road touring in a play, she once again had to rush home to a California hospital to be at her son's side, when John was seriously injured in an automobile accident. The strain of these two events, and the fact that Mercedes was still in the depths of her alcoholism, led her to once again attempt suicide by taking an overdose of sleeping pills. She had gone home exhausted after her breathless cross-country flight to be with John, and the twenty-four continuous hours she had spent at his bedside at the hospital. She awoke the next day in the same hospital that John was in, remembering nothing about the previous day, her stomach having been pumped clean of its contents once again. "Nobody loves life more than I do," Mercedes lamented several years after the event. "But [at that time] there was just … no more will in me. I wanted to be out … away! I just closed it all off, I guess. As the doctor said, I was emotionally bankrupt." Both John and Mercedes survived these ordeals, and John eventually went back to college while Mercedes resumed her acting career.

It was a doctor at Mt. Sinai hospital in New York City, Dr. Stanley N. Gitlow, who proved instrumental in Mercedes finding her way out of her alcoholic abyss. While at Mt. Sinai recovering from a severe case of bronchitis (brought on by her excessive drinking and heavy cigarette smoking), Dr. Gitlow told her, very directly, that he believed that she was an alcoholic, something Mercedes certainly had suspected but could never quite admit to herself. He assured her that he did not think that she was a bad person because of this, since he believed alcoholism was an illness as serious as diabetes or any other potentially fatal disease. Dr. Gitlow urged her to commit herself to a treatment center for alcoholics located in Lima, Peru. Mercedes, hopeful that she could indeed overcome her drinking problem, took his advice and

went to Lima, which was located well out of the public spotlight, to receive treatment. Amazingly, the woman in charge of the alcohol treatment center in Lima was "Snookie" Meyer, whom Mercedes had gone to grade school with and who had become a nun, Sister Mary Arthur. "God works in mysterious ways," Mercedes later said of her chance encounter with Sister Mary Arthur, who became instrumental in helping her control her disease. At the clinic, Mercedes learned that

One of the last big-budget films in which Mercedes had a major role was the 1960 remake of the epic Western *Cimarron*. McCambridge played a raw-boned pioneer woman named Sarah Wyatt, the wife of a crusty-but-good-natured man (played by Arthur O'Connell). The couple had a whole passel of kids to keep under control as the family ventured West, encountering numerous hardships.

84 percent of all alcoholics came from families with a history of abnormal drinking. Researchers, she was told, had reported that persons with such a family history faced odds of four-to-one at birth that they would become alcoholics if they drank at all. Mercedes became convinced that she had indeed been born with a predisposition to the disease; her family had all been heavy drinkers.

In her autobiography, Mercedes wrote about some of the insights she received concerning her own addiction to alcohol in that treatment center in Lima, Peru. "I believe I had little chance," she said, "of avoiding my disease. For me, caffeine, nicotine, Novocain, aspirin, Valium, Librium, and alcohol are all not the oral magic that erases pain for other people. For me the results are disastrous. I lose all control after two drinks of anything. People used to tell me that I would spend a whole evening with them, behaving no more foolishly than anyone else, but the following morning I would not remember anything that happened after the first two drinks were served. I would have gone on drinking with the rest of them, but it was a total blackout time for me. I was trying to drink like everybody else. I couldn't make it."

After her disease was brought under control, Mercedes did not talk publicly about her drinking problem. She had decided it would be best to remain quiet about her disease if she intended to continue working as an actress. "Alcoholism can, and has, enhanced *other* actors' careers," Mercedes later stated in her autobiography. "John Wayne's drunken brawls were considered part of his charm. The terribly sick John Barrymore became a spectacle for public glee as he snorted and staggered his way across the stage to his death. Alcoholism for males is macho. But a woman alcoholic who is a performer has a rough row to hoe. How often does anybody say, 'Why can't you drink like a woman?'"

In November 1966, just when Mercedes was beginning to get her personal and professional life back on track, she suffered a setback. Her beloved father, John Patrick McCambridge, died at the age of 73. In her autobiography, Mercedes wrote about the love and affection she had always felt for her father, whom she knew she was, in many ways, so like in his desire for attention and his love of storytelling (and his enjoyment of a good laugh every now and then with a favored group of friends). John Patrick and Marie McCambridge had moved to California to be near their daughter, and one of their sons and their families, several years before. Mercedes arranged to have her father's body prepared for burial in California and then shipped back to Kanakee, Illinois, for an Irish wake held at Clancy's Funeral Home, so that all of his many friends in the Chicago area could attend the event and share stories about their fun-loving former friend. When Mercedes said her final farewell to her father before he was laid to rest, she thought, as she looked down at his body lying in his coffin, that he looked like a young man in his early forties. His features were still sharp and handsome, and he had a slight smile on his lips and laugh lines at the corner of his eyes, which made him look as if he were sharing an amusing little secret with his daughter. Before the lid of the coffin closed for the final time, Mercedes, left alone with him to say "Goodbye," leaned over and kissed him on the forehead and thanked him for her life.

Mercedes made four very bad films in 1965, 1968, and 1969, three of which it probably would have been better had she turned them down. They were *Run Home Slow* (1965); *Counterfeit Killer* (1968), a made-for-television film and the best of the four; the dreary, heavy-handed sexploitation movie *Marquis de Sade* (1969)*;* and a picture that offered unflattering lesbian overtones, *99 Women* (1969), which was shot inexpensively in Europe.

The real high points of her acting career in the 1960s, however, were not in films or on television, but on the stage. In 1963, Mercedes returned to stage acting after a fifteen-year absence when she replaced actress Shelley Winters in an Off Broadway production of Lewis John Carlino's somewhat avant garde play *Cages*. Mercedes received some of the best reviews of her stage acting career for her performance in *Cages*; but, unfortunately, the size of the audiences were not as impressive as she would have wished. "People gripe about there being nothing new in the theater," she complained after she opened in the play and the audiences remained sparse. "But when there is, they don't come."

Her real stage acting triumph occurred, however, shortly after she had gained control over her drinking problem. On January 14, 1964, Mercedes replaced actress Uta Hagen as Martha in Edward Albee's successful play, *Who's Afraid of Virginia Woolf?* on Broadway, and then played the role in a subsequent national tour. *Who's Afraid of Virginia Woolf?* is set in the living room of a middle-aged couple named George and Martha. They have just come home from a faculty party at the college where George teaches biology and Martha's father serves as college president. They are drunk and very argumentative. During a long night of painful games, nasty comments, embarrassing humiliations, painful confrontations, and bitter humor, they reveal secrets about themselves (as well as about a young couple they have invited back to their home for a nightcap). Both couples' illusions are viciously shattered during the course of a long evening of drinking. At play's end, George and Martha realize several truths about themselves and their relationship, and the play ends quietly, with the two of them understanding and sharing their pain. Mercedes gave what many people consider one of the best performances of her career as Martha. She continued to appear in the play, was first seen on Broadway in 1962, until it ended its Broadway run on May 16, 1964 after 664 performances.

Critic Norman Nadel of New York's *Morning Telegram and Sun* compared the performances of Donald Davis, who played George in the play, and Mercedes McCambridge, as Martha, with those of the original George and Martha, Arthur Hill and Miss Hagen. He commented that "Hill and Hagen were a force of evil the instant that you met them, whereas the new players [Mercedes and Mr. Davis] do not provide this instant uneasiness ... they prefer to build into the tensions and tortures, using comedy as a deception to make the audience more vulnerable later." Nadel went on to describe Mercedes as having "a good range of emotional response, plus a deadly effective way of holding herself in check for a few seconds before triggering her anger. It's like," the critic said, "the good back-swing of a golf club."

In the May 1965 issue of *Films in Review*, Mercedes said of *Who's Afraid of Virginia*

Woolf?: "Anybody would drop dead to play a part like that. I couldn't wait to get to the theater. Think of being paid to vent spleen and venom, all your pent-up monstrosities, every night. People pay thousands of dollars to psychoanalysts to let go that way."

While Mercedes was appearing in *Who's Afraid of Virginia Woolf?* on Broadway, she began a relationship with another older man, one who, like Adlai Stevenson, became an important part of her life. The man's name was Billy Rose. Billy owned the theater in which *Who's Afraid of Virginia Woolf?* was being performed, and he frequently visited her backstage during the show's run. Mercedes and Billy would often go to Sardis' restaurant after an evening's performance for a bite to eat. Gradually, an ever-closer friendship developed between the unlikely couple. Billy Rose was a show business tycoon who produced Broadway spectaculars like

Replacing Uta Hagen and Arthur Hill, the actors who originated the roles on Broadway in 1962, Donald Davis played "George" and Mercedes McCambridge played "Martha" in Edward Albee's *Who's Afraid of Virginia Woolf?* until the play ended its Broadway run at the Billy Rose Theater in New York on April 16, 1964. McCambridge received some of the most glowing reviews of her entire career for her work in *Who's Afraid of Virginia Woolf?*, and she played the role of "Martha" in the subsequent national touring company production of the play (Photofest).

the Aquacade. He was also a songwriter and a collector of fine art, as well as a millionaire investor and an all-around financial genius. According to Mercedes, in addition to his business expertise, Billy Rose was "a wonderful conversationalist." He was well known as a "lady killer," and was considered very attractive to many women, even though he was a small, dumpy and certainly not-very-handsome man. Rose had been married to comedienne Fanny Brice from 1929 until 1938, when the couple divorced because of his many extra-marital affairs. Soon after Fanny and Billy divorced, he married the beautiful swimming star Eleanor Holm, but they divorced in 1954. He then married actress and model Joyce Matthews in 1956, whom he divorced and then remarried in 1965 after his relationship with Mercedes had ended. In between marriages to Joyce Matthews, Billy married Doris Warren Vidor, whom

Show business tycoon, songwriter, and producer Billy Rose owned the Broadway theater (named after him) in which Mercedes appeared in Edward Albee's *Who's Afraid of Virginia Woolf?* in the 1960s. Mercedes and Billy developed a close relationship that lasted until Mercedes decided to end their affair in the late 1960s. Mercedes claimed Rose, a well known philanderer as well as philanthropist, was "one of the kindest and most generous men" she had ever known (Photofest).

he also divorced shortly after the wedding. None of this mattered very much to Mercedes, who enjoyed his company enormously, whatever his domestic arrangements were. The feisty, short (five-foot-two) Russian-Jewish man and the feisty, short (also five-foot-two) Irish Catholic woman became an unusual, but apparently compatible, couple-about-town. Mercedes said that the best times she spent with Billy were when they talked the night away about all manner of subjects. She once asked Rose if there had been "a continuing motivation that had persisted throughout his life." "When you find yourself in a tunnel," Billy answered, after he thought about what she had asked him for a long time, "don't turn back. Keep going until you see a steady gleam of light at the other end, and go for it with all your might, knocking down everything that stands in your way." In her autobiography, Mercedes admitted that she really loved little Billy Rose — "Perhaps not enough, but quite a bit."

Billy Rose was born William Samuel Rosenberg on September 9, 1899, to Jewish-American parents on the Lower East Side of New York City. He always said that he regretted never having gone to college, and was embarrassed by the fact that he only had a high school education. Billy was, however, a very ambitious young man, and when he graduated from high school he went to his family and friends — and his family's friends — and asked them to invest in his future … at five dollars apiece. He guaranteed them a profit. Billy received enough money from people to enroll in a business college, where he learned stenography and typing and became a "cracker-jack" secretary. He was hired by the man who had invented the Gregg shorthand system to prove its efficiency, and this was followed by a position as a chief stenographer for the celebrated and very wealthy investor, city planner, and philanthropist Bernard Baruch in 1918. Since it was during World War I, Rose's duties included the reorganization of the War Manpower Commission's stenographic corps for its chairman, Bernard Baruch. His exceptional abilities did not go unnoticed, and Baruch decided to take Billy under his wing and guide him with his finances, eventually making Rose a very wealthy man.

When Mercedes' son, John Lawrence Markle, who was an Economics major at U.C.L.A. and was about to receive his Doctor of Economics degree at the time, heard about his mother being seen in public with Billy Rose, he called her on the telephone from California and berated her for dating that "infamous, notorious, little man who has been married *twenty-five* times." Mercedes told John that Billy was "a marvelous person … a brilliant and terribly lonely man." Astutely aware of John's interest in money and financial matters, she then added, "You know Mr. Rose is one of the richest men in America and he has no children of his own." After a long pause, John finally asked, "Mom, do you mean he has no children at all?" That ended any further criticism of little Billy Rose by John Lawrence Markle. Eventually, Mercedes decided that, "the boat they had embarked upon together was bound to sink like the Titanic," and ended the relationship "before things got out of hand."

Mercedes was shocked when she heard about Billy's death at the age of sixty-four on February 10, 1966. She mourned his loss and wrote in her 1981 autobiography: "He was one of the kindest and most loving men I have ever known."

Another of Mercedes' most treasured companions was a little white Scottish ter-
rier that her friend Adlai Stevenson had given her in 1963. Mercedes doted on the
little dog, whom Stevenson had dubbed "Sir Malcolm Percy." In 1967 Mercedes took
a case before the Canine Review Board in New York City on behalf of her beloved
pet, Sir Malcolm. Mercedes brought charges against a New York City policeman
whom she claimed had chased her dog across Central Park in a police car so fast that
he had almost run the animal down. "The dog's tail," she told the judge, "was just
inches in front of the police car. If my dog had panicked, he would have been killed."
She called the chase "the worst kind of Storm Trooper action; it was cruel; it was like
a scene from a bad movie of Hitler's day!" She continued, "I know it was wrong to
let my dog go without a leash in Central Park and I am willing to pay the five dollar fine, but that was the most blatant example of cruelty I've ever seen!" The policeman who had harassed Sir Malcolm was reprimanded for his behavior, and Mercedes
left the hearing with her dog, satisfied that justice had indeed been served.

In 1969 Mercedes received a phone call from Senator Hughes of Iowa, who was
the Chairman of the Senate Subcommittee on Alcoholism and himself a recovering
alcoholic. Senator Hughes asked her to testify on national television about her bout
with alcoholism before his committee in Washington, D.C. Mercedes was perplexed
by his request because she had never made a public issue of her problem with alcohol. "Why me?" she asked Senator Hughes. "I am a very private person."

"Why not you?" Senator Hughes replied. She thought about this and then decided,
"Indeed, why not!" and agreed to speak before the committee. Her speech, published
in the Congressional Record, became a landmark for people seeking understanding
from the public about their disease, alcoholism, and also revealed a great deal about
what she had personally undergone during her life as an alcoholic. The speech stated:

> I am a recovered alcoholic person, a recovered alcoholic of the protected Bel Air
> type. The American Medical Association tells me that my alcoholism is a disease. The
> American Medical Association tells me that my alcoholism is the third, if not fourth,
> largest killer of people in this country. Therefore, with those statistics, I must be con-
> vinced that my disease can be terminal.
>
> I am equally convinced that my disease can be arrested. My own disease is in
> that state now and has been for some considerably rewarding, splendid, and truly
> awesome time.
>
> I say "awesome" because the remarkable thing about my disease, which could
> be terminal, is that I, in a certain sense, hold jurisdiction over it. I can choose to
> accelerate my disease to one or two inevitable conclusions ... an alcoholic death or
> incurable insanity, or I can choose to live within my thoroughly human condition. I
> submit that is a remarkable thing.
>
> It has never been more remarkable to me than it is at this moment when I am
> aware that perhaps my own survival, when so many have died, is for that purpose,
> so that I can sit with you at this level with utmost respect and talk to you about this
> matter of life or death ... my life or death.
>
> As I sit here, scores of women like me are being arranged on slabs in morgues
> throughout this country with tickets on their toes that read "acute alcoholism," or if

they have been protected as I was, those tags may read "liver ailment," "pneumonia," "chronic bronchitis," "massive hemorrhage," but the mother of all of those veiled, protective tickets may well be alcoholism, pure and simple.

I drank, like everybody else, for a while ... until this structure that is my body began its rejection, its refusal to absorb physiologically the alcohol that I put into it. My body lacks certain faculties, certain vitally needed faculties that most people have, to burn off and throw off alcohol.

This delicious chemical, this social amenity, this medicine that puts people at their ease because merely being together without it makes them uncomfortable, this medicine became my poison. The insidious diabolical evil, the viciousness of my disease, is that the poison sets up its own craving for more of itself...

So I would get sick. A doctor would be summoned, as doctors are being summoned this afternoon to fine homes all over this country to minister to ladies who are crouching in corners in the master bedroom suite, and the doctor will

Once she had overcome her addiction to alcohol in the late 1960s, McCambridge became one of the most active spokespersons on behalf of recovering alcoholics. She fulfilled countless speaking engagements for various organizations, promoting understanding that alcohol was a disease that could be controlled but never cured, all over the country until her retirement in the mid–1990s (Photofest).

administer to this lady by injecting her buttocks with something that will put her to sleep, and he will leave on the dressing table two or three prescriptions to get her over the rough times that will follow.

I can unequivocally state that if I had taken one-tenth of all of the prescriptions prescribed for me, for me to recover, I would be long since dead. Senators, I am absolutely convinced of that. I never did take much medicine, I don't like to take medicine, thank God. But the woman who wakes up and the doctor has left a little something called a calm-downer and she has that. Then he has left something else called a psychic energizer and she has that, according to his prescription, and then she goes out into the living room and, "Oh, well," says her protective family, "a martini never hurt anybody," so she has a martini.

She has two, maybe, maybe no more than two in the beginning. Dinner, desultorily done, something to make her sleep, she wakes up in the morning, she feels badly, I submit this is the onset of alcoholism in its most disastrous fashion. The fat race had begun.... There is only one way for this woman to go...

I had been at the University of Mississippi in Oxford, working on a production with the students. Word came that a great and brilliant woman had died tragically and alone in a bathroom in a foreign country. This woman had been very good to me at a time when I needed a friend. I was in Mississippi and she was dead in London. She was Judy Garland.

All day long I thought about two doctors who understood people like me ... and I telephoned these two doctors, one a psychiatrist and one an internist. I had to say to them, "You must feel when you read this morning [about Judy's death] that you can't be doing much that is right, because in such a short recent time three of your patients, brilliantly, exciting special people who made this planet a better place for their having been on it, are dead, alone. [The other two patients were Montgomery Clift and Nicky Hilton.]

I wanted these doctors to know that I realized I could have been any one of these people. I know that sitting here now. There is no question in my mind. Nobody need die of this disease. We are eminently salvageable. We are well worth the trouble. We are eminently equipped to enrich this world. We wrote poetry, we paint pictures, we compose music, we build bridges, we head corporations, we win the coveted prizes for the world's greatest literature, and too often too many of us die from our disease, not our sin, not our weakness ...

If you think along with our Puritanical ancestors, that the alcoholic is a spineless weakling, a morally culpable wreck, I would remind you from Shakespeare's *Measure for Measure:*

> Go to your bosom;
> Knock there, and ask your heart what it doth know
> That's like my brother's fault: if it confess
> A natural guiltiness such as is his,
> Let it not sound a thought upon your tongue
> Against my brother's life. Go gentle, my lord.

At the end of her testimony before the committee, Mercedes concluded:

Lastly, I would remind you, probably on your way to your office this morning you saw what has become known as a skid-row bum asleep on a park bench. That man and I *are* the same person. There is a difference between us. I am sitting here addressing you with my own sense of dignity, with a certain pride, an enormous gratitude and my priceless sense of self esteem, because I know I have my right to my life.

The bum need only be shown that he has his right to his.

Thank you.

When she rose to leave the committee room, Mercedes received a thunderous round of applause from those attending the hearing. Senator Yarborough, a member of the committee, said, "Miss McCambridge, I vote you another Oscar, this time for public service."

For all intents and purposes, Mercedes' career throughout the 1960s was, as previously stated, most rewardingly spent on the stage, touring the country in productions of such celebrated plays as *The Madwoman of Chaillot* (playing the title role), a play about an eccentric Frenchwoman who cannot accept the fact that the world is not as beautiful a place as it once was; *The Little Foxes*, by Lillian Hellman (with McCambridge playing Regina Giddons), which is about a greedy Southern family who plot against each other to increase their personal fortunes; *The Glass Menagerie*, by Tennessee Williams (with Mercedes as Amanda Winfield, a role her good friend, actress Laurette Taylor, had originally essayed on the Broadway stage), a play about a mother trying to live in the past — to the dismay of her single son, who considers himself a failure, and her daughter, who is crippled and love-starved; and *The Miracle Worker* (playing Helen Keller's teacher Annie Sullivan), a factually-based play about a teacher who breaks through to a deaf and blind girl, Helen Keller, and helps her communicate with others.

In 1969, soon after she testified before the Senate Subcommittee on Alcoholism, McCambridge appeared in a production of the play *The Show Off*, which co-starred comedian-actor Dick Shawn, Linda Bennett, Monroe Arnold and Donald Buka. The play was presented at the John Kenley Theater in Warren, Ohio. The brief biographies supplied by performers for a play's printed program, in addition to listing their past theatrical credits, occasionally gave information about their off-stage activities as well. These biographical sketches usually revealed only what the performer wanted the reader to know — or what they *wished* had happened (to make them sound more interesting). Accordingly, from play to play (as the reader of this book might have noticed from McCambridge's previously mentioned theater program "bios") the entries changed over the years. When she appeared in *The Show Off* at the Kenley Theater, Mercedes' biography stated, "Her real love has always been the Theatre and recently she has concentrated her efforts almost exclusively on the stage. In addition to *Who's Afraid of Virginia Woolf*, she has appeared extensively throughout the country in *The Miracle Worker, Candida, The Little Foxes, The Glass Menagerie,* and *The Subject Was Roses.*" The program also stated, "She is currently at work on a concert tour presenting 'The World's Greatest Actress,' which is her study and interpretation of Sarah Siddons. She is also at work on a book about Mrs. Siddons [no such book is known to have been published] for which she is under contract to her British publishers who published her first book, 'The Two of Us.'" In addition, the Kenley Theater program mentioned that she had "been honored three times for her work on behalf of hospitals and has been cited by the National Hemophilia Foundation, having enlisted as members Mr. and Mrs. Richard Burton [Elizabeth Taylor], who have been enormously generous toward this charity."

In spite of the personal setbacks Mercedes faced throughout the 1960s, her acting career

This atypical, overly glamorized photograph of Mercedes McCambridge appeared on the back of the program for the Warren Ohio, John Kenley Theater production of *The Show Off* in 1969. It depicts Mercedes in an almost unrecognizable pose, which was, perhaps, more in character with the part she was playing in *The Show Off* than the actress herself.

never faltered. In 1965, *Films in Review* published an article about her work that had nothing but praise for the actress' career. "It is true," the article stated, "her low, vibrant voice is her most distinctive asset, but there is a directness about her character interpretations which gives them a force audiences feel and are subliminally moved by." Mercedes herself, in the same article, was quoted as saying, "Film director Walter Huston once said that learning to act was 'a matter of looking and listening.' Like every truism, it sounds simple but means more than it says. Looking and listening requires honesty, alertness, dedication, energy, concentration, no prejudices, and few inhibitions." The actress had learned a great deal about herself during those difficult, only occasionally fulfilling, years of the 1960s, and she had undergone several major changes in both her personal and professional life.

In the same article, when asked what she thought her future as an actress was going to be like, she answered, "Who knows? We have no control over it anyway. Just get up in the morning and lead with your chin."

4. The Seventies and After

The 1970s, although they offered less of the heady success Mercedes McCambridge had experienced in the 1930s, '40s and '50s, were certainly kinder and gentler years than the 1960s had been for the actress. She appeared in several films, was featured on many television series, and continued acting on the stage. She also fulfilled numerous speaking engagements, talking on behalf of "recovered alcoholics." Mercedes' work in the 1970s included major supporting roles in *The Last Generation* (1971), the made-for-television films *Killer by Night* and *Two for the Money* (both 1972), the feature films *Sixteen* and *Other Side of the Wind* (also in 1972), the made-for-TV movie *The Girls of Huntington House* (1973), the feature film *The President's Plane Is Missing* (1973), the made-for-TV movie *Who Is the Black Dahlia?* (1975), the feature film *Thieves* (1977), the made-for-TV movie *The Sacketts* (1979), and as a Russian gymnastics instructor in the film *The Concorde: Airport '79* (1979). Television appearances on such series as *Bonanza*, *Medical Center*, *The Name of the Game*, *Gunsmoke*, and *Charlie's Angels* also kept her busy in the 1970s.

In February 1972, Mercedes returned to Broadway in Romulus Linney's play *The Love Suicide at Schofield Barracks*. The play, although not the success she had hoped it would be, was called "strong theater and frequently striking" by *New York Daily News* critic, Douglas Watt. "Set in an Army barracks in Hawaii," wrote Watt, "the play attempts to examine the American conscience." *Love Suicide* concerned an inquiry into the mysterious deaths of an Army barrack's commanding general and his wife. In his review, Watt also said that, "McCambridge gave an incisive and beautifully poised account as a New England poet who was befriended by the general and his wife." In a post script to his review, Watt added, "Miss McCambridge is quite an actress, in case anyone has forgotten." Theater critic Clive Barnes, in his *New York Times* review of the play, said, "I very much liked Mercedes McCambridge as the slightly butch woman poet," but he was not particularly enthusiastic about the production itself. Mercedes was nominated for an Antoinette Perry (Tony) "Best Actress" award in 1972 for her performance in *Love Suicide at Schofield Barracks*, but she failed to win the treasured Tony. The next project the actress became involved

Top: Two for the Money, a made-for-television film from 1972, was one of Mercedes' more satisfying film vehicles in the 1970s. Her character, Mrs. Castle, was also one of the better roles she played on television in the '70s. *Bottom:* McCambridge appeared in Viacom's made-for-TV film *The Girls of Huntington House* in 1973, playing a character names Miss McKenzie.

Universal Studio's *The Concord: Airport '79* was one of several disaster films that surfaced in the 1970s. It offered a star-studded cast that included Robert Wagner, Alan Delon, Cecily Tyson, Martha Raye, George Kennedy, and Susan Blakely. In the film, Mercedes played a Russian gymnastics coach named "Nelli," one of the many victims of a missile attack during the Concorde's trans–Atlantic flight.

with did not prove quite as fulfilling an experience as Mercedes had expected it to be.

Mercedes claimed that her relatively happy and fulfilling days of acting on radio was the reason she accepted an assignment to supply the voice of the demon/devil Pazuzu for the film *The Exorcist* in 1973. Mercedes was hired to portray the evil-sounding voice of "the Prince of Darkness" when he demonically possesses the body of a young girl. The job turned out to be one of the most physically demanding and difficult assignments of her career. To approximate the sound of the demon vomiting on two priests in the film, Mercedes swallowed mushy apples and a dozen raw eggs and then regurgitated them. The microphone in front of her in the studio recorded all of the sounds she produced with astounding clarity. As she watched the image of the grotesquely made up, demon possessed child Regan, played by Linda Blair, throw up on the priests, Mercedes produced the sound of vomiting over and over again until it was perfectly timed with the actions on the screen. Mercedes had been a heavy smoker, but had given up the habit ten years before she began working on *The Exorcist*. In order to make her voice sound as husky as she thought it should be for reading the part of the Devil, she began smoking three packs of cigarettes a day again. Mercedes' naturally husky voice, already ravaged by habitual smoking and chronic bronchitis, easily sounded like the voice of the Devil when she read the lines, which included a great deal of shockingly vulgar profanity. When she returned home to Brentwood, where she was living at the time, after a day's recording session, she was totally exhausted and fell into bed to sleep the sleep of the dead each night.

Warner Brothers Studios, and the film's director, William "Billy" Friedkin, insisted, for some unknown reason, that Mercedes' participation in the film be kept a secret. Nobody on the Warner Brothers lot was to know that she was dubbing the Devil's voice for the child actress Linda Blair. Mercedes was promised a credit at the end of the film's cast list which would read, "And Mercedes McCambridge as the voice of the Demon." At the movie's Hollywood premiere, Mercedes sat in the audience waiting for the applause she was sure was coming when her name appeared on the screen at the end of the film. But her name was not included on the list of credits. Everyone else who had anything to do with the film received credit, but not Mercedes McCambridge. Mercedes stormed out of the theater, furious that she had been denied the credit for her work that she had been promised. *The Exorcist* was one of the most publicized, and she knew it was going to be one of the most successful, films of the year. As she was leaving the theater, she ran into the director, Billy Friedkin, who saw her rage and said, "Let me explain, please. There wasn't time to work it out.... I told you we wouldn't have a film without your work. You made it go, for Christ's sake." Mercedes walked right by him and, forgetting that she had not arrived in her own car for the premiere, got into someone else's vehicle, which had the keys in the ignition, started it up, and sped away from the theater. When she realized her mistake, she sheepishly returned the car to the spot where she had found it. Fortunately, no one had come to claim it yet.

The next day Mercedes began a campaign to obtain the recognition she felt her contribution to the film most certainly deserved. Much later, she heard from inside sources at Warner Brothers that Billy Friedkin had not wanted anything to detract from Linda Blair's performance in the film, which he felt could win the coveted Academy Award as Best Supporting Actress for Blair the following March if everyone thought that she herself had performed all of the stunts and vocal effects seen and heard in *The Exorcist*. Of course, this would have been near impossible. The truth was that not only had Mercedes been the voice of the demon in the film, two other actresses, Eileen Dietz (who played the possessed girl in many of the film's more lurid scenes) and Linda Rae Hager (who served as Linda Blair's stand-in and occasional photo and stunt double), had also been used in several of *The Exorcist*'s important possession and exorcism scenes.

Soon after the film's premiere, numerous articles appeared in various magazines and newspapers informing the public that several women had played the Demon, in addition to the thirteen-year-old Linda Blair. In one magazine, the headline blared: "Mercedes McCambridge Demands Apology from Exorcist Director." The article stated, "Mercedes McCambridge ... the husky voiced actress who 'portrayed' the voice of the devil in *The Exorcist* is giving Warner Brothers 'a devil of a time' with the studio's plans to issue an album of dialogue excerpts from the controversial movie." The article continued, "In a statement filed with Screen Actor's Guild, the organization Ms. McCambridge had asked to arbitrate the situation, Mercedes declared, 'I will not at the hands of Mr. Friedkin [the film's director] or Warner Brothers, sink into senility with shame.'" The article concluded, "According to the Oscar-winning actress, after her initial hassle over her billing with Friedkin, 'I suffered to the point where my physician suggested I be hospitalized. Consequently, I cannot permit the further abuse, the misuse, the insult. It is a matter of self respect.'" The proposed record album of the sound track from the film was never released, and Mercedes had her revenge for Friedkin's insensitivity.

Even the prestigious *New York Times*, in their weekend Arts and Leisure section, printed an article titled "Will the Real Devil Speak Up? Yes!" and declared, "Perhaps the most terrifying feature of *The Exorcist* is the sound track: director William Friedkin and his experts used the cries of pigs being driven to slaughter to produce the scream of the Demon when it is exorcized from the 12 year old Regan's body. Although Warner Brothers has not made the fact public, Mercedes McCambridge, the Lady Macbeth of Orson Welles's *Mercury Theater of the Air* [although this author could find no record that such a radio performance had ever been broadcast] and Oscar winning actress of *All the King's Men* hair-raisingly spoke the aural role of the Demon itself." The caption under her picture read, "Mercedes McCambridge, the voice of the Devil in *The Exorcist*."

In another article, titled "A New Row Over *The Exorcist*: Who Was That Body?" published in *The New York Post*, actress Eileen Dietz also decided to go public about her contribution to the film. Warner Brothers and Friedkin finally decided to give in to Mercedes' demand for the billing she had been promised, and added her name to the list of credits at the film's end. Eileen Dietz, however, did not fare as well as Mercedes, and remained anonymous as far as the picture's credits were concerned.

Mercedes' good friend and ofttimes advisor Orson Welles told Mercedes that he thought *not* receiving credit for her work in *The Exorcist* was actually the best thing that ever could have happened to her. If she had been credited, Welles said, everyone would have expected her to do a decent job because she had been in the business (show business) practically all of her life. The fact that she hadn't received credit, Welles told her, led to everyone *knowing* that she had worked on the film, because the fact was certainly well publicized, and that surely had been a good thing for her. Years later, when a young reporter rather foolishly asked her how she could have played such a repulsive role as the Devil so convincingly, Mercedes patiently answered the young man by saying: "There has not been a human being who does not have a dark side. To me that's a very interesting side. That's why it was so easy to do *The Exorcist* ... to play the devil. I was honest enough to admit there's a devil in me, probably as heinous as Lucifer himself." She then gave the young reporter a somewhat wicked smile and bade him "Good evening" in a manner befitting the host of the old *Inner Sanctum* radio mystery series she had worked on so often in the mid–1940s.

According to Mercedes, the most professionally rewarding activity she became involved with in the 1970s, in spite of her obvious enjoyment at all of the attention her performance in *The Exorcist* had given her, was a brand new radio drama program called *The CBS Mystery Theater* that made its debut in 1974. At the helm of the new radio drama series was Mercedes' old friend, radio director and producer Himan Brown, who was the driving force behind the new syndicated radio series. Produced at CBS, but heard on many different independent radio stations across the country, *The CBS Radio Mystery Theater* placed many actors from radio's Golden Age (the

1930s, '40s and '50s), including Mercedes, back in front of the radio microphones again.

In a publicity release issued by CBS in February 1975, Mercedes said, "Radio has always been my favorite medium." The press release went on to state that, "It will be the fifteenth time Ms. McCambridge has starred on the Peabody Award winning *Mystery Theater* [then] in its second year.

This portrait of Mercedes McCambridge was used by the Michael Hartig Agency, Ltd., when the actress' name was being submitted to casting directors and producers in the 1970s. It was taken when the actress was fifty-four years old. At the time, McCambridge was dubbing the voice of the devil Pazuzu for the film *The Exorcist*.

Mercedes returned to radio, the medium that had introduced her to the public in the late 1930s, for Himan Brown's *CBS Mystery Theater* radio series in the mid–1970s. The actress starred in over twenty radio plays on *Mystery Theater*, several of which were written by her long-time friend Elspeth Eric. This photograph was taken during a broadcast of "The Horse That Wasn't for Sale," which originally aired on February 24, 1974. It was her first appearance on the program.

'Just think,' [Mercedes said in the release], 'a few minutes ago I stood in front of a microphone opposite a man I've known for about 30 years, Leon Janney, looking into his eyes for the support I need and he is looking into my eyes for the same support he needs. There is a mutual vulnerability, a trust, a certain kind of reliant love in radio that you just don't get anywhere else. We rely on each other ... and it's great. Nobody is on a starvation diet, nobody has to worry about getting their noses fixed, no leading man is standing there with the makeup man fixing the spit curl in front of his forehead the way some of them do in films. I can't get used to that. But it doesn't happen in radio ... talent is either there or it isn't and the audience is getting nothing more than what you convey with one sense, speech. Everything has to be behind that, literally everything. And it requires an accelerated, even an enlarged, amount of adrenaline and concentration. Two years ago I was artist-in-residence at Catholic University. I kept touting radio and all those young people in the graduate school kind of pooh-poohed it as being a lesser sister of the arts. So I asked permission to do *Under Milk Wood* by Dylan Thomas, which was a radio show originally, and, after some persuasion, I got the time and worked with the students who half-heartedly went at it and recorded it as a radio show. When they listened to it as a group afterwards they wanted to jump off the Washington Monument. They had no idea that they were as false, as slow, as colorless, as vapid, as uninteresting as they came out on the tape. You can't go half-way on radio. They did it again and they learned a lot and they don't pooh-pooh radio any more. It was a marvelous training thing. I wish there were more of it for young actors and actresses.'"

Mercedes admitted in her 1981 autobiography that in order to work on Brown's *Mystery Theater* radio series in the 1970s she had had to juggle her film and television schedule. She then described the regimen the cast had to follow for each show produced — and there were five (and sometimes more) shows released each week. It began with the cast, producer-director Himan Brown, and the sound man all gathered around a long table in Studio B at 485 Madison Avenue, where CBS had its offices and studios. After no more than fifteen minutes chatting, Brown started the rehearsal. Mercedes has often said of Himan Brown, "I would kill for this man who has always been my number one life supporter. He is determined that radio drama will be kept alive if it kills him, and one day it probably will, right in the middle of throwing a cue at one of us doddering old actors." The rehearsals for *The CBS Mystery Theater*, Mercedes continued, always commenced at exactly 9:15 a.m. Brown gave out the scripts to the actors and told them what character they were to play. None of the actors knew while they were reading one page of the script what they would be called upon to say or do on the next page, and that, Mercedes felt, was great fun for all involved. They enjoyed watching each other discover where they were going as characters in the play. After the first reading of the script, Brown gave them cuts (to accommodate the exact timing needed for the broadcast), and made suggestions to the actors and sound man. Finally, the cast went to the microphones to tape the show. The experienced professionals usually got everything right the first time out. "It was," Mercedes said, "always a wonderful and exhilarating acting experience."

The CBS Radio Mystery Theater made its on-air debut on January 6, 1974. The last new broadcast of the series was heard on December 7, 1982 (it finally ended its long and successful continuous original run on December 31, 1982, after a series of eighteen rebroadcasts aired). Mercedes was heard on 25 original broadcasts of *The Mystery Theater*, several of them written by her long-time friend, actress-writer Elspeth Eric, who also occasionally appeared on the series as an actress. Many other actors who had worked with Mercedes in radio decades earlier in New York (and even in Chicago and Hollywood) also appeared on *The CBS The Mystery Theater*. Among these were Agnes Moorehead, Claudia Morgan, Robert Dryden, Leon Janney, Hans Conried, Grace Matthews, Mary Jane Higby, Stefan Schnabel, Arnold Moss, Rosemary Rice, Bryna Raeburn, Ian Martin, Ralph Bell, Larry Haines, Santos Ortega, Mandel Kramer, Court Benson, and Mason Adams.

One of the most interesting and original scripts Mercedes enacted on *The Mystery Theater* was a radio play written by Elspeth Eric entitled, "General Laughter."

Himan Brown's *CBS Mystery Theater* series (1974–1981) reunited many performers Mercedes had worked with on radio thirty years (and more) previously. Pictured above are actors Robert Dryden, Arnold Moss, and Kevin McCartthy during a performance of Edgar Allan Poe's "Fall of the House of Usher," broadcast on the *Mystery Theater* series on March 14, 1974.

The story was about a distraught actress who decides to tape record a suicide message rather than write a final suicide note. Mercedes gave a tour de force performance as the actress in this drama, heard on February 25, 1976.

Even Mercedes' ex-husband, Fletcher Markle, managed to get back on the radio bandwagon via the *CBS Mystery Theater* when a script he wrote, "Blood, Thunder, and a Woman in Green," was presented on the program on April 4, 1977.

Because of the success of the *CBS Mystery Theater*, several other new radio drama series turned up on commercial radio in the 1970s, including *The CBS Radio Adventure Theater* and *The Sears Radio Theater* proved (also called *The Mutual Theater* in syndication). None, however, proved as successful as Brown's *CBS Mystery Theater* series, and they only enjoyed brief runs on the airwaves. The *Sears* program broadcast from the West Coast, spearheaded by the former radio producer, director and actor Elliot Lewis. *The Sears Radio Theater* also involved Fletcher Markle, who enjoyed a brief comeback on radio as the series' director and occasional performer. Markle even directed Anne Burr, one of the actresses who had been heard on his *Studio One* radio series in the 1940s, on two *Sears Radio Theater* programs. Mercedes, the reader will remember, had replaced Burr as the resident leading lady on *Studio One*.

Another hour-long, New York–based midday syndicated radio drama series, called *The Radio Playhouse*, surfaced in the mid–1970s. This series presented four fifteen-minute daytime dramas, that included: Peg Lynch's comedy sketches, *The Little Things in Life*, which starred Miss Lynch and Mercedes' frequent radio acting cohort Robert Dryden; two new soap operas—*To Have and to Hold* and *The Faces of Life;* and a series called *The Author's Playhouse*, which offered serialized versions of such classic works of literature as *Becky Sharp*. Many actors who worked with Mercedes during radio's "Golden Years" in the 1940s and 1950s worked on these programs as well, including Charita Bauer, Rosemary Rice, Larry Haines, and Joyce Gordon. These series, however, proved short-lived and did not enjoy the longevity of *The CBS Mystery Theater*.

In spite of Himan Brown's valiant attempts to keep his program on the air, CBS lost interest in the project in the early 1980s and decided that, even though the series was breaking even financially, there was far more money to be made with their television endeavors. Without CBS's support, Brown had no choice but to suspend production of the popular series. Nevertheless, Brown never gave up trying to revive radio drama, and as of this writing he is still trying to convince the powers that be that radio drama remains a viable commodity which the public would listen to and support, if given the chance.

In the mid–1970s Mercedes was touring the country in a Chicago-based Drury Lane Theater production of *The Madwoman of Chaillot* when she was interviewed on a PBS radio talk show about her radio acting career. As stated above, she had already been working, whenever her schedule permitted, on Himan Brown's *CBS Radio Mystery Theater*. "Radio," she said, "is still my favorite of all of the branches of show business. It is the most imaginative … the most involving. On the stage, there are a great many things for an actress to consider, as there are in films and on television. But radio … it has its own particular disciplines … its own particular set of rules and principles and they are as rigorous as any other medium. There is only one sense, however, that you can use to communicate … sound. You have to call up all sorts of things in your bag of tricks and experiences, in order to make what you are trying to convey felt. In radio, you can do so many things … so very many, many things … if you risk the amount of imagination you have and trust the imagination of the listeners."

During this same interview Mercedes was asked if she had any particular favorites among the many radio directors she had worked with. "There were many great directors and there were a lot of mediocre ones and many useless ones," she answered. "A radio director has to have a keen ear and those who do are very rare birds. I have been extremely fortunate with mentors on radio—Orson Welles, Carlton E. Morse, Arch Oboler, and Hi Brown, who is, as we speak, directing the new *CBS Radio Mystery Theater* series. They were all very good to me. They indulged me in all of my whims as far as acting was concerned."

Mercedes enjoyed an interesting, but not totally successful, career change-of-pace in August 1975 when she agreed to play the starring role of Minnie Marx in a stage production revival of the musical comedy *Minnie's Boys*, which was to begin a tour of the country at a summer theater in New Buffalo, Michigan. The musical was about the early careers of the famous comedy team of the Marx Brothers—Groucho, Harpo, Chico and Zeppo—and their domineering stage mother, Minnie Marx, who guided the early years of the brothers' show business careers. *Minnie's Boys* had made its debut on Broadway five years earlier in 1970, starring actress Shelley Winters as Minnie. The production only lasted 65 performances on the Great White Way, and it was not particularly well received by theater critics or theater-goers. (Mercedes, it will be remembered, had previously replaced Shelley Winters eight years earlier in the Off Broadway play *Cages* in 1963.) *Minnie's Boys* had a score composed by Larry Grossman, with lyrics by Hal Hackady, and a book by Arthur Marx (Groucho's son) and Robert Fisher. The difficulty of performing in a musical comedy, and especially of having to sing several challenging songs each night (and at several matinee performances each week), proved too much for Mercedes, who had not been trained as a singer. She was, however, saved from what might have been a disastrous experience at the New Buffalo Summer Theater (and subsequent national tour) when she mysteriously developed "blood poisoning" and was hospitalized, forcing her to withdraw from the production.

Between working on Himan Brown's *Mystery Theater* radio program, making films, and appearing in stage plays, Mercedes had little time for an active social life. In the late 1970s, Mercedes' first husband, Bill Fifield, who was on a business trip to his publisher in New York, asked if he could stay in Mercedes' Manhattan apartment while she was out of town touring in a production of *The Madwoman of Chaillot*. Fifield had, by that time, fulfilled his promise as a writer and had penned several well-received books, including the definitive biographies of the artist Modigliani and the oceanographer Jacques Cousteau. He had also written numerous short stories and articles that appeared in various periodicals, and was a contributor to Alex Lichine's massive, *The New Encyclopedia of Wines and Spirits*. Mercedes told Fifield that she would be happy to have him stay in her apartment while she was away on tour.

Fifield was finished with his business in New York by the time Mercedes returned to the city, but she recalled opening the door to her apartment and "sensing that the place felt like Bill." She found a bottle of Dior perfume that he had left for her on her dresser, and a "thank-you" note from him that was written on the back of a blank laundry list from the Melia Apartohel in Alicienda, which was on the Costa De Oro. In the note, Fifield told Mercedes that he had read one of the books on her bookshelf, recalled their "aloneness" (he was in between wives at the time), congratulated them both on their son, and lamented at their having been born in an age which had "too little space to hold [their] excellence." When she went to bed that night Mercedes admitted in her autobiography that she thought of Bill for a long time, before she eventually fell asleep.

Mercedes admitted in her autobiography that her feelings about her second husband, Fletcher Markle, were not quite as forgiving as they were for her first spouse, Bill Fifield. On a flight from Alaska to Los Angeles, as she returned from a speaking engagement on alcoholism in the late 1970s, Mercedes heard the pilot's voice coming

Throughout the 1970s and 1980s Mercedes McCambridge received numerous awards during her speaking engagements to make people more aware that alcoholism is a disease, a serious illness that can be treated, if not cured. In the late 1970s, Mercedes, pictured above with her son, John Lawrence Markle (né Fifield), arrives at a tribute in her honor.

over the plane's loudspeaker, announcing that below the airplane was the famous Universal Studios, beautiful downtown Burbank, and Pasadena (where Mercedes knew her second husband was living with his third wife, Dorothy). At this, Mercedes couldn't help cursing him as she looked down on the twinkling lights of Pasadena. "You son of a bitch!" she thought to herself. She wrote in her autobiography that she liked to think Fletcher had actually heard her that night. The actress had, apparently, never gotten over Markle's callous rejection of her when she was at one of the lowest points of her life and in the depths of her alcohol abuse. Markle had married another woman shortly after he divorced Mercedes, but she had remained single. She drew a certain amount of satisfaction, however, from knowing that although he had gone on to direct episodes of such TV series as *Father of the Bride, Thriller* and *Julia*, and produced the TV series *Telescope*, he had never approached the prominence in the television or motion picture industries that his early career in radio had won him, and he certainly had never come near to matching the degree of world-wide recognition McCambridge enjoyed during her long and distinguished show business career. That was, perhaps, her greatest revenge. Fletcher had always actively sought the spotlight and basked in its brightness, even if that spotlight was usually on someone else.

Mercedes candidly admitted in her autobiography that she knew she had failed to keep her two marriages together — and she was not, you will remember, a lady who liked to fail. All things considered, however, the 1970s were relatively calm and productive years for Mercedes McCambridge, as she went about the business of living and making a living for herself.

On December 20, 1978, Mercedes' mother, Marie Mahaffry McCambridge, died after a long and painful illness. Just as she had done before with her father, Mercedes had her mother's body prepared for burial in California and sent east to the Clancy Funeral Home in Kanakee, Illinois, where her father's wake had been held twelve years earlier. The actress accompanied her mother's body back to Illinois in an airplane, just as she had done with her father's remains. During the flight back to Illinois, Mercedes thought about her strained relationship with her disapproving and often reproachful mother. "The only thing that ever really stood between us, mother," she thought as she sat next to her mother's coffin, "was a mirror." They too, like Mercedes and her father, had been very much alike — if not physically, then certainly emotionally.

All her life Mercedes had been well acquainted with death. Her father, her grandparents, her infant sister, various aunts, uncles and other relatives, and, of course, several good friends had all passed away before her mother died. In a 1981 radio interview, Mercedes recalled that as a child she had often made frequent treks to visit various cemeteries with her family. She admitted that even as an adult, one of her favorite pastimes was to visit cemeteries in the towns and cities that she happened to be in while on tour with a play or fulfilling a speaking engagement, and she said she enjoyed reading the inscriptions on the tombstones. When she was on the board of directors, and then the President and CEO for five years, at the Livengrin Foundation's treatment center for drug abuse and alcoholism (located on a farm in Bucks County, Pennsylvania), she often observed families visiting the small graveyard that adjoined the Livengrin property. She said she would watch the cemetery visitors gesturing about where certain markers were on family plots, just as she remembered she had done with her family while growing up in Chicago. "I think," she said at an interview shortly after her mother died, "that there is a great deal of that still going on in suburban and rural areas in America. People go to the cemetery and visit the dear departed on Sunday afternoon. When I was in Elmira once, I visited the cemetery where author Mark Twain is buried. I don't think that's morbid. I like to have been that close to what was greatness, even if it's in decomposition."

In the late 1970s, and into the first year of the 1980s, Mercedes was very busy writing her memoirs. In 1981 her book, titled *The Quality of Mercy*, was published by Time Books. The notices she received for the autobiography were, for the most part, favorable, especially those written by her show business colleagues. Actress Susan Strasberg, the daughter of Paula and Lee Strasberg (of the famed Actors Studio school), said of Mercedes' book: "It made me laugh and cry. It was inspiring, and totally unique and beautifully written. Mercedes is a real writer. Thank you, Mercedes, for your courage and honesty. People across the country are hungry for this kind of book, and it is far too rare."

Orson Welles called Mercedes "a hugely gifted artist, a passionately true-hearted original, who has written a book which, wonderfully enough, does justice to its subject. I read it with delight." *Publishers Weekly* labeled the book "a bravura performance. This vibrant story holds the reader fast by revealing the private woman behind the façade." Liz Smith, a show business columnist for *The New York Daily News*, said in her March 20, 1981, column, "Mercedes McCambridge: Write on!" Smith continued, "She is a full-fledged talent on stage, screen, or typewriter, and her writing is offbeat and provocative." The most prestigious newspaper in the country, *The New York Times*, reviewed Mercedes' book in their March 29, 1981, *Book Review Section* of the Sunday edition of *The Times*, and, to Mercedes' disappointment, proved less than enthusiastic. The review, written by Gina Mallet (a critic for the *Toronto Star* who frequently wrote show business profiles for *The Times*), although not totally negative, said that the book was "rendered in a spattershot style reminiscent of a Jackson Pollock action painting, and [was] equally so. It starts, stops and jumps, disconcertingly in place and time. Within the first 25 pages, Miss McCambridge had me winded." She went on to say, "*The Quality of Mercy* is full of funny, shamefaced anecdotes, told in the confiding tones of someone trapped in a confessional booth." Later in Ms. Mallet's review she observed, "Increasingly, anger seems to have been her spur. To say Miss McCambridge is angry as the devil [in a reference to her work in *The Exorcist*] is an understatement." The book proved only moderately successful financially, and Mercedes plowed ahead with her acting career, which was becoming less and less productive (with the exception of her praiseworthy work on the stage). Age, and perhaps a certain lack of enthusiasm for appearing in less than admirable films and television shows, were beginning to wear down the vibrant actress.

On March 16, 1981, on her sixty-third birthday, Mercedes appeared on WOR Radio's *Arlene Francis Show* in New York City to talk about her newly published autobiography. Arlene Francis and Mercedes had known each other for over forty years, since the time both were active radio actresses in New York in the 1940s. Arlene began her interview by introducing Mercedes as a woman who had lived "a rich life filled with tragic things and wonderful things." She then asked Mercedes why she had decided to write her autobiography at that time. After stating that her book was about a person and people connected with that person, Mercedes answered, "*The New York Times* [Time Books] decided it for me. I didn't want to do it. I kept insisting I didn't want to do it. They kept insisting I did. Somehow or other, they won and I'm glad. They have been very indulgent and long suffering ... especially my editor Leonard Schwartz."

In an interview with Mercedes that appeared in the January 6, 1985, Sunday Arts section of *The New Haven Register*, the actress gave a clearer indication as to why she had decided to write her autobiography, in addition to giving a very vivid account of her interest in "all things literary." "I do think it's rather pompous when actors do such books, so I said 'no,' to *The New York Times*," she told *New Haven Register* interviewer Markland Taylor. "But the editors insisted. After I'd written four chapters, I told them I didn't want to continue and I returned their advance. I'd written one book years before. It was about my world-wide tour with my son. They continued to insist, and then they promised to give me two Shaw [the celebrated playwright and critic George Bernard Shaw] letters if I finished the book. I did finish the book and I'm glad I did. One of the letters was written to Mr. Brentano [Shaw's publisher]. It's rather funny. Shaw talks about taxes and asks Mr. Brentano not to deduct U.S. taxes from his royalties on that side of the Atlantic [the U.S.], because all that was being 'seen to' on his side of the Atlantic [England]. He also mentions working on a large project, though he doesn't know whether anything will come of it. The 'project' was Shaw's critically acclaimed *Back to Methuselah*. The other letter isn't really a letter. It's one of Shaw's calling cards, on which he's written, 'I shall write you a longer letter as soon as I find the time.' It's not addressed to anyone, so it's not known for whom it was meant. Oh, yes, I have both of those letters framed, at home in La Jolla, California. I have a whole collection of things like that. Such as a shingle from the gazebo [a famous American novelist] William Faulkner built at his home in Roanoke, Mississippi. He fancied himself as a carpenter. I sat at the desk he made. He wasn't much of a carpenter."

In Arlene Francis' 1981 radio show interview, Arlene said to Mercedes, "It's a great day for you ... your birthday, St. Patrick's Day, and it's the day your book is coming out. In your book, you talk a good deal about alcoholism. One can't help but notice the parade that's going on outside [the St. Patrick's Day Parade was in progress]. My first impression after the parade is over, is that the kids are drunk! I wonder what you think about that after your experience with alcoholism."

In her typically emphatic, somewhat self-righteous way of addressing a serious social or political issue that she perceived as unjust or morally wrong, Mercedes answered, "It's so horrendous! Coming down now to be with you ... 59th Street looked like a direct bomb hit in front of the Plaza Hotel. Nobody is paying any attention to the parade. They're all marching along with their pompoms and their music and their costumes and their zest and their banners and that's not what the kids are watching. They're all being bombed and stoned a block away, not caring anything about St. Patrick or the celebration. And I think that what should happen ... and this is a terrible thing for me to say because it is my birthday and the St. Patrick's Day Parade has always been *my* parade ... I think we better cancel it! I think there is no need to perpetuate this dreadfully, disgusting, insulting insolence that we see of the kids! Vomiting! I saw a young man falling down on our way here ... and young women ... some of those young women will end up pregnant and won't remember it, and God knows what else! What has that to do with the celebration of St. Patrick's Day? I think they have ruined a New York tradition, and I think we ought to put it right smack in their lap. That's how I feel! Six out of ten young people who die this year will die drunk, you know!"

Arlene added, "I think that if some of the people that are out there would hear your experience and what happened to you as far as alcoholism is concerned, it would be a powerful lesson."

"Yes, indeed," Mercedes replied.

Towards the end of the broadcast, Arlene said that she was looking at a "gorgeous picture" of Mercedes and her granddaughters and daughter-in-law. She then asked, "Where's a picture of John ... your lovely son?" Mercedes answered, "There's no picture of John. He just takes the pictures of the women in his life." As Arlene looked at the picture she said, "Beautiful ... beautiful children. Where do they live?" Mercedes answered, "They live in Little Rock, Arkansas, where my son is a banker with Stephens, Inc. They just bought a one-hundred-year-old Victorian house ... and they're doing everything to it. I talked last night, being Sunday, to all of them, and little Suzanne, who is just three, was the last to talk, so I said to her, 'And how did your Sunday go, dear?' and she said, 'Well, I go to the church ... I cry a little bit ... and then I come home.'" Mercedes, the proud grandmother, laughed and said, "Well, what do you do when you're three and it's Sunday?" The genuine love and affection that the actress felt for her family was very obvious to anyone listening to Arlene Francis' show that day.

During the publicity tour to promote her book, Mercedes also appeared on NBC's *Today Show*. She was supposed to be interviewed by Barbara Walters, but at the beginning of the interview, Walters introduced Mercedes as "a fine actress who was once an alcoholic." Mercedes immediately took over the spot, saying, "Not *was* an alcoholic — It's 'an alcoholic!'" She then went on to deliver a spirited monologue about her battle with alcoholism that took up the entire time she had been allotted to promote her book. Walters, who was none-too-shy about cutting off an interviewee, did not dare interrupt Miss McCambridge's emphatic tirade. When Mercedes finished, Walters simply said, "Thank you, Miss McCambridge," and went on to her next order of business. Walters' opening and closing remarks were all that she had managed to utter during that particular interview.

Mercedes continued to tour in stage productions in the 1980s, and was seen in such plays as *Agnes of God* and *'night, Mother*. John Pielmeier's *Agnes of God* is a story of three women that played on Off Broadway in 1979. In the play, a psychologist, Dr. Martha Livingstone, tries to determine, for legal reasons, why a convent novice named Agnes, who is apparently a total innocent, gave birth to a baby that was later found dead in a wastepaper basket at the convent. In the touring production in which Mercedes featured, Dr. Livingstone was played by actress Elizabeth Ashley, who had originated the role in New York. Assisting Dr. Livingstone in her investigation of the novice nun, Sister Agnes (played by Maryann Plunkett), is the Mother Superior of the convent, Mother Miriam Ruth, played by Mercedes McCambridge. McCambridge's performance in this play earned high praise from theater critics for its honesty and dignity. Mercedes was sixty-five years old in 1983 when she toured in the play.

Among the tour venues was Boston's Shubert Theatre. The theater's Playbill program published a brief biography of McCambridge that, although certainly more accurate than McCambridge's 1948 Playbill program notes for *The Young and the Fair*, contained several errors. It did, however, offer information about the actress that few members of the public were aware of. *Agnes of God*'s program stated that McCambridge had been called, "the world's *finest* radio actress," by Orson Welles, when indeed he had hyperbolically called her "the world's *greatest* living radio actress." The bio also stated that Mercedes had appeared in "two TV series of her own … *Defense Attorney* and *Wire Service*." *Defense Attorney*, the reader will remember, was a radio, not a television, series. The honors and awards the actress had received over the years, which were listed in the *Agnes of God* program, was most impressive. The biographical sketch also stated that she had appeared on Broadway, which she certainly had done, and "in theaters in 44 states." It also mentioned that she had been Artist-in-Residence on many college campuses, and held, "a half dozen honorary degrees from colleges and universities from Oregon to Texas to Ohio and Minnesota to Pennsylvania," which was certainly true. In addition, the biography said that she had received "two Foreign Correspondents Awards, the *Look*, *TV/Radio Mirror* and *Photoplay* magazine awards and [had been] honored by three Presidents, the Senate, and the Governors and Mayors of all sections of the country for her devotion to her work in the field of alcoholism." The program of the *Agnes of God* Boston production ended by saying, "Miss McCambridge has been awarded the Gold Key of the National Council on Alcoholism," and said that she was "working on a book about Arkansas," which apparently was never published.

The play, *'night, Mother*, by Marsha Norman, which Mercedes also extensively toured with in the 1980s, is a play in one long act. Like *Agnes of God*, it had its New York premiere in the late 1970s. It is a two character play about a disillusioned

'Everyone pays lip service to the idea that alcoholism is a disease, but no one really believes it.'

During her many speaking engagements on behalf of alcoholics throughout the 1960s, 70s, and 80s, people who attended her lectures received a photograph of the actress as a souvenir. The photograph at left is from the 1980s. During her lifetime, the actress made hundreds of appearances speaking up for greater understanding that alcoholism is a disease and not a choice.

woman in her late thirties who lives with her mother, Thelma, played by Miss McCambridge. The play opens with the daughter, Jessie, asking her mother where a particular gun is kept. Jessie finds the weapon with Thelma's help, cleans it, and then quietly announces that she is going to kill herself at the end of the evening. Thelma spends the night trying to convince her daughter that life is indeed worth living, and in the process reveals truths about a great number of issues that have affected both of their lives. Again, Mercedes' performance as Thelma won her high praise from theater critics, and the actress stated during the tour that she was pleased with both the vehicle and her costar, Phyllis Sommerville, whom she generously praised in a newspaper interview. "Phyllis is absolutely wonderful as my daughter in the play," Mercedes said in a January 6, 1985, interview that appeared in *The New Haven Register* when *'night, Mother* played in that city. "And I don't use those words lightly. She's superbly trained and is an absolute rock on stage … cooperative and generous." The "Who's Who in the Cast" biography that appeared in the November 1984 Wilmington, Delaware, Playhouse Theater's *'night, Mother* Playbill program contained similar information to that found in the *Agnes of God* program. "Mercedes McCambridge," this biography began, "is one of America's finest actresses whose career encompasses theatre, film, television and radio."

In the same *New Haven Register* interview, the actress gave an interesting, if somewhat defensive, answer when reporter Markland Taylor asked if she thought the Oscar she had won at the beginning of her film career in 1950 had been a hindrance, rather than a help, as it seemed to have been for so many actors who had won Academy Awards. "Why?" Mercedes answered with a nervous chuckle. "My salary went way up, I can tell you that. I think I'd been making about $350 a week in my last Broadway role, before the Oscar. When I got it [the Oscar], that very day my salary in Hollywood went up to $6,000. Tell me about an Oscar being a hindrance!"

In addition to her tours in stage plays in the 1980s, Mercedes appeared in just one motion picture. It was an unusual film entitled *Echoes*, which was released while she toured in *Agnes of God* in 1983. *Echoes*, directed by Arthur Allan Seidelman, was about an artistic young man in Africa trying to find his way in a troubled environment. The cast of the film included Richard Alfieri, Nathalie Neil, Ruth Roman (whom McCambridge had first worked with in 1950 in the film *Lightning Strikes Twice*), and Gale Sondergaard, who, like Mercedes, had won a "Best Supporting Actress" Academy Award for her performance in the 1936 film *Anthony Adverse*. (Interestingly, Mercedes' first major appearance on her ex-husband Fletcher Markle's radio series, *Studio One*, had her playing the female lead in an adaptation of *Anthony Adverse* in 1947.)

In the mid–1980s, when a newspaper interviewer insensitively asked Miss McCambridge why she thought her film career seemed to have faltered in recent years, she answered defensively, "I was available to films. Nobody cared that much about hiring me. Well, so? There are other things to do. I've done a lot of plays, all kinds. I've appeared on stage in all but two states in the country. I've done a lecture tour, written two books, gone around the world twice by myself and raised my family. Am I to be considered lost? Oh no, no, no!"

Then, when asked which actresses she had admired most during her lifetime, she answered without hesitation, "Laurette Taylor, who was good friend of mine, Vanessa Redgrave and Glenda Jackson," all of whom she gathered under the mantle of Sarah Siddons. Interestingly, Redgrave and Jackson were both champions of the underdog and decidedly outspoken about their liberal political beliefs, just as Mercedes had always been.

When asked which form of acting, stage, film, television or radio, was the most difficult, she thought for a moment and then answered, "My friend, actor Walter Huston, once said, 'Acting is acting is acting. It is all just a matter of projection … more intimate projection for radio, films and television … and bigger for the stage.' While you are acting, you open the door and let the light in … as far as necessary … according to the medium you are working in. A stage director I once knew told me that he would never want to be an actor because he could never take the pain. Director Elia Kazan said that when he was an actor and received a particularly bad review from theater critic Brooks Atkinson, he said, 'That's it! I'll never take that again,' and he decided to concentrate on directing. And my actor friend Theodore Bikel once said, 'An actor has to have the ability to be hurt over a long period of time.'" Sighing, Mercedes concluded, "It's all hard. Acting is an extremely rough way to go, if you have any kind of sensitivity or feeling. You get hurt a lot, but you work and you work and you work and you just try to get the job done."

Shortly after this 1985 interview, Mercedes heard that her old friend, Orson Welles, had died. Once again, Mercedes was devastated by the news of her good friend and mentor's death. This, however, paled next to the loss she was to suffer less than a year later.

Mercedes was featured on just three television program episodes in the 1980s: *Magnum, PI*, playing a character named "Agatha Kimble" on an episode of the show titled "Don't Say Goodbye" (telecast on March 26, 1981); *Amazing Stories*, on which her voice was heard as a character named "Miss Lestrange" in an episode called "Family Dog" (February 16, 1987); and *Cagney and Lacy*, on an episode titled "Land of the Free," playing a nun named "Sister Elizabeth" (February 23, 1988). It was apparent that her career was, most assuredly, winding down. Then, just as her work life seemed to reach one of the lowest points of her long career, one of the worst things that could possibly happen occurred in her personal life.

On November 16, 1987, Mercedes received what was surely the most horrific news of her entire life. Her beloved son, John Lawrence, who was just 45 years old, was dead. As if the news of his death was not terrible enough, Mercedes learned that John had reportedly killed his wife and two daughters and then committed suicide. Three days before the murders and suicide, which occurred in Little Rock, Arkansas, on Friday the thirteenth while a furious storm raged, John purportedly had reserved a video tape of the horror film *Nightmare on Elm Street* at a local video rental store. *Nightmare on Elm Street* is a movie about a supernatural psychopath who kills young people while they sleep. John's wife and daughters had been murdered in their bedrooms at the Markle home in Little Rock, where John had been working for the prestigious investment firm of Stephens and Company. He was said to have used three different handguns that he purchased shortly before the murders and suicide, and had shot each family member many times while wearing a Halloween mask of a wrinkled old man. The Little Rock police found the mask, covered with blood, next to his body in the living room of his house. In a local Little Rock newspaper account of the tragedy, John Lawrence Markle was described as "a brilliant PhD in Economics, who had received the third highest average in the history of his department when he was graduated from U.C.L.A." John Markle, the article stated, had joined the Stephens and Company firm eight years before the events being investigated, after having established a solid reputation as a clever financial genius at the Salomon Brothers financial institution. While working for Stephens and Company, Markle apparently had a lot of money to "play with," and he held a position that had no limitations, at least none that he knew about. "They're [the limitations] at least $800 million, because I once had that much at risk and nobody stopped me," Markle had told *Forbes* magazine on March 31, 1987. John traded exclusively for the house account — essentially for the personal profit of the two Stephens brothers, "Witt" and "Jack" Stephens, who were the only stockholders in the company. The brothers controlled an empire that included the investment bank Stephens, Inc., the multi-bank holding company of Worthen Banking Corp., the Capitol Hotel of Little Rock, the software firm Systematics, the nursing home operator Beverly Enterprises, the insurance holding company ICH Corporation, and the enormously profitable natural gas company Stephens Production Company. "The Stephens brothers have so much money it scares you," a Merrill Lynch vice president told *Time* magazine shortly before the tragic events of 1987. "Markle, who was a futures trader, could put much of the Stephens brothers' wealth at risk, could bet it on the rolls of the market dice, and he liked to think that he could predict the future. Quite suddenly, it was announced that John Lawrence had been fired from Stephens and Company after being questioned about an unidentified out-of-state brokerage account he controlled and its relationship to a Stephens' corporate account." Rumors began to circulate that John had been putting profitable trades in a secret account and sticking the Stephens Company with unprofitable ones, and he was accused of "mishandling the firm's accounts, specifically his mother's." John was, it was said, deeply distraught at having been fired. The Associated Press reported shortly after the tragic deaths occurred that John "had created an account in his mother's name and was using his power of attorney to transfer funds from one account that he had established in her name at Gelderman, Inc. in Chicago, to an account controlled by him at another financial institution." A five million dollar lawsuit was filed against Mercedes and her son's estate, but she was subsequently cleared of any wrongdoing.

Before John reportedly killed his wife and children and then committed suicide, he was said to have written a bitter, thirteen-page suicide letter that he addressed to his mother. The letter ended with the phrase, "night, Mother," in a reference to the play Mercedes had appeared in a few years before. The play, as stated previously, was about a woman who commits suicide in spite of her mother's futile attempt to understand and help her.

As one can only imagine, Mercedes was devastated by the news of this tragedy, and she went into total seclusion for several months. In all of the interviews that followed this terrible incident, she always referred to the tragedy in veiled terms, saying such things as, "It happened. It's been just too hard and very, very cruel." But she never explained what "it" was in any published interview. Kevin Kelly, in an article appearing in *The Boston Globe* in 1991, said, "Perhaps she tried to minimize what happened by placing it beside more readily comprehended grief, such as the unexpected cancer death of her brother a short time before, and the death of her parents many years prior to the tragedy. She tried to alleviate her agony by repeated references to the Blessed Virgin Mary, the poetry of Joyce Kilmer, and to the wisdom of Sarah Siddons, the legendary eighteenth century actress who Miss McCambridge considers a soul mate."

As the news of their murders and suicide reached her many fans and personal friends, hundreds of letters and phone calls from people offering their condolences began finding their way to her home. After several months passed, Mercedes sent everyone who had offered her their sympathy a printed note, many containing a brief personal message, and all signed, "Mercedes." The note read:

> After weeks of attempting to find the courage, the strength and the wisdom to answer individually the letters and cards and phone calls that came to me in a torrent of compassion and tenderness, I realize that I have no endurance for the unspeakable pain such an endeavor would bring.
>
> Please accept this simpler, albeit less proper way and know beyond all question that your reaching out to me was (and continues to be) all that makes any sense to me.
>
> About what happened ... that's all there is to say ... it happened. A Greek tragedy ... a cast of four beautiful people. The play closed.
>
> Thank you for caring.

In spite of the dreadful emotional consequences Mercedes suffered because of her son's unfortunate actions, one final triumph lay ahead for the actress before she settled down into a well-earned retirement. In 1990, at the age of 74, Mercedes was signed to replace Irene Worth in a Broadway production, followed by a national tour, of Neil Simon's play *Lost in Yonkers*. The play was about a family that "suffered with laughter" as one way to survive, one way to "get through" life. Mercedes played a character called Grandma Kurnitz. Grandma Kurnitz's son Eddie, a widower saddled with debts, leaves his two young sons in his mother's care while he looks for work down South. The play is set during World War II, and Eddie's mother, a German-born Jewish woman, lives in a small, dingy apartment located above the family's "Kurnitz Kandy Store" in Yonkers, New York. Living with Grandma Kurnitz, in addition to Eddie's two sons, is her good-hearted but somewhat simple-minded single daughter, Bella, a grown woman who never really matured into womanhood and remains almost childlike in her behavior. The story is related through the memories of one of Grandma Kurnitz's grandsons. To the boys, Grandma Kurnitz is a

Mercedes McCambridge's final acting triumph before she quietly settled into a well deserved retirement was playing Grandma Kurnitz in Neil Simon's play *Lost in Yonkers* in 1991. The actress played the role both on Broadway and during its long national tour, receiving critical and public acclaim for her performance in the Pulitzer Prize–winning play.

distant, cold, unaffectionate woman, but as the play progresses, the audience gradually comes to understand that Grandma Kurnitz's hostile and removed behavior is the result of a repressive upbringing in Europe and a less-than-supportive husband.

Irene Worth's performance as Grandma Kurnitz when the play originally opened on Broadway earned nothing but glowing reviews from the drama critics, and Mercedes knew that she had quite a job ahead of herself convincing people that her portrayal of Grandma Kurnitz was as good as the original. Both Worth and her co-star, Mercedes Ruehl, who played Bella on Broadway, had, after all, been nominated for Tony Awards in 1990. The New York theater critics, however, proved to be equally as impressed with Mercedes' performance when she stepped into the role in 1991. The review Mercedes received in *The Boston Globe*, written by Kevin Kelly when the play was on tour in that city, best represents what most of the critics said about her performance: "Mercedes McCambridge doesn't erase the memory of Irene Worth, who originated the role, but she gives it a similar dimension of terrible pain. Eyes downcast … as though she's seen too much … and tapping her cane, she limps around the stage dragging a terror she can never outdistance." There was, of course, startling similarities between many of the horrors in the actress' own life and that of Grandma Kurnitz. Apparently, audiences everywhere could sense the reality of her heartfelt performance and responded to it accordingly, awarding her numerous curtain calls as each performance ended.

Lost in Yonkers was the final major accomplishment of Mercedes McCambridge's long and diversified career as an actress. In an interview that appeared in *The New Haven Register* during her 28-city national tour, Mercedes told reporter Robert Viagas how much she enjoyed playing the role of Grandma Kurnitz in the play: "I love Grandma Kurnitz for her strength, for her truth, for her honesty, and for her adherence to her own principals. Grandma is tough and she expects everyone to be as tough as she is. She knows that if you're not tough, you don't make it in this world. You have to be like steel. Every teacher has always told you that. Your best teachers … weren't they the toughest ones? The ones who demanded the most of you, rather than the ones who patted you on the back and said, 'You're just doing a beautiful job.'"

While Mercedes was appearing in *Lost in Yonkers* on tour and in New York, many of her friends and long-time fans paid homage to the actress by attending a performance of the play. In Boston, actress Julie Harris, who had appeared on Broadway with Mercedes in the late 1940s in *The Young and the Fair*, and had been, like McCambridge, a close friend of actor James Dean, visited her backstage at the Shubert Theater after the show one evening. Long-time friends Joan Kroc (the widow-owner of the founder of McDonald's), Helen Copeley (chairman of the board of Copley Press), and Maureen O'Connor (the mayor of San Diego) flew across the country to New Haven, Connecticut, from California to see their friend Mercedes toward the end of her *Lost in Yonkers* tour. She was leaving the play after playing Grandma Kurnitz for 560 performances. "It's time," Mercedes announced at a press conference when the play was ending its run in New Haven, Connecticut. "Besides," she added, "I've made plans to go whale-watching in two weeks … and that's about as far as I care to look ahead at the moment."

Just before her tour in *Lost in Yonkers* ended, Mercedes received the news that her former husband, Fletcher Markle, had died of a heart attack in California. It was May 23, 1991, and her performance that evening, according to people who saw it, was poignant and moving, especially during the scene when Grandma Kurnitz talks about her deceased husband. Bronwyn Drainie, the daughter of Canadian actor John Drainie, who had worked with Markle for many years, wrote an article about Markle shortly after he died that appeared in the "Arts" section of the Canadian newspaper *The Globe and Mail*. "Nothing in the second half of Markle's career," Ms. Drainie stated, "ever quite lived up to the promise and energy of the first half." The article concluded, "Ill health, in the form of diabetes, slowed him down a great deal; he no longer had the stamina to sustain the long hours and grueling tensions of a directing career. He lived his last years, quietly writing, in Pasadena, California." An obituary, published in the Toronto newspaper, stated, "Mr. Markle leaves his third wife, Dorothy, and son, Stephen, from his first marriage. His body is to be cremated and his ashes will be scattered in the sea." There was no mention of Markle's eleven-year marriage to Mercedes McCambridge, or of his adopted son, John Lawrence. The actress had by that time, however, forgiven Markle for his abandonment of her in the early 1960s, and her friends say that she was sincerely saddened by the news of his death.

Then, just as Mercedes gave her final performance as Grandma Kurnitz in *Lost in Yonkers* in 1992, she received the news that her dear friend, Marlene Dietrich, had died of a kidney infection in Paris, France. Marlene was ninety-one years old when she died, and had been a recluse for many years, rarely seen by anyone and cloistered in her apartment in Paris for the last several years of her life. The two women had remained good friends for almost fifty years, and Mercedes and Marlene kept in frequent telephone contact with one another since their Hollywood days in the 1950s. As she did when she heard about the death of Orson and Fletcher, Mercedes deeply mourned the loss of her good friend Marlene Dietrich. Marlene was the last of the many famous folk who had befriended Mercedes McCambridge over the years, and the film star had certainly enriched Mercedes' life immensely with her kindness, helpful career advice, and genuine friendship.

When she returned home from the whale-watching vacation that followed her tour of *Lost in Yonkers*, Mercedes retreated to the sanctity of her home in La Jolla, California. "It's beautiful," she had said when she first announced her retirement. "It's heaven," she added with a chuckle. "Why, I can look across the Pacific and see China from my lawn."

In 1993, Mercedes came out of retirement briefly to narrate Dr. Seuss' (Theodore S. Geisel) children's story *Thidwick, the Big-Hearted Moose* for a book and audio cassette package released by Random House. It seems appropriate, somehow, that her enchanting audio performance should have been one of the last of her memorable career, since that career had begun many years before as a radio actress. The story, originally published in 1948 when the actress was at the height of her radio acting career, was about a moose named Thidwick who doesn't know what he is in for when he lets a "Bingle Bug" hitch a ride on his antlers. The ungrateful guest subsequently invites a spider, and then some birds, and then various other animals to ride on Thidwick's antlers as well. Before long, there are more animals on Thidwick's head than he can manage. In some ways, the story paralleled Mercedes McCambridge's own life experience. Her parents, two ex-husbands, son, a host of friends, and even, in one sense, her fans had certainly taken refuge on Mercedes' broad shoulders over the years. At one point in the story, the narrator says, "A host has to put up with all kinds of pests. For a host, above all, must be *nice* to his guests." Interestingly, as if she had been anticipating her taped performance of *Thidwick*, Mercedes had written a caption for a smiling photograph of herself in her early sixties that appeared in her autobiography, *The Quality of Mercy*, which was published twelve years before the *Thidwick* edition and cassette was released. The captain under the photograph in her autobiography read: "Can't you see, I want you to love me. I'm so nice."

Afterword

At the 70th annual Academy of Motion Picture Arts and Sciences Awards in 1998, Mercedes McCambridge and an impressive number of well-known film personalities were assembled on the stage of the Shrine Auditorium in Los Angeles to receive a special tribute. During the course of the evening's activities, they were recognized and applauded as former Academy Award–winning actors. The previous winners gathered on the stage that evening included some of the all-time great stars of the Motion Picture Industry: Anne Bancroft, Kathy Bates, Ernest Borgnine, Red Buttons, Michael Caine, George Chakiris, Sean Connery, Geena Davis, Michael Douglas, Richard Dreyfuss, Faye Dunaway, Robert Duvall, Louise Fletcher, Brenda Fricker, Whoopie Goldberg, Cuba Gooding, Jr., Louis Gossett, Jr., Charlton Heston, Dustin Hoffman, Celeste Holm, Holly Hunter, Angelica Huston, Jeremy Irons, Claude Jarman, Jr., Jennifer Jones, Shirley Jones, George Kennedy, Ben Kingsley, Martin Landau, Jack Lemmon, Walter Matthau, Frances McDormand, Rita Moreno, Patricia Neal, Jack Nicholson, Jack Palance, Anna Paquin, Estelle Parsons, Gregory Peck, Joe Pesci, Sidney Poitier, Luise Rainer, Cliff Robertson, Geoffrey Rush, Harold Russell, Eva Marie Saint, Susan Sarandon, Maximilian Schell, Mira Sorvino, Rod Steiger, Shirley Temple, Marisa Tomei, Claire Trevor, Jon Voight, Denzel Washington, Shelley Winters, Teresa Wright … and Mercedes McCambridge. As the TV camera panned the faces of each of the actors and actresses seated in several rows on the stage, and their names were read by an off-camera announcer, each of them acknowledged his or her applause with a polite smile or a gentle nod of the head. When the camera came to rest on Mercedes McCambridge, and her name was announced, the eighty-two-year-old actress raised her clasped hands above her head in a self-congratulatory manner and then led the applause for herself. It was as if she was saying, "Yes. It's me. I am still here and I have survived it all." Most of the people Mercedes had cherished and relied upon for support over the years were dead by then … her parents, her brothers, her son, her daughter-in-law, her two granddaughters, both of her ex-husbands, Marlene and Orson, Adlai and Billy, James Dean and Monty Clift … all gone. But there she was at the 1998 Academy Awards, sitting on a stage in front of six thousand people, surrounded by many of the most famous motion picture personalities of all time, as television cameras transmitted her image to millions and millions of people all over the world. And yet, in spite of all of the attention she received that evening, Mercedes McCambridge was exactly where she always seems to have been, both during her professional as well as private life: she was veritably alone, applauding her own vibrant and exceptional self amidst a group of similar, attention-needing people.

On March 2, 2004, the vibrant and talented woman who was born Carlotta Mercedes McCambridge on March 16, 1916, and enjoyed well-deserved success and celebrity as an actress, as well as enduring numerous personal hardships, died quietly of natural causes at the age of 87 at an assisted-living facility located near her La Jolla, California, home. Her death came just fourteen days before her 88th birthday and fifteen days shy of St. Patrick's Day, the holiday she always liked to claim was the day of her birth. Newspapers and television news anchormen and women all over the country paid tribute to the Academy Award–winning performer whom Orson Welles had once called "the world's greatest living radio actress." In his Associated Press obituary, Bob Thomas said of Miss McCambridge: "The Oscar-winning actress honed her vocal skills in radio. McCambridge's strong voice made her an ideal film portrayer of hard-driving women. She acquired a reputation as a strong-willed, outspoken woman [both] on and off the screen." Indeed she did. As the story of her life and career illustrates, she did that, and then some!

Perhaps no one has summed up what every human being's life, no matter how successful they have been, is ultimately all about better than William Shakespeare in Act Two, Scene Seven, of his play *As You Like It*.

> All the world's a stage
> And all the men and women merely players;
> They have their exits and their entrances,
> And one man in his time plays many parts,
> His acts being seven ages. At first, the infant
> Mewling and puking in his nurse's arms.
> Then the whining schoolboy, with his satchel
> And shining morning face, creeping like snail
> Unwillingly to school. And then the lover,
> Sighing like a furnace, with a woeful ballad
> Made to his mistress' eyebrow. Then a soldier,
> Full of strange oaths and bearded like a pard.
> Jealous in honour, sudden and quick in quarrel,
> Seeking a bubble reputation
> Even in the cannon's mouth. And then the justice,
> In fair round belly with good capon lined,
> With eyes severe and beard of formal cut,
> Full of wise saws and modern instances;
> And so he plays his part. The sixth age shifts
> Into the lean and slippered pantaloon
> With spectacles on nose and pouch on side;
> His youthful hose, well saved, a world too wide

For his shrunk shank, and his big, manly voice,
Turning again toward childish treble, pipes,
And whistles in his sound. Last scene of all,
That ends this strange eventful history,
Is second childishness and mere oblivion,
Sans teeth, sans eyes, sans taste, sans everything.
William Shakespeare

Postscript

If, as C.C. Colton (1780–1832) said, "Imitation is the sincerest flattery," Mercedes McCambridge would certainly have been flattered to learn that a staged musical comedy version of her 1954 film *Johnny Guitar*, which has become a cult classic, opened at the Off Broadway Century Center for the Performing Arts on March 23, 2004. The musical features Ann Crumb as Emma (the role Mercedes essayed in the film) and Judy McLane as Vienna, and the two actresses reportedly play the cat fight between the two characters—and McCambridge and Crawford—to the hilt in their over-the-top performances. The lesbian overtones of the original film have apparently not been overlooked in this stage adaptation, which was written by Nicholas van Hoogstraten and features music by composer Martin Silvestri. One can only hope that Miss McCambridge at least heard about this production before she closed her eyes for the last time on March 2, 2004, a mere twenty-one days before the musical opened Off Broadway. She certainly would have loved the flattery of being imitated.

PART II

Her Performances

Radio, Television, Film and Theater Log

The title of the film, play, or radio or television series (or individual radio or television episode) is followed by the name of the character McCambridge played (in parentheses). Next are listed the broadcast/release/performance date(s) of the series, film or play. Names of other performers follow, as well as the names of those appearing on individual episodes. Directors are included where the author felt it appropriate due to their prominence, or if the name was not mentioned in the text. The dates indicate the years Mercedes McCambridge was heard on the program and not always the total run of the show. The total number of years the program was on the air, however, is listed for especially long-running series.

*   indicates one (or more) sustained, regular short- or long-running roles on a radio or television series
+   indicates one or more single performances on a radio or television series

---

1936–1941

RADIO (as an NBC contract actress in Chicago)

NBC Variety Show, 1936, Soloist with Mundelein College's Verse Speaking Choir.

Dan Harding's Wife (Donna Harding), *1936, with Isabel Randolph, Merrill Fugitt, Cliff Soubier, Carl Hanson, Alice Goodkin, Gladys Heen, Herb Nelson, Templeton Fox, Judith Lowry, others. This was the first daytime serial drama series Mercedes McCambridge was featured on at NBC when she first began working as a contract actress in 1936. She played the young daughter of the program's heroine on this series, which was about family life in Middle America.

141

Timothy Makepeace, *1936. Mercedes played a supporting role on this short-lived domestic comedy daytime series with Dickensian overtones. It remained on the air for less than two months before NBC dropped it from their schedule after it failed to attract an audience of listeners. The series revolved around a young man coming of age in Middle America, with Mercedes playing the hero's love interest.

Lights Out, +January 1, 1936–August 30, 1939. This series broadcast for one half-hour a week on NBC's Red network. The stories on this series were all eerie horror tales specifically designed to frighten people out of their wits. Written and directed by Arch Oboler, *Lights Out* often featured Joseph Kearns, Hans Conried, Raymond Edward Johnson, Betty Winkler, Earle Ross and others. McCambridge was heard on (among many others):

"Sakhalin," March 3, 1937
"Murder Castle," February 16, 1938, with Joseph Kearns
"It Happened," May 11, 1938
Five radio shows with Boris Karloff, March–April, 1938
"The Author and the Thing" September 28, 1943

(These four named episodes are available from Old Time Radio show vendors.)

Arch Oboler Theater, +March 25, 1939–March 30, 1940, with Joseph Kearns, Raymond Edward Johnson, Hans Conried and others. This dramatic anthology program offered all sorts of stories, from adventure tales to comedies to mysteries. The program was directed by Arch Oboler.

    Note: Mercedes McCambridge was heard on many more broadcasts of Arch Oboler's programs between 1936 and 1941 that originated at NBC Red network's studios in Chicago.

The Guiding Light (Mary Rutledge), *1937–1941, with Arthur Peterson, Ed Prentiss, Sam Wanamaker, Marvin Miller, Raymond Edward Johnson, Willard Waterman, Murray Forbes, Eloise Kummer, Charlotte Manson, Bret Morrison, Betty Lou Gerson, Peggy Fuller, Gertrude Warner, and others. This soap opera series first aired as a fifteen-minute inspirational drama heard five days a week. It centered on the domestic problem-solving activities of a Protestant clergyman named the Reverend Rutledge. McCambridge played the widower minister's young daughter, Mary.

Betty and Bob (Betty), *1936–1941, with Les Tremayne, Van Heflin, Ned Wever, Alice Hill, Elizabeth Reller, others. This was one of Frank and Anne Hummert's first soap opera series. Betty and Bob Drake, a young newlywed couple, were the main characters on this soap opera series heard five times a week, Monday through Friday. The series focused on the problems most young married couples face in their relationship.

Girl Alone (Patricia Rodgers), *1936–1940, with Raymond Edward Johnson, Willard Waterman, others. This soap opera series was one of the first to revolve around a woman who faces the world without a partner. It led the way for the many serial dramas about independent women that followed.

Amanda of Honeymoon Hill, +1940–1941, with Joy Hathaway, Boyd Crawford, George Lambert, Cecil Roy, Helen Shields, Reese Taylor, Florence Malone, others. Frank and Anne Hummert produced, and sometimes directed and wrote, this five-day-a-week soap opera series about a poor young girl trying to adjust to young womanhood as the wife of a wealthy young man in the southern United States.

Backstage Wife, +1936–1938, also called *Mary Noble, Backstage Wife*, with Vivian Fridell, Ken Griffith, Claire Niesen, James Meighan, Ethel Owen, Eloise Kummer, others. This soap opera series (heard five days a week) about a woman married to a celebrated Broadway star was mainly concerned with the various adjustments she had to make as the wife of a famous and handsome actor. A spoof of this series became one of talk show hosts Bob and Ray's most popular running gags. It was called "Mary Backstayge, Noble Wife" on *The Bob and Ray Show*.

The Carters of Elm Street, +1939–1940, with Virginia Payne, Vic Smith, Ginger Jones, Ann Russell, Herb Nelson, Bill Rose, Harriette Widmer, others. A typical middle class American family made up the central characters on this soap opera series heard five days a week on NBC's Red network.

David Harum, +1936–1941, with William Walter, Gertrude Warner, Peggy Allenby, Cameron Prud'Homme, Charme Allen, Lawson Zerbe, others. Frank and Anne Hummert were responsible for this soap opera series heard five days a week on NBC's Blue, and then Red, network. This serial drama focused on a kindly small-town banker with "all–American" values who spent as much time helping his friends and family with their problems as he did working in his bank.

Don Winslow of the Navy, +1937–1940, with Bob Guilbert, Betty Lou Gerson, Raymond Edward Johnson, Edward Davidson, others. This five-day-a-week children's series followed the exciting adventures of a naval officer and his friends.

Ellen Randolph, +1939–1941, with Elsie Hitz, Macdonald Carey, John McGovern, Jay Meredith, Jackie Jordan, Florida Friebus, Bart Robinson, others. The title character on this NBC Red network soap opera series, heard Monday through Friday, was a young married woman who, with her husband, George and son Bobby, must deal with the usual domestic problems faced by many young couples in Middle America.

The First Nighter, +1936–1941, with Bret Morrison, Don Ameche, June Meredith, Betty Lou Gerson, Barbara Luddy, Les Tremayne, others. Each week offered a different drama, said to originate from a "little theater off Times Square," on this popular, long-running series, heard as early as 1930 on the NBC Blue, and then Red, network. The series was narrated by a character called Mr. First Nighter. Supporting casts varied, and McCambridge occasionally played supporting roles on this series in the late 1930s.

Jane Arden, +1938, with Ruth Yorke, Florence Freeman, others. This short-lived soap opera series centered on a young single woman trying to find love as she attempts to make a living for herself.

John's Other Wife, +1936–1942, with Adele Ronson, Luis Van Rooten, Hanley Stafford, Matt Crowley, Erin O'Brien Moore, others. Heard on the NBC Blue and Red networks, this serial drama often became the butt of jokes because of its title. The "other wife" in the series was John's secretary, but there was never anything "going on" between John and his employee; John was a happily married man. Frank and Ann Hummert were responsible for this series.

Lone Journey, +1940–1943, with Claudia Morgan, Les Damon, James Meighan, Betty Winkler, Eloise Kummer, Reese Taylor, Olive Deering, John Hodiak, others. Set in a small town in Montana, this five-day-a-week NBC Red network serial drama was about the social and domestic difficulties people faced by those in a remote rural community.

Lorenzo Jones, *+1937–1938, with Karl Swenson, Betty Garde, Nancy Sheridan, Elliott Reid, Mary Wickes, Frank Behrens, Chester Stratton, others. The title character on this Monday-through-Friday soap opera series was a mechanic in Jim Baker's garage. A kind-hearted, simple working man, Lorenzo, with his wife Belle, faced many good and bad times together as a working class married couple. Lorenzo, a dreamer, is a would-be inventor, and this series offered a good deal of humor along with its drama, due to Lorenzo's always-hopeful character. McCambridge played several short-lived running characters on this series in the late 1930s. The program was broadcast from both Chicago and New York.

Ma Perkins, +1937–1942, with Virginia Payne, Charles Egelston, Murray Forbes, Rita Ascot, Laurette Fillbrandt, Margaret Draper, others. The five-day-a-week soap opera *Ma Perkins*, heard on NBC's Red network for several years, focused on an elderly widow with two daughters who owned a lumber yard in a town called Rushville Center. Good-natured and caring, Ma, in addition to doing whatever she could to help her daughters, also became involved in the problems of others who lived in her town.

The Man I Married, +1939–1940, with Vicki Vola, Van Heflin, Gertrude Warner, Dorothy Lowell, Betty Winkler, others. This NBC Red network Monday-through-Friday serial drama followed the marital problems of a character named Evelyn Waring, who was married to a rather weak-willed man.

Midstream, *(Midge), 1939–1941, with Hugh Studebaker, Betty Lou Gerson, Fern Persons, Russell Thorson, others. *Midstream*, a soap opera heard on NBC's Red and

Blue networks, revolved around a middle-aged married couple named Charles and Julia Meredith, who had "reached the halfway mark between the distant shores of birth and death."

Modern Romances, +1937–1939, with Gertrude Warner, narrator. This program told fifteen-minute-a-day, week-long stories that involved romance and featured different casts each week.

Mr. District Attorney, +1937–1941, with Dwight Weist, Vicki Vola, Walter Kinsella, Len Doyle, and others. Heard on NBC's Red and Blue networks, *Mr. District Attorney* was a weekly crime drama series in which Mr. District Attorney (whose name was never given) solved a different mystery each week.

Mr. Keen, Tracer of Lost Persons, +1937–1942, with Phil Clarke, Arthur Hughes, Jim Kelly, Florence Malone, others. *Mr. Keen*, the "kindly old investigator" who each week for a half-hour tracked down a missing person with the help of his assistant Mike Clancy, originated on NBC's Blue network.

Mrs. Wiggs of the Cabbage Patch, +1936–1938, with Betty Garde, Robert Strauss, Andy Donnelly, Alice Frost, Agnes Young, Bill Johnstone, Marjorie Anderson, others. This five-day-a-week series, based upon Alice Caldwell Rise's popular novel of the same name was about a kindly country woman who found time to help various members of her community in any way she could. The program was heard on NBC's Red network from 1936 to 1938.

Orphans of Divorce, +1939–1942, with James Meighan, Margaret Anglin, Effie Palmer, Richard Gordon, Claire Wilson, Patricia Peardon, Warren Bryant, others. This half-hour weekly series on NBC's Blue network focused on four orphaned children and the woman who adopted them. The stories dealt with the children of divorced parents, who were considered "orphans" because they only had one parent.

The Parker Family, +1940–1942, with Michael O'Day, Roy Fant, Linda Carlton Reid, Leon Janney, Jay Jostyn, others. A typical American teen, Richard Parker, was the hero of this weekly series on NBC's Blue network that was both amusing and thought provoking. Richard dealt with all of the usual problems facing a teenaged boy, such as dating, school, and parents.

Pepper Young's Family, +1936–1942, with Lawson Zerbe, Bill Adams, Betty Wragge, Elliott Reid, Tess Sheehan, Jack Raleigh, others. Originally titled *Red Adams*, and then *Forever Young*, *Pepper Young's Family* dealt with a typical American family, centering on the son Red, later called "Pepper." Over the years, Pepper married, had children, and faced the usual problems encountered by young married men and their wives.

Stella Dallas, +1937–1941, with Anne Elstner, Joy Hathaway, Frederick Tozier, Julie Benell, Harold Vermilyea, Frank Lovejoy, Michael Fitzmaurice, others. Stella Dallas was a down-to-earth, somewhat common woman whose daughter Laurel (or "Lolly Baby," as she called her) married into wealth and society. It was "the story of mother love and sacrifice," according to the series' opening. The program made its debut on NBC's Red network and was heard five days a week for fifteen minutes a day.

The Story of Mary Marlin, +1937–1941, with Anne Seymour, Raymond Edward Johnson, Joan Blaine, Eloise Kummer, Robert Griffin, Raymond Edward Johnson, Art Kohl, Murray Forbes, others. On this 15-minute, Monday-through-Friday soap opera series (heard on NBC's Red and Blue networks), Mary Marlin took over her husband's Senate seat when she thought he was dead (he actually suffered from amnesia after an airplane accident). Mary proved how independent a woman could become when she really had to.

A Tale of Today (Flora Little), +1936–1939, with Luise Barclay, Laurette Fillbrandt, Raymond Edward Johnson, Ethel Owen, others. Originally a ten-minute segment on *The Princess Pat Players* program, *A Tale of Today* became a regular five-day-a- week daytime series on NBC's Blue network. It told the story of the Houstons, an average, middle-class American family.

Today's Children, +1936–1938, with Helen Kane, Forrest Lewis, Judith Lowry, Irna Phillips, others. Another of NBC's daytime serial dramas broadcast on their Red and Blue networks, *Today's Children* was about an immigrant family, the Schultzes, and the problems they encountered trying to settle in a new country.

Valiant Lady, +1938, with Florence Freeman, Bill Johnstone, James Meighan, Richard Gordon, Bill Johnstone, Kate McComb, others. Joan Hargrave-Scott was the "valiant lady" in this daytime serial drama, who "struggles to help her unstable husband keep his feet on the ground on the pathway to success."

Woman in White, +1938–1942, with Luise Barclay, Betty Ruth Smith, Betty Lou Gerson, Willard Farnum, Harry Elders, others. Karen Adams was a caring, hardworking nurse on this five-day-a-week serial drama, who works in a big city hospital and tries to balance her job and home life.

Young Dr. Malone, +1939–1940, with Alan Bunce, Carl Frank, Elizabeth Reller, Barbara Weeks, Euince Howard, Bill Redfield, others. On this long-running five-day-a-week soap opera series, physician Jerry Malone, with his ever-patient wife at his side, faces professional and personal problems (ranging from a patient's death to troubling financial difficulties).

Young Widder Brown, +1938–1942, with Florence Freeman, Ned Wever, Jimmy McCallion, Helen Shields, Marilyn Erskine, others. As the opening of this daytime soap opera stated, "Young Widder Brown is the story of the age-old conflict between a mother's duty and a woman's heart." The problems the young widow faced while trying to balance the start of a new personal life and a career was the focus of this NBC Red network series.

Your Family and Mine, +1938–1939, with Raymond Edward Johnson, Joan Tompkins, Bill Adams, Lucille Wall, others. This daytime series revolved around the all–American Wilbur family and their everyday problems.

1939–1942

RADIO (as an NBC contract actress in Hollywood)

I Love a Mystery, *1939–1941, with Michael Raffeto, Barton Yarborough, Walter Paterson, Gloria Blondell, others. Private detectives Jack Packard, Doc Long and Reggie Yorke of the A-1 Detective Agency solved weekly adventures on this memorable and popular radio series heard on NBC's Red and Blue networks. McCambridge was a regular player on this program and performed *all* of the female roles in the adventures on which she was featured. This was the first time (but not the last) McCambridge was heard on the series, which was re-introduced to the listening public, with a different cast, in the late 1940s and early 1950s (and which featured Mercedes once again on several multi-episode adventures).

"Yolo County — Battle of the Century" (18 episodes) McCambridge played Jacqueline "Jack" Dempsey Ross 9/6/39–9/29/39
"Blue Phantom" (15 episodes) 10/2/39–10/20/39
"Castle Island" (20 episodes) 10/23/39–11/17/39
"Hollywood Cherry" (15 episodes) 11/20/39–12/8/39
"Bury Your Dead, Arizona" (15 episodes) 12/11/39–12/29/39
"Eight Kinds of Murder" (8 episodes) 5/12/41
McCambridge continued to work on the *I Love a Mystery* series from time to time while in Hollywood until 1942, when she went to New York to star on NBC's *Abie's Irish Rose* program. She featured on *I Love a Mystery*'s well-remembered 12 episode adventure "The Pirate Loot of the Island of the Skulls," playing Florence Sedgewick from April 1942 through June 19, 1942.
(It is unknown whether the following broadcasts emanated from Hollywood or New York. They may have been broadcast from the Big Apple, or McCambridge may have briefly returned to California temporarily to work for Morse. Most of McCambridge's radio work during these years was in New York.)
"The Decapitation of Jefferson Monk" (25 episodes) 8/30/43–10/1/43
"You Can't Pin a Murder on Nevada" (15 episodes) 10/13/44–6/2/44

NBC sponsored a 30-minute special broadcast written and produced by Carlton E. Morse which was called "The Knock on the Door." The special was part of California's United States Bond Pledge Drive to promote sales of Defense Savings Bonds. The program was broadcast May 5, 1942. In addition to Mercedes McCambridge, the cast included Sam Edwards, Jr., and Sr., Elliot Lewis, Wally Maher and Jay Novello.

The Rudy Vallee Sealtest Show, +1941–1942, starring Rudy Vallee. The January 1 and January 16, 1941, shows are available from several Old Time Radio vendors. This weekly musical variety program often included comedy. McCambridge appeared as an occasional supporting player.

Arch Oboler's Everyman's Theater, +October 4, 1940–March 28, 1941, with Joseph Kearns, Hans Conried, guest stars, others. This anthology program featured different half-hour dramas once a week. Mercedes played the female lead in: "Papa Jonathan," January 17, 1941, with Howard Duff.

The Jack Benny Show, +1941–1942, starring Jack Benny, Mary Livingstone, Don Wilson, others. This half-hour comedy program heard on NBC's Red network featured guest stars and sketches, as well as a situation comedy segment. McCambridge was an infrequent featured player on the show.

The Bing Crosby Show, +1941–1942, starring Bing Crosby, guest stars. This NBC RED Network program offered occasional comedy skits, and McCambridge played featured roles in them.

The Bob Hope Show, +1941, starring Bob Hope, with Vera Vague (Barbara Jo Allen), Jerry Collona, others. This half-hour comedy program sometimes featured comedy sketches and spoofs, and was heard on NBC's Red network.

Suspense, +1942. Joseph Kearns was the regular host, "The Man in Black," in the early episodes of this series. This half-hour program presented stories "well calculated to keep [an audience] in suspense." Famous Hollywood guest stars appeared in different tales each week, and a cast of radio actors supported them.

"Till Death Do Us Part," December 15, 1942, with Peter Lorre, Alice Frost, David Gothard

This Is Judy Jones (Judy Jones), *August 21, 1941–October 9, 1941. McCambridge starred on this short-lived, half-hour situation comedy series that dealt with the problems of a girl attempting to accept her new responsibilities as a young adult.

Arch Oboler's Plays for America, 1942. This half-hour weekly drama series presented plays that usually carried patriotic messages or themes. It was heard on NBC shortly after World War II began. McCambridge was featured on:

"The Welburns—A Confidential Report," April 26, 1942, with Elliott Lewis
"Gangster in the House," May 31, 1942

1942–1949

RADIO (as a freelance actress in New York)

Abie's Irish Rose (Rose Murphy—leading role), *NBC, 1942–1943, directed by Axel Gruenberg, with Richard Coogan, Alan Reed (Teddy Bergman), Walter Kinsella, Menasha Skulnick, Anna Appel The half-hour situation comedy series centered on a young Jewish man, Abie Levy, his new wife, an Irish girl named Rosemary Murphy, and their families, friends and neighbors. McCambridge was still under contract to NBC as an actress when she appeared on this series. The following *Abie's Irish Rose* broadcasts featuring McCambridge as Rose are available from Old Time Radio collectors and vendors:

"Solomon and Pat Try to Buy Back Abie's Contract," January 13, 1943
"Rose and Abie's Anniversary," August 31, 1943

Lights Out (reprised), +NBC. Mercedes starred, with Arch Oboler playing himself, on the program's final show. This eerie series of half-hour horror stories featured rebroadcasts of many of the same radio plays that had originally been heard when the series first aired in Chicago in the 1930s. New scripts were also presented on this series as well. McCambridge was heard on:

"The Execution," April 27, 1943
"Murder Castle," August 3, 1943, with Joseph Kearns
"The World," September 14, 1943
"The Author and the Thing," September 28, 1943
"The World," September 14, 1945
"Prelude to Murder," June 15, 1953, with Hans Conried

(Several of these shows were rebroadcasts from the 1930s series. They are available from Old Time Radio collectors and vendors.)

Famous Jury Trials, +NBC Red, with Maurice Franklin as the Judge, and Roger DeKoven and DeWitt McBride as the Narrator. This series presented half-hour dramatized courtroom trials and featured different casts each week. McCambridge was heard on several of these programs, which were broadcast from NBC's third floor Blue network studio at 30 Rockefeller Plaza in New York.

The Big Story, +1947, NBC, with Robert Sloane, Ernest Chappel. The series dramatized newspaper stories of ace reporters in half-hour weekly radio plays. At the end of the program, the actual reporter whose story had been adapted was introduced to the listening audience. On *The Big Story*, and the shows that followed, McCambridge worked as a freelance actress and was no longer under contract to NBC.

Gangbusters, +1942–1946, CBS, NBC, ABC, and Mutual This series often featured Elspeth Eric, Alice Reinheart, Robert Dryden, Frank Readick, Santos Ortega, Leon Janney, and others, as well as McCambridge. Based upon both true and fictional events, this half-hour series focused on crime-busting G-Men (Government Men) and the criminals they tracked down. It was produced by Phillips H. Lord. McCambridge was heard on "Triple Theater Bandits" (also known as "Broadway Bandits").

Inner Sanctum Mysteries, +1941–1952, CBS, with Raymond Edward Johnson, Paul McGrath, Ann Shepherd, Anne Seymour, Arnold Moss, Everett Sloane, Karl Swenson, Larry Haines, Mason Adams, and others, produced and directed by Himan Brown). Introduced by a spooky host with a chilling greeting ("Good evening, friends of the Inner Sanctum; this is your host, welcoming you through the squeaking (creaking) door to hear another exciting tale of mystery and suspense"), this half-hour weekly series presented horror stories about murders and ghosts, and usually ended with the evil-doers coming to an appropriate end. A partial list of shows featuring McCambridge includes:

"Blood of Cain," January 29, 1946
"Murder Always Comes at Midnight," April 30, 1946
"Detour to Terror," May 21, 1946, with Mason Adams, Berry Kroeger, Santos Ortega, Donald Dane
"Bury Me Not," June 11, 1946
"I Want to Report a Murder," June 18, 1946, with Santos Ortega, Lawson Zerbe
"One More Murder," July 29, 1946, with Berry Kroeger, Santos Ortega
"Asleep in the Deep," August 5, 1946
"The Dead Laugh," September 23, 1946, with Berry Kroeger, Lawson Zerbe, Santos Ortega
"Death's Old Sweet Song," November 4, 1946, with Luis Van Rooten, Alice Frost, Jackson Beck
"But the Dead Walk Alone," December 2, 1946
"A Time to Die," October 6, 1947
"'Till Death Do Us Part," November 27, 1947, with Everett Sloane
"The Doomed," January 26, 1948, with Karl Swenson
"The Magic Tile," March 8, 1948, with Everett Sloane
"Death Rides a Riptide," September 6, 1948, with Arlene Blackburn, Everett Sloane
"The Phantom Dance," October 25, 1948
"Death Wears a Lonely Smile," April 4, 1949, with Robert Sloane
"The Death Deal," April 19, 1949, with Arnold Moss, Everett Sloane, Alan Devitt
"The Curious Corpse," June 13, 1949
"Dead Heat," August 15, 1949, with Everett Sloane, Karl Swenson

"Murder Rides the Carousel," September 5, 1949

"Honeymoon with Death," September 19, 1949, with Mason Adams and Arlene Blackburn

"A Corpse for Halloween," October 21, 1949, with Larry Haines, Berry Kroeger

"Beyond the Grave," December 4, 1950, with Mason Adams

"The Hitch-Hiking Corpse," January 23, 1950, with Ken Lynch, Everett Sloane

"Beyond the Grave," December 4, 1950, with Mason Adams, Lester Coppel

Big Sister (Ruth Wayne — leading role), *1943–1947, CBS, with Arnold Moss, Peggy
Conklin, Fran Carlon, Elspeth Eric, Paul McGrath, Martin Gabel, Arlene Francis,
many others. Ruth Evans, the "big sister" of this five-day-a-week soap opera series,
guided her two younger sisters as they attempted to adjust to their lives as young
adults, as well as trying to live a life of her own. Mercedes played the primary character on this serial drama for many years.

Arch Oboler's Everything for the Boys, January 18, 1944–June 13, 1944, NBC, with
actor Ronald Colman (as host) and singer Dick Haymes. This half-hour dramatic
anthology series presented stories designed to help members of the military, as well
as people on the home front, forget about the war they were fighting for a while. The
weekly dramas usually offered some sort of inspirational or uplifting message. Among
the episodes featuring McCambridge were:

"Lost Horizon," February 1, 1944, with Janet Blair, Norman Field

"The Women Stayed at Home," February 22, 1944

"The Loving Book," April 4, 1944, with Dennis Day, Robert Bailey, Lou Merrill

"Blithe Spirit," May 16, 1944, with Loretta Young, Edna Best

Arch Oboler's the Devil and Mr. O, 1943. These were rebroadcasts of shows previously aired on *Lights Out* and *Arch Oboler Theater*. Among the episodes featuring
Mercedes were:

"Ancestor" with Hans Conried

"Where Are You?"

Arch Oboler's Plays, April 5, 1946–October 11, 1945, NBC. Recreations of many of
Oboler's previously heard radio plays were presented on this half-hour series.

Orson Welles' Mercury Summer Theater, +1946, CBS. This hour-long summer
replacement series based upon Orson Welles' previously successful Mercury Theater
of the Air program presented adaptations of classic works of literature, as well as original plays. McCambridge featured on the following broadcasts:

"Life with Adam," by Fletcher Markle, July 19, 1946

"The Moat Farm Murders," July 26, 1946

"Golden Honeymoon — Romeo and Juliet," August 2, 1946, co-starring Orson Welles.

Arch Oboler's Your Radio Hall of Fame (*Arch Oboler Plays*), +NBC. This dramatic anthology series presented half-hour plays written and directed by Arch Oboler. McCambridge was heard on:

"Alter Ego," April 22, 1945, with Ann Shepard, Clifton Fadiman (host)

"The House I Live In," April 26, 1945, with Raymond Massey, Alfred Ryder, Ann Shepard, Hester Sondergaard

Cavalcade of America, +1947–1949, NBC. This series offered half-hour plays with American themes, or stories about famous or newsworthy American characters. McCambridge was heard on "Us Pilgrims," November 24, 1947, and November 22, 1949, with George Tobias

Columbia Presents Corwin, +1944, CBS. Classic radio plays by Norman Corwin were presented on this half-hour series. McCambridge was featured on "Carl Sandburg–Part 2," June 6, 1944, with Harry Bartel, Hans Conried, Charles Laughton, Joan Lorring, Lurene Tuttle, Will Wright

Studio One, +April 24, 1947–July 27, 1948, CBS, produced and directed by Fletcher Markle (all of these shows are available on cassette, reel-to-reel or MP3 CDs from vendors). This was an hour-long dramatic anthology series that presented classic works of literature and the theater, and occasional original plays written for radio. The shows on which Mercedes McCambridge featured include:

"An Act of Faith," September 23, 1947, with Frank Behrens, Anne Burr, Robert Dryden, Miriam Wolfe and Fletcher Markle

"Anthony Adverse," October 14, 1947, with Bud Collyer, Miriam Wolfe, Robert Dryden, Hedley Rennie, Ronald Liss

"Kitty Foyle," November 4, 1947, with Fletcher Markle, Miriam Wolfe, Elspeth Eric, Amanda Randolph

"Let Me Do the Talking," November 11, 1947, with John Garfield, Raymond Edward Johnson

"Young Man of Manhattan," November 18, 1947, with Robert Mitchum, Anne Burr, Joe DeSantis, Miriam Wolfe, Robert Dryden

"Payment Deferred," November 25, 1947, with Charles Laughton, Hester Sondergaard, Miriam Wolfe, Robert Dryden, Hedley Rennie

"Earth and High Heaven," December 2, 1947, with Geraldine Fitzgerald, Raymond Edward Johnson, Miriam Wolfe, Robert Dryden, Hedley Rennie

"To Mary, with Love," December 9, 1947, with Gene Kelly, Everett Sloane, Miriam Wolfe

"Painted Veils," December 23, 1947, with James Mason, Eileen Farrell, Everett Sloane

"Confidential Agent," January 6, 1948, with Raymond Massey, Miriam Wolfe, Robert Dryden, Hedley Rennie

"King's Row," February 24, 1948, with Robert Young, Leon Janney, Robert Dryden, Everett Sloane, Miriam Wolfe

"The Thirty Nine Steps," March 23, 1948, with Glenn Ford, Kathleen Cordell, Everett Sloane, Miriam Wolfe, Robert Dryden, Hedley Rennie

"Babbitt," March 30, 1948, with Walter Huston, Everett Sloane, Miriam Wolfe, Robert Dryden, Hedley Rennie

"The Kimballs," April 6, 1948, with Franchot Tone, Everett Sloane, Miriam Wolfe

"Private Worlds," May 4, 1948, with Madeleine Carrol, Michael Fitzmaurice, Fletcher Markle, Miriam Wolfe, Robert Dryden, Hedley Rennie

"Wine of the Country," May 11, 1948, with Robert Mitchum, Everett Sloane, Miriam Wolfe, Robert Dryden

"The Last Tycoon," May 19, 1948, with Fletcher Markle, Betty Field, Everett Sloane, Miriam Wolfe, Robert Dryden, Hedley Rennie

"Spanish Bayonet," July 20, 1948, with Burgess Meredith, Ian MacAlister, Everett Sloane. Gertrude Warner, Miriam Wolfe, Robert Dryden, Hedley Rennie

The Ford Theater, +October 8, 1948–July 1, 1949, CBS. This hour-long dramatic anthology series followed the same format as the above listed *Studio One* series. Mercedes McCambridge was heard on:

"Madame Bovary," October 8, 1948, with Marlene Dietrich, Claude Rains, Van Heflin, Miriam Wolfe, Robert Dryden, Ronald Liss, Hedley Rennie

"Double Indemnity," October 15, 1948, with Burt Lancaster, Joan Bennett, Miriam Wolfe, Robert Dryden, Joe DeSantis, Hedley Rennie, Myron McCormick

"The Horn Blows at Midnight," March 4, 1949, with Jack Benny, Claude Rains, Hans Conried, Jane Morgan, Anne Whitfield, Jeanette Nolan, Miriam Wolfe, Robert Dryden

"Intermezzo," April 29, 1949 with Frederick March.

("Madame Bovary," "Double Indemnity," and "The Horn Blows at Midnight" are available from Old Time Radio show collectors and vendors.)

The Adventures of Bulldog Drummond, +1942–1946, Mutual, with Ned Wever, Everett Sloane, others. British private detective "Bulldog" Drummond, "in his American adventures," was the main character on this half-hour, crime/adventure series. Detective Drummond was assisted by his valet, Denny, in his crime solving activities. Among the Bulldog Drummond shows McCambridge appeared on in the 1940s (exact dates unknown) were:

"The Claim Check Murders"
"The Book Store"
"The Case of the Atomic Murders" "Death Loops the Loop"
"The Geiger Counter"
"The Penny Arcade Story"

Dick Tracy, +McCambridge played several sustained female characters on this series, including "Snowflake" (imitating actress Katharine Hepburn) on "The Case of the

Firebug Murders" and "The Case of the Dark Corridor" episodes in 1946. The program was heard Monday through Friday on ABC for fifteen minutes each day. Ned Wever, and then Matt Crowley, played Tracy. The series, produced and directed by Himan Brown, was based on Chester Gould's popular comic strip, *Dick Tracy, Detective.*

Superman, +1943–1945, Mutual, with Bud Collyer, Joan Alexander, Robert Dryden, others. Superhero, "Superman" (aka Clark Kent), who was first seen in the *Action* comic books, was the main character on this children's adventure serial heard five days a week on the Mutual network. McCambridge played several supporting roles on this series, and also featured on a children's recording of the program released in the late 1940s.

The Adventures of the Thin Man, +1943–1946, CBS, with Claudia Morgan, Les Damon, David Gothard, Joseph Curtin. Nick and Nora Charles, the husband-and-wife team who solved various mysteries on this half-hour weekly series, were based on characters created by author Dashiell Hammett. Before it became a radio program, it was a popular motion picture series that starred William Powell and Myrna Loy. McCambridge featured in several adventures from the radio show.

Grand Central Station, +1942–1946, CBS, produced and directed by Himan Brown, with Arnold Moss, Charlotte Manson, Elliott Reid, Nancy Coleman, Elaine Kent, others. This weekly, half-hour dramatic anthology series offered stories that always began at New York City's Grand Central Station train terminal. The dramas ranged from comedies to mysteries, and featured different casts each week.

Quick as a Flash, +1944, Mutual, with Win Elliot and Ken Roberts as hosts, and Elspeth Eric, Julie Stevens, Mandel Kramer, Joan Alexander, Charles Webster, Santos Ortega, McCambridge, and others. This half-hour weekly quiz show had contestants try to beat their opponents by being the first to answer a question. The show always ended with a guest radio show detective (like the Shadow, Mr. Keen, Bulldog Drummond, Mr. and Mrs. North, or Ellery Queen) introducing a short, dramatized mystery drama that guest contestants had to try to solve.

Armstrong Theater of Today, +1941–1942, CBS. This half-hour dramatic anthology series cast celebrated guest stars (such as Bette Davis, Jane Wyman and others), in different stories each week, with support provided by veteran radio actors. McCambridge co-starred with Burgess Meredith in a radio play on this series.

Carrington Playhouse, +1946, Mutual. This short-lived dramatic anthology series was written by Elaine Sterne Carrington, the creative force behind such soap operas as *Pepper Young's Family*, *Rosemary*, and *When a Girl Marries*. This series featured different casts in half-hour dramas each week. McCambridge was heard on "Portrait of a Girl," May 23, 1946, and repeated August 15, 1946.

(This was the program featured in the September 23, 1946, *Life* magazine photo story on Mercedes McCambridge.)

The Romance of Helen Trent, *1944–1946, CBS, with Julie Stevens, David Gothard, Marvin Miller, Carlton Kadell, Vivian Fridell, Alan Hewitt, Lesley Woods, Don MacLaughlan, Helene Dumas, Ed Latimer, others. The fifteen-minute-a-day soap opera series was "the story of a woman who sets out to prove ... that romance can live on at thirty-five ... and even beyond." This show was on the air continuously for twenty-seven years. McCambridge played several long-running roles on this series.

This Is Nora Drake (Peg Martinson),* 1947, NBC, with Charlotte Holland, Everett Sloane, Bob Readick, Elspeth Eric, Leon Janney, Mary Jane Higby, Charlotte Manson, Joan Lorring, Roger DeKoven, Everett Sloane, Ralph Bell, others. This soap opera series set in a small Midwestern town revolved around the domestic affairs of the long-suffering Nora Drake and her husband Arthur, who had difficulty avoiding designing women.

The Second Mrs. Burton, *1946, CBS, with Sharon Douglas, Dwight Weist, Claire Neisen, Jan Miner, Larry Robinson, Karl Weber, Joan Alexander, Evelyn Varden, Ethel Owen, Elspeth Eric, Gary Merrill, Les Tremayne, Alice Frost, Bob Readick, others. "The Second Mrs. Burton" referred to Terry Burton, the wife of Stan Burton. The "first" Mrs. Burton was Terry's meddlesome mother-in-law, who tried to control Terry's life, as well as Terry's husband and son, Brad.

The Adventures of Nero Wolfe, +1943–1946, Mutual, with Santos Ortega, Luis Van Rooten, others. Orchid-loving, heavy set gourmet private detective Nero Wolfe, and his assistant Archie Goodwin, were the central characters on this half-hour weekly mystery series.

The Adventures of Philo Vance, +1945–1946, Syndicated, with Jackson Beck, Maurice Mells, George Petrie, Joan Alexander, Humphrey Davis, others. Philo Vance was a debonair private detective who specialized in solving mysteries in fashionable homes, theaters, or other high-toned paces, but sometimes became involved in less sophisticated cases when they proved of interest to him.

Joyce Jordan, Girl Intern (aka *Joyce Jordan, MD*), +1944–1945, NBC, with Betty Winkler, Elspeth Eric, Ann Shephard, Myron McCormick, Jack Grimes, John Raby, Alan Devitt, Amanda Randolph, Joseph Julian, Charlotte Holland, Raymond Edward Johnson, others. This daytime drama series, which originated in Chicago in the late 1930s, began its life as *Joyce Jordan, Girl Intern*, but changed its name to *Joyce Jordan, MD* when Joyce finally became a doctor. It followed the trials and tribulations of Joyce at both the hospital where she worked and at home.

John's Other Wife, +1943–1946, NBC, with Richard Kollmar, Mary Jane Higby, Florence Freeman, Matt Crowley, Joseph Curtin, Luis Van Rooten, others. This soap opera followed the same format in New York that it had when it made its debut in Chicago in the 1930s. John still remained loyal to his wife, while the "other wife" in the series title was still his loyal secretary.

David Harum, +1943–1946, NBC, CBS, with Craig McDonnell, Gertrude Warner, Bennett Kilpack, Charme Allen, others. Frank and Ann Hummert's soap opera series, *David Harum,* remained unchanged when it moved its broadcast base from Chicago to New York. The character did not move from his small town in the Midwest, however, and remained the benevolent banker who tried to help solve the problems of his many friends and neighbors. Many of the same actors who worked on the show when it emanated from Chicago continued to play their roles when the series transferred its operations to New York.

Murder at Midnight, +1946–1947, Syndicated. This half-hour mystery series presented different stories each week, and starred many of radio's most distinguished actors, including Elspeth Eric, Berry Kroeger, Lawson Zerbe, Abby Lewis, James Monks, Ed Begley, Santos Ortega, Charlotte Holland, and others. The story usually featured gruesome murders. "The Man with the Black Beard"(September16, 1946) featured Mercedes McCambridge.

Theater of Romance, +1944–1946, Syndicated. This half-hour weekly series featured stories of love and romance. Many Hollywood stars starred on this series, including Bonita Granville, Ralph Bellamy, Shirley Booth, Mary Astor, Cary Grant, Shirley Temple, and Claude Rains. Mercedes appeared in "Casablanca" (December 19, 1944), with Victor Jory, Santos Ortega and Dooley Wilson. (In this radio adaptation of the Academy Award–winning film, McCambridge essayed the role of Ilsa, which had been played in the film by actress Ingrid Bergman.)

I Love a Mystery, *1949–1953, Mutual. Mercedes played all of the female roles in several ongoing, serialized adventures on this series. These shows were revivals of the previously successful radio series. It was broadcast from WOR in New York. Her co-stars on these programs were Russell Thorson, Jim Boles and Tony Randall, who played Jack, Doc and Reggie, the detectives who ran the A-1 Detective Agency. On the following serialized adventures, McCambridge played the only female roles heard on the program.

"The Thing That Cries in the Night" (15 episodes), 10/31/49–11/18/49
"Bury My Dead, Arizona" (15 episodes), 11/21/49–12/9/49
"The Million Dollar Curse" (15 episodes), 12/12/49–12/30/49
"The Temple of the Vampires" (20 episodes), 1/2/50–1/27,50
"The Battle of the Century" (18 episodes), 1/30/50–2/22/50

FILMS (Hollywood)

All the King's Men (Sadie Burke), 1949, with Broderick Crawford, Joanne Dru, John Ireland, Shepperd Strudwick. This award- winning film exposed the corruption of Deep South politics. McCambridge won an Academy Award for her portrayal of the assistant and rejected lover of a once-poor, ruthlessly ambitious politician.

TELEVISION (Hollywood)

Carlton E. Morse's One Man's Family, (Beth Holly),* 1949–1950, 1954–1955, with Russell Thorson, Marjorie Gateson, Bert Lytell, Eva Marie Saint. This was a TV version of a long-running radio drama series that made its debut on radio in the early 1930s. McCambridge played the Barbour family's oldest son's girlfriend for one season.

THE STAGE (New York)

The Hasty Heart, by John Patrick (Sister Margaret), pre–Broadway, 1944, with Richard Basehart. Set in a military hospital in the Far East, a proud and defensive Scottish soldier discovers that he has only a short time to live, and finally makes friends and allows himself to become attracted to a nurse at the hospital. McCambridge was originally signed to play the nurse, but was replaced by actress Anne Burr before the play reached Broadway.

Hope for the Best, by Marc Connolly, pre–Broadway, 1944.

A Place of Our Own, by Eliott Nugent, April 2, 1945, eight performances, with Franchot Tone.

Twilight Bar, by Arthur Koestler, 1945.

Woman Bites Dog, by Sam and Bella Spewack, 1946, with Frank Lovejoy, E. G. Marshall and Kirk Douglas.

The Young and the Fair, by N. Richard Nash (Frances Morfitt), 1948, with Julie Harris, Rita Gam, Doe Avedon. This play, set at the Brook Valley Academy (a Junior College for women, not far from Boston), featured a large, all-female cast.

1950–1959

RADIO (Hollywood)

Carlton E. Morse's Family Skeleton, *June 8, 1953–March 5, 1954, NBC. Four episodes of this five-day-a-week series (September 4, 18, 24, and 29, 1953) are available from Old Time Radio vendors. Mercedes played the lead role of a spinster school-teacher on this short-lived soap opera.

Defense Attorney (Mary "Marty" Ellis Bryant), *August 31, 1951–December 12, 1952, ABC. This program was also called *The Defense Rests*, which was the original NBC audition recording for the series. It co-starred Howard Culver as the reporter/boy-friend of defense lawyer Mary Ellis Bryant (played by McCambridge). Two of the shows from this series are widely available from Old Time Radio show collectors:

"Man in the Death Cell," August 31, 1951
"Sixteen Year Old Hit and Run," September 14, 1951

Suspense, 1957–1958. This long-running CBS series remained on the air from 1942 until 1962, with just one year off the air, 1960–1961. A half-hour, weekly program, it featured major Hollywood film stars in roles they would not ordinarily get a chance to play. During its last several years on the air, veteran radio performers played the major roles. The well written series remained one of radio's most popular programs over the course of its entire run. McCambridge starred in the following two *Suspense* programs:

"America's Boyfriend," July 21, 1957
"The Diary of Sophronia Winters," August 10, 1958

Screen Director's Playhouse, +1951, NBC. On this once-a-week series, a different film director would introduced one of the movies he had directed, which was then presented as a radio play. Major Hollywood stars always featured among the cast of supporting radio actors. McCambridge co-starred on:

"Spellbound," January 25, 1951, with Joseph Cotten
"Back Street," May 24, 1951, with Charles Boyer

The Screen Guild Theater (Players), +1951, CBS, NBC. This popular half-hour weekly program presented abbreviated versions of popular motion pictures, and starred various popular Hollywood film actors alongside a supporting cast of radio actors. The series remained on the air from 1939 until 1951.

"The Guilt of Janet Ames," March 1, 1951. (McCambridge, a motion picture star at this time, was the featured "star" performer on the program.)

Hollywood Star Theater, +1947–1952, NBC. Hollywood films, as well as original plays written for radio, were adapted on this half-hour-a-week series. Film stars usually featured in major roles. Mercedes McCambridge appeared in "Death Takes a Honeymoon," September 11, 1950, and "Not the Nervous Type," July 13, 1952.

FILMS

Screen Snapshots: Hollywood Awards, 1951 (Herself). A newsreel film.

Warner Pathe News, Issue #87, 1955 (Herself). A newsreel film.

The Scarf (Connie Carter), 1951, with John Ireland. This well-received film is about an innocent man accused of murder. McCambridge plays a kind waitress who tries to help him clear his name.

Lightning Strikes Twice (Liza McStringer), 1951, with Ruth Roman, Richard Todd, Zachary Scott, Darrel Hickman. A man just released from prison (for murder returns home. McCambridge plays a deranged woman who was in love with the man.

Inside Straight (Ada Stritch), 1951, with David Brian, Barry Sullivan. Set in California in the late 19th century, this film tells the story of a corrupt and ambitious family who destroy themselves with greed. McCambridge plays the matriarch of the family.

Johnny Guitar (Emma Small), 1954, with Joan Crawford, Sterling Hayden, Ward Bond. A glamorous woman tries to open a saloon and gambling palace somewhere out West. A jealous cattle woman, played by McCambridge, tries to stop her, and even intends to see her hung.

Giant (Luz Benedict), 1956, with Elizabeth Taylor, Rock Hudson, James Dean, Jane Withers, Chill Wills, Sal Mineo. In this sprawling epic film that covers three decades in the marriage of an Eastern girl and a rich Texas ranch owner, McCambridge plays the crusty, bitter sister of the ranch owner. She won a second Academy Award nomination for her work in this film.

A Farewell to Arms (Miss VanCampen), 1957, with Jennifer Jones, Rock Hudson, Elaine Stritch. This epic remake based on an Ernest Hemingway novel tells the story of a couple's love affair during World War I. McCambridge played the small role of a stern nurse.

Suddenly Last Summer (Mrs. Holly), 1959, with Elizabeth Taylor, Montgomery Clift, Katharine Hepburn. A girl is traumatized by an event she cannot remember and therefore reveal, and is treated by a psychiatrist, who helps her discover the truth about the incident. McCambridge plays the girl's inept and weak mother.

Touch of Evil (Gang Member), 1958, with Orson Welles, Charlton Heston, Marlene Dietrich, Janet Leigh. McCambridge plays the cameo role of a masculine-looking gang member who terrorizes the wife of the hero in a motel room in this Orson Welles film set on the border between the U.S. and Mexico.

TELEVISION

The Chevrolet Tele-Theater, 1950. This "live" television dramatic anthology series made its TV debut in 1948. McCambridge featured in a tele-drama entitled "The Chirp of the Cricket," telecast on January 16, 1950.

The 22nd Annual Academy Awards, 1950 (as herself). McCambridge accepted a Best Supporting Actress award (from actor Ray Milland) for her performance in *All the King's Men*.

Ford Television Theater. On this "live" television dramatic anthology series that presented hour-long plays each week, McCambridge appeared in "Crossed and Double Crossed" on December 11, 1952, with Louis Hayward.

The 26th Annual Academy Awards, 1954 (as herself a presenter)

Lux Video Theatre. This live television dramatic anthology program presented adaptations of motion pictures (occasionally featuring the film's original star, but usually starring another player). The series also presented many original television plays as well. McCambridge appeared in:

"The Lovely Menace" (Marie), December 11, 1950
"The Hill" (Chris), November 24, 1952

What's My Line (Episode #47), 1951, usually featuring panelists Arlene Francis, Bennett Cerf, Dorothy Kilgallen, and Fred Allen or Steve Allen, and host John Daly. Miss McCambridge was a guest panelist on this popular TV quiz-panel show.

Climax. This half-hour weekly series presented mystery, adventure and domestic drama. McCambridge starred in the episode "Sailor on Horseback," on September 19, 1955.

Ed Sullivan's the Toast of the Town (guest), 1953, with Ed Wynn, Patachou, Jack Cassidy. Mercedes McCambridge made a special guest appearance on this TV variety show.

Letter to Loretta. Film star Loretta Young had a popular dramatic anthology series on television in the 1950s. She was usually the star of each week's drama. The casts on her TV plays varied from week to week. McCambridge appeared on "Father Hope," as a character named "Cissy Brackett."

Wire Service (Kate Wells), *1956–1957. McCambridge, George Brent and Dane Clark starred as three international reporters for the fictional "Trans Globe Wire Service" on this weekly TV series. The three stars alternately appeared on every third episode of the series. McCambridge was seen in:

"Conspiracy," November 8, 1956, with Shepperd Strudwick and Katherine Wells
"Until I Die," November 29, 1956, with Ralph Volrian
"High Adventure," December 20, 1956, with Scott Marlowe, Sarah Selby, and Michael Landon
"World of the Lonely," January 10, 1957, with Robert Cornthwaite, Virginia Gregg and Carla Merey

"The Comeback," January 31, 1957, with Bart Burns and John Smith
"Profile of Ellen Gale," February 25, 1957, with Beverly Garland
"No Place in Lo Dao," March 18, 1957, with Keye Luke
"The Indictment," April 8, 1957, with Rhodes Reason
"Run, Sheep, Run," April 29, 1957, with Don Beddoe, James Lydon and Parley Baer
"The Last Laugh," May 13, 1957, with Ann Codee, Rodolfo Hoyos, Lisa Montell and Robert Hutton
"The Washington Story," June 10, 1957, with Barry Atwater, Anthony Eustral and Eugene Borden

Tales of Tomorrow, 1953. This half-hour weekly science fiction television series, although popular with some viewers, failed to remain on the air for very long. McCambridge guest starred in an episode called "Read to Me Herr Doktor" (as Patricia) on March 20, 1953.

Studio One. This series was one of television's most popular weekly, one-hour, live dramatic anthology programs. It presented original plays written especially for television, as well as adaptations of current novels and classic works of literature and the theater. McCambridge starred in:

"Shadow of the Devil," April 6, 1953
"Fly with the Hawk," May 24, 1953
"A Public Figure," January 23, 1956

Four Star Playhouse. This was another live TV dramatic anthology series. McCambridge starred in the episode "The House Always Wins," broadcast April 28, 1955.

Front Row Center. This live, dramatic anthology series featured adaptations of popular works of literature, as well as original dramas written for television. Fletcher Markle directed Miss McCambridge in productions of "Tender Is The Night" (Nichole Warren), September 7, 1955, and "Pretend You Belong to Me" (Vivian Donfield), April 25, 1956

Wagon Train. This was a popular filmed Western adventure series about a wagon train traveling across the Great Plains of the U.S. in the late 1800s. McCambridge featured in "The Emily Rossiter Story" (as Emily), broadcast on October 30, 1957.

Rawhide, 1959–1966. This hour-long weekly TV series was about the cattlemen who drove cattle from North Texas to Sedalia in Kansas in the latter part of the nineteenth century. Eric Fleming and Clint Eastwood were the series' stars. McCambridge appeared in the episode "Incident of the Curious Street," broadcast on April 10, 1959.

The Jane Wyman Show (aka *The Fireside Theater*), 1955–1958, film actress Jane Wyman appeared as the hostess and sometimes star on this weekly dramatic anthology series. *Fireside Theater* was one of the first shows filmed. McCambridge appeared on the episode "On the Brink" in 1958, as "Aunt Hannah."

Riverboat, 1959–1961. Darren McGavin starred in this series set on a 100-foot-long stern-wheeler that went up and down the Mississippi River in the 1840s. McCambridge was seen in "Jessie Quinn" on December 6, 1959.

RECORDINGS

"While We Danced, Danced, Danced" (Song), Decca. The Gordon Jenkins Orchestra and Chorus, with Soloist Mercedes McCambridge, 1951.

1960–1969

FILMS

Cimarron (Mrs. Sarah Wyatt), 1960, with Maria Schell, Glenn Ford, Arthur O'Connell. Pioneers venture West during the nineteenth century to find their American dreams in this epic film. McCambridge plays a stalwart pioneer woman with a large family in this spectacular.

Angel Baby (Sarah Strand), 1961, with George Hamilton, Salome Jens, Joan Blondell, Henry Jones. McCambridge plays the alcoholic wife of a much younger man who promotes a young female evangelist in this critically acclaimed but mostly ignored film set in the rural South.

Run Home Slow (Nell Hagen), 1965 (filmed in 1963), with Linda Gaye Scott, Tim Sullivan Allan Richards, Gary Kent. A woman avenging her father's hanging organizes relatives into a band of murderous bank robbers.

The Counterfeit Killer (aka *Crackshot*) (Frances), 1968, with Jack Lord, Shirley Knight, Jack Weston. This is a made-for-television film about a secret service man who infiltrates a counterfeit syndicate.

Marquis de Sade (aka *Justine*, aka *Deadly Sanctuary*) (Madame Dusbois), 1968–1969, with Klaus Kinsky, Jack Palance. This confusing sexploitation film shot in Europe, despite its sensational subject matter, failed to hit with either the public or film critics. McCambridge plays an eccentric Frenchwoman.

99 Women (aka *Island of Despair*) (Thelma Dietz), 1969, with Maria Schell, Herbert Lom. Lesbianism in a women's prison was the subject matter of this less-than-successful film.

TELEVISION

Overland Trail (1960). This unsuccessful TV series (which failed to last even one full season) was about the opening of the Overland Trail, one of the major stage-coach routes in the West in the late 1800s. The series starred William Bendix and Doug McClure. McCambridge appeared on the May 8, 1960, episode "Sour Annie" (as Sour Annie Tatum).

Rawhide, 1959–1966. These were McCambridge's second, third and fourth appearances on this series, which starred Eric Fleming and Clint Eastwood (she previously featured on an episode in the late 1950s):

"Incident of the Captive" (Martha Mushgrove), December 16, 1960
"The Greedy Town" (Ada Randolph), February 16, 1962
"Hostage for Hanging" (Ma Gafler), October 19, 1965

Bonanza, 1959–1972. This hour-long TV Western series was one of the most popular shows on television in the 1960s. The series, starring Lorne Greene, Michael Landon, Dan Blocker and Pernell Roberts, centered on the Cartwright family — a widower and his three sons — which owned a huge ranch. McCambridge appeared in the episode "The Lady from Baltimore" (as Deborah Banning), on January 14, 1962.

The Dakotas (1963). This short-lived TV Western series depicted the adventures of a U.S. marshal and his three deputies as they try to maintain order in the Black Hills and Badlands of the Dakota Territory. The series starred Larry Ward, Jack Elam, and Chad Everett. McCambridge appeared in the January 23, 1963, episode "Trouble at French Creek" (as Jay French).

The Nurses, 1962–1965, with Shirl Conway, Zina Bethune, Edward Binns, Michael Tolan. This hour-long series set in a large urban city hospital revolved around the nursing staff at the hospital. McCambridge was seen in "Credo," on January 9, 1964.

The Defenders, 1961–1965, with E. G. Marshall, Robert Reed, Joan Hackett. The father-and-son law firm of Preston and Preston was the setting for this hour-long TV series. McCambridge was seen in "The Man Who," on October 29, 1964.

Dr. Kildare, 1961–1966, with Richard Chamberlain, Raymond Masscy. Based on an MGM film series, this hour-long TV drama was about a young doctor at a large metropolitan hospital and his elderly doctor-mentor. McCambridge was seen on:

"Rome Will Never Leave You — Part One" (Sister Teresa), November 12, 1964
"Rome Will Never Leave You — Part Two" (Sister Teresa), November 19, 1964
"Rome Will, Never Leave You — Part Three" (Sister Teresa), November 26, 1964

Lost in Space, 1965–1968, with June Lockhart, Guy Williams, Angela Cartwright, Mark Goddard, Jonathan Harris, others. This science fiction series followed the adventures of a family of space travelers who are indeed lost in outer space and meet up with some strange aliens on various distant planets. McCambridge appeared in "The Space Croppers" (as Sybilla) on March 30, 1966.

Bob Hope Presents the Chrysler Theater, 1963–1967. Bob Hope was the host of this hour-long anthology program that presented a different drama each week. McCambridge was seen on "The Faceless Man" in 1966.

ABC Stage 67, 1966–1967. This TV series presented various "specials," including dramas, variety shows, etc. McCambridge was featured on "The People Trap" in 1966.

Bewitched, 1964–1972, with Elizabeth Montgomery, Dick Sargent, Agnes Moorehead, Maurice Evans, others. This was a situation comedy series about a witch with special powers who marries an ordinary man and tries to live the life of a normal housewife. McCambridge substituted for the ailing actress Agnes Moorehead, playing an eccentric witch named Carlotta in "Darrin Gone! And Forgotten" broadcast on October 17, 1968.

THE STAGE

Cages, by Lewis John Carlino, Off Broadway, 1963. This was an experimental off–Broadway play that originally starred actress Shelley Winters in the role Mercedes McCambridge subsequently played.

Who's Afraid of Virginia Woolf? by Edward Albee (Martha), Broadway, also on national tour (with Jack Heller), 1964. This play about a professor and his wife, who is the daughter of the college president, takes place during a long night of drinking, soul searching and nasty game playing with a younger couple at the professor's home.

The Show Off, by George Kelly, 1969. McCambridge appeared in a production of this play that co-starred Dick Shawn, Linda Bennett, Monroe Arnold and Donald Buka. It was performed at the John Kenley Theater in Warren, Ohio, among other places.

*Note: Throughout the 1960s, 1970s, and 1980s, McCambridge toured in national companies of such celebrated plays as *The Madwoman of Chaillot*, *The Little Foxes*, *The Glass Menagerie*, *The Miracle Worker*, *Candida*, *The Subject Was Roses*, *'night, Mother*, *Agnes of God*, and others.

1970–1979

RADIO

Himan Brown's CBS Radio Mystery Theater, +1974–1978, Syndicated. This hour-long radio mystery program heard five (sometimes more) days a week was a valiant attempt to revive radio drama in the 1970s. It remained on the air from 1972 until 1982.

All of the programs listed below starred Mercedes McCambridge and are available from Old Time Radio show vendors.

"The Horse That Wasn't for Sale," February 24, 1974, written by Henry Slesar, with Arnold Moss, William Redfield, Earl Hammond

"All Things Must Die," April 4, 1974, written by Elspeth Eric, with Ralph Bell, Larry Haines

"Dracula," May 2, 1974, written by George Lowthar, with Michael Wager, Stefan Schnabel, Marian Seldes

"The Secret Doctrine," June 20, 1974, written by Elspeth Eric, with Nick Pryor, Robert Dryden, Mildred Clinton, William Johnstone

"Yesterdays Murder," June 27, 1974, written by Sam Dann, with Leon Janney, Patricia Wheel, Robert Maxwell

"Murder to Perfection," September 30, 1974, written by George Lowthar, with John Newland, Joe Carpenter

"Stephanie's Room," December 16, 1974, written by Bob Juhren, with Robert Dryden, William Redfield, Mary Jane Higby

"Give Him His Due," December 23, 1974, written by Nancy Moore, with Ian Martin, Bryna Raeburn, Joe Silver, Peter Donald

"A Death of King," January 16, 1975, written by Sam Dann, with William Redfield, Robert Dryden

"The Flowers of Death," January 24, 1975, written by Sam Dann, with Larry Haines, Robert Maxwell, Gilbert Mack

"Death Is a Dream," February 26, 1975, written by Sam Dann, with Michael Wager, Jack Grimes, Bryna Raeburn, Robert Kaliban

"Key to Murder," March 28, 1975, written by George Lowthar, with Mary Jane Higby, Robert Dryden, Robert Maxwell

"The Devil's Leap," June 4, 1975, written by Ian Martin, with Ian Martin, Kristoffer Tabori, Robert Dryden

"Frame-Up," June 18, 1975, written by George Lowthar, with Leon Janney, Bryna Raeburn, Ian Martin

"The Triangle," July 8, 1975, written by Sam Dann, with Robert Dryden, Paul Hecht, Bryna Raeburn

"Carmilla," July 31, 1975, written by Ian Martin, with Marian Seldes, Martha Greenhouse, Court Benson, Staats Cotsworth

"Person to Be Notified," August 25, 1975, written by Sam Dann, with Ian Marin, Russell Horton, Gilbert Mack, Bryna Raeburn

"The Other Life," September 8, 1975, written by Sam Dann, with Elliott Reid, Ralph Bell, Bryna Raeburn

"The Man Who Ran Away," October 2, 1975, written by Elspeth Eric, with Martha Greenhouse, William Redfield, Robert Dryden

"Castle Kerfal," January 30, 1976, written by Murray Burnett, with Ian Martin, William Redfield, Guy Sorel

"General Laughter," February 25, 1976, written by Elspeth Eric, with Mandel Kramer, Sam Gray

"The Unborn," October 29, 1976, written by Ian Martin, with Robert Dryden, Robert Kaliban

"The Star Killers," February15, 1977, written by Sam Dann, with Court Benson, Judith Light, Norman Rose

"Silent Shock," September 7, 1977, written by Elspeth Eric, with Ralph Bell, Ian Martin, Teri Keane

"Death and Desire," May 8, 1978, written by Elspeth Eric, with Arnold Moss, Robert Dryden, Joen Arliss

FILMS

The Last Generation, 1971. This made-for-television movie focused on the generation gap.

Killer by Night (Sister Sarah), 1972, with Diane Baker, Theodore Bikel, Robert Lansing, Robert Wagner, Greg Morris. A fugitive killer may be a vital link to a citywide diphtheria epidemic in this made-for-television film.

Two for the Money (Mrs. Castle), 1972. This made-for-TV movie focuses on two greedy killers plotting the murder of a wealthy widow.

Sixteen (Ma Erdly), 1972, with Parley Baer, Beverly Powers, Simone Giffith. A backwoods girl comes of age in the Deep South. Mercedes plays a cantankerous Southern woman in this film.

The Other Side of the Wind (Maggie), 1972. A made-for-television film.

The Girls from Huntington House (Doris McKenzie), 1973. This made-for-TV horror movie is about a group of girls terrorized by a stalker.

The President's Plane Is Missing (Hester Madigan), 1973. The title of this made-for-television film tells it all.

The Exorcist (Voice of the demon Pazuzu), 1973, with Linda Blair, Ellen Burstyn, Jason Miller, Max Von Sydow, Kitty Wynn. McCambridge provided the voice and various vocal effects for the demon Pazuzu, who has taken over the body of a twelve-year-old girl.

Who Is the Black Dahlia? (Grandmother), 1975, with Lucy Arnaz, Richard Crenna. The unsolved murder of a would-be Hollywood actress turned call-girl is the subject of this made-for-TV film. McCambridge played the girl's grandmother.

Thieves (Street Lady), 1977, with Marlo Thomas, Charles Grodin. This film adaptation of a Broadway play by Herb Gardner centered on a couple who try to recapture their youth in a New York City that has, like the couple, lost its innocence. McCambridge plays the cameo role of a homeless woman who lives on the street.

The Sacketts (Ma Sackett), 1979, with Sam Elliot, Tom Selleck, Glenn Ford, Ruth Roman. This made-for-TV movie follows three brothers, all veterans of the Civil War, who go West in the post-war years. McCambridge plays their mother.

Concorde: Airport '79 (Nelli), 1979, with Alan Delon, Susan Blakely, Robert Wagner, Bibi Anderson, Martha Raye, Charo, Dennis Weaver, Cicily Tyson, Jimmie Walker, George Kennedy. When the huge transatlantic airplane finds itself disabled by a terrorist's missile, the crew try to save the plane and their passengers from certain death. McCambridge plays a Russian gymnastics instructor on her way to a competition in the U.S.

Television

Bonanza, 1959–1973, This series about a rancher and his three sons was a long-running success on television. It starred Lorne Green, Pernell Roberts, Dan Blocker and Michael Landon. McCambridge appeared in "The Law and Billy Burgess" (as Matilda) on February 15, 1970 (the second time the actress had guested on the series).

Medical Center, 1969–1976, with James Daly, Chad Everett, Audrey Totter. The medical center in this hour-long weekly TV series was located in a large university. McCambridge was seen on "A Matter of Tomorrow," February 25, 1970.

The Name of the Game, 1968–1971, starring Robert Stack, Tony Franciosa, Gene Barry. This one-and-a-half-hour TV series starred one of these three actors alternately each week. McCambridge was seen in "A Capitol Affair" on February 12, 1971.

Gunsmoke, 1955–1975, with James Arness, Amanda Blake, Dennis Weaver, Milburn Stone. This long-running TV Western series focused on a United States marshal named Dillon and his friends in Dodge City, Kansas, in the latter part of the nineteenth century. McCambridge was seen in "The Lost" (as Mrs. Mather) on September 13, 1971, with Royal Dano.

Charlie's Angels, 1976–1981, with Jaclyn Smith, Farrah Fawcett-Majors, Kate Jackson, David Doyle. This popular TV series featured three pretty female private detectives who worked for a man named Charlie Townsend, whose voice was heard but whose face was never seen. The voice was supplied by John Forsythe. McCambridge appeared on the episode "Angels in the Springtime" (as Norma) on October 11, 1978.

THE STAGE

The Love Suicide at the Schofield Barracks, by Romulus Linney (Lucy Lake), Broadway, February 1972. A General and his wife are murdered at an Army Barracks in Hawaii. McCambridge played a poetess befriended by the couple. (Mercedes was nominated for a "Best Actress" Tony Award for her performance in this play.)

Minnie's Boys (Minnie), August 1975. This was Mercedes McCambridge's only foray into musical comedy. The musical had originally been seen on Broadway in 1970, and was about the early career of the Marx Brothers comedy team and their indomitable stage mother, Minnie Marx. This revival of the Broadway show was first presented at a summer theater in New Buffalo, Michigan, and was scheduled for a subsequent national tour.

Flagstaff Festival of the Arts, North Arizona University. Miss McCambridge was a guest artist during the summers of 1979 and 1980. In the summer of 1979, she starred in two plays that were presented at the festival: *Butterflies Are Free* and *Shadowbox*. In the summer of 1980, she appeared in *Blythe Spirit* and *Buried Child*.

1980–1997

RADIO

WUGA-FM (University of Georgia): Himan Brown's Audio Production Workshop — Theater of the Mind production, 1989. "Madeleine's and Harry's Story," with McCambridge and Paul Hecht in the leading roles.

TELEVISION

Magnum P.I., 1980, with Tom Selleck, John Hillerman. Private Investigator (and Vietnam War veteran) Thomas Magnum is the house guest of a wealthy man named Robin Masters (whose voice was provided by Orson Welles for the first few years the series aired) on a luxurious Hawaiian estate. McCambridge played Agatha Kemble, a blind friend of Magnum's, on the March 26, 1981, episode, "Don't Say Goodbye."

Amazing Stories, 1985–1987. Steven Spielberg produced this series of unusual tales, which were similar to those seen on the popular *Twilight Zone* and *The Outer Limits* series. McCambridge was heard as the voice of Miss LeStrange on the "Family Dog" episode broadcast February 16, 1985.

Cagney and Lacy, 1982–1988, with Tyne Daly, Sharon Gless. Female police detectives Mary Beth Lacey and Chris Cagney were partners who worked on various cases together on this one-hour-a-week series. McCambridge guest starred on the episode "Land of the Free" (as Sister Elizabeth) on February 23, 1988.

70th Annual Academy Awards (Past Oscar Winners Tribute) (as herself), 1998.

FILMS

Coming of Age, 1982, with Ford Rainey. A poor rural family's way of life is threatened when a highway comes through their property in this made-for-television film that starred McCambridge as an impoverished farm woman.

Echoes (Lillian Gerben), 1983, with Richard Alfieri, Ruth Roman, Nathalie Nell, Gale Sondergaard. An art student becomes obsessed with a dream he has about a twin brother who died at birth, but is trying to kill him.

Amazing Stories (Book Two–"Family Dog"). McCambridge had previously been heard in the same role on the television series *Amazing Stories*. In this 1992 made-for-TV film, she repeated her vocal performance as Miss LeStrange.

THE STAGE

Lost in Yonkers, by Neil Simon (Grandma Kurnitz). McCambridge appeared in this play on Broadway in 1991 and on a national tour with Jane Kazmarek (Broadway) and Brooke Adams. Two young boys are left with their seemingly indifferent and unemotional grandmother while their single father looks for work down South in this Neil Simon semi-biographical play. McCambridge played the world-weary, born-in-Europe immigrant Grandma Kurnitz.

RECORDINGS

Thidwick, the Big-Hearted Moose, by Dr. Seuss. This audio cassette (with accompanying picture book) published by Random House in 1993 features Mercedes

McCambridge as the story's narrator. The children's book, first published in the 1940s, is about a good-hearted moose named Thidwick whose good nature allows others to take advantage of him.

Frank Sinatra: An American Legend, 1995. This two-cassette audio package, narrated by Sinatra's daughter Nancy, contains interviews and various recorded events relating to the life of singer-actor Frank Sinatra. It included his first professional appearance on the *Major Bowes Original Amateur Hour* radio show, conversations and performances with fellow entertainers Bob Hope, Bing Crosby, Sammy Davis, Jr., and others, and famous political friends like John F. Kennedy. On the eleventh track, Mercedes McCambridge reads Frank's Academy Award acceptance speech, which he had given when he won the "Best Supporting Actor" Oscar for his work in the 1953 film *From Here to Eternity*.

Bibliography

Books

Abramson, Albert. *The History of Television, 1942–2000.* Jefferson, NC: McFarland, 2003.

Allen, Robert C. *Speaking of Soap Operas.* Chapel Hill: University of North Carolina Press, 1985.

Ansbro, George. *I Have a Lady in the Balcony: Memoirs of a Broadcaster.* Jefferson, NC: McFarland, 2000.

Archer, Gleason L. *The History of Radio.* New York: American Historical Society, 1938.

Arnheim, Rudolph. *"The World of the Daytime Serial." Radio Research 1942–1943.* New York: Duell, Sloan and Pearce, 1944.

Bach, Steven. *Marlene Dietrich: Life and Legend.* New York: Da Capo, 2000.

Bannerman, R. LeRoy. *Norman Corwin and Radio: The Golden Years.* Tuscaloosa: University of Alabama Press, 1986.

Barabas, Gabor, and SuzAnne Barabas. *Gunsmoke: A Complete History.* Jefferson, NC: McFarland, 1990.

Barnouw, Erik. *Radio Drama in Action.* New York: Farrar and Rinehart, 1945.

Benny, Joan. *Sunday Nights at Seven.* New York: Warner, 1990.

Berg, Chuck, and James M. Welsh and Thomas Erskine (eds.). *The Encyclopedia of Orson Welles (Great Filmmakers Series).* New York: Facts on File, 2002.

Bernardoni, James. *The New Hollywood: What the Movies Did with the New Freedoms of the Seventies.* Jefferson, NC: McFarland, 2001.

Bobbitt, David G. *World Radio TV Handbook.* Watson-Guptill, 2000.

Boemer, Marilyn Lawrence. *The Children's Hour: Radio Programs for Children.* Metuchen NJ: Scarecrow Press, 1989.

Bordman, Gerald. *American Musical Theater: A Chronicle.* Expanded edition. New York and Oxford: Oxford University Press, 1986.

Brooks, Tim, and Earle Marsh. *The Complete Directory to Prime Time Network and Cable and TV Shows.* New York: Ballantine, 1999.

Brown, Gene (ed.). *The New York Times Encyclopedia of Film, Volumes 1–13.* New York: Times Books, 1988–present.

Bushnell, Brooks. *Directors and Their Films: A Complete Reference, 1893–1990.* Jefferson, NC: McFarland, 1993.

Buxton, Frank, and Bill Owen. *The Big Broadcast.* Lanham, MD: Scarecrow Press, 1997.

Campbell, Robert. *The Golden Years of Broadcasting.* New York: Scribner's, 1976.

Capua, Michelangelo. *Montgomery Clift: A Biography.* Jefferson, NC: McFarland, 2002.

Carlile, John S. *The Production and Direction of Radio Programs.* New York: Prentice-Hall, 1939.

Chase, Francis, Jr. *Sound and Fury: An Informal History of Broadcasting.* New York: Harper and Brothers, 1942.

Chernow, Barbara A., and George A. Vallasi. *The Columbia Encyclopedia*, 5th edition. New York: Columbia University Press, 1993.

Chester, Gerard, and Edgar R. Garrett. *Television and Radio*, 3rd edition. New York: Appleton Century Crofts, 1963.

Conrad, Peter. *Orson Welles: The Stories of His Life*. New York: Faber & Faber, 2003.

Cox, Jim. *The Great American Soap Operas*. Jefferson, NC: McFarland, 1999.

____. *Radio Crime Fighters*. Jefferson, NC: McFarland, 2002.

Cuthbert, Margaret (ed.). *Adventures in Radio*. New York: Howell, Siskin, 1945.

DeLong, Thomas A. *Radio Stars: An Illustrated Biographical Dictionary of 953 Performers, 1920 through 1960*. Jefferson, NC: McFarland, 1996.

Donaldson, Charles E. *Radio Stars: Brief Biographical Sketches of More Than One Hundred Best Known Actors, Musicians, Commentators, and Other Stars of Radio Programs*. Washington, D.C.: Newspaper Information Services, 1942.

Douglas, George H. *The Early Days of Radio Broadcasting*. Jefferson, NC: McFarland, 2001.

Dunning, John. *Tune in Yesterday: The Ultimate Encyclopedia of Old-Time Radio, 1927–1976*. Englewood Cliffs, NJ: Prentice-Hall, 1976.

Edmondson, Madeleine, and David Rounds. *The Soaps: Daytime Serials of Radio and TV*. New York: Stein and Day, 1973.

Fetrow, Alan C. *Feature Films, 1950–1959: A United States Filmography*. Jefferson, NC: McFarland, 1999.

Gaver, Jack, and Dave Stanley. *There's Laughter in the Air*. New York: Greenberg, 1945.

Gazetas, Aristides. *An Introduction to World Cinema*. Jefferson, NC: McFarland, 1999.

Goldsmith, A. N., and A. C. Lescaboura. *This Thing Called Broadcasting*. New York: Henry Holt, 1939.

Gowdy, Curt. *Cowboy at the Mike*. New York: Doubleday, 1966.

Grams, Martin, Jr. *A Comprehensive Chronicle of American Network Programming*. Jefferson, NC: McFarland, 2000.

____. *The I Love a Mystery Companion*. Churchville, MD: OTR Publishing, 2003.

____. *Inner Sanctum Mysteries: Behind the Creaking Door*. Kearney, NE: Morris Publishing, 2002.

____, and Gordon Payton. *The CBS Radio Mystery Theater: An Episode Guide and Handbook to Nine Years of Broadcasting, 1974–1982*. Jefferson, NC: McFarland, 1999.

Halliwell, Leslie. *The Filmgoers Companion*. New York: Hill and Wang, 1967.

Harmon, Jim. *The Great Radio Heroes*. New York: Doubleday, 1967.

Harrington, Ann M., and Prudence Moylan (eds.). *Mundelein Voices: The Women's College Experience, 1930–1991*. Chicago: Loyola Press, 2001.

Hickerson, Jay. *The Ultimate History of Network Radio Programming and Guide to All Circulating Shows*, 3rd edition. Hamden, CT: J. Hickerson, 1996.

Higby, Mary Jane. *Tune in Tomorrow*. New York: Cowles, 1968.

Holley, Val. *James Dean: The Biography*. New York: St. Martins, 1996.

Inman, David M. *Performers' Television Credits, 1948–2000*. Three volume set. Jefferson, NC: McFarland, 2001.

Jennings, Peter, and Todd Brewster. *The Century*. New York: Doubleday, 1998.

Katz, Ephraim, and Fred Klein. *The Film Encyclopedia: The Most Comprehensive Encyclopedia of World Cinema in a Single Volume*, 4th edition. New York: Macmillan, 2001.

Kittnos, John M., and Christopher H. Sterling. *Stay Tuned: A Concise History of American Broadcasting*. Belmont, CA: Wadsworth, 1975.

Lackmann, Ron. *The Encyclopedia of American Radio*. New York: Facts on File, 2000.

____. *The Encyclopedia of 20th Century American Television*. New York: Facts on File, 2000.

LaGuardia, Robert. *From Ma Perkins to Mary Hartman: The Illustrated History of Soap Opera*. New York: Ballantine, 1977.

Lamparski, Richard. *Whatever Became of...* series. New York: Crown, 1967–1989.

Lawrence, Jerome. *Off Mike*. New York: Essential Books, 1944.

Lenberg, Jeff. *The Encyclopedia of Animated Cartoons*, second edition. New York: Facts on File, 1999.

Lloyd, Ann (ed.) and Graham Fuller, with consultant editor Arnold Desser. *The Illustrated Who's Who of the Cinema.* New York: Portland House, 1987.

MacDonald, J. Fred. *Don't Touch That Dial: Radio Programming in American Life 1920–1960.* Chicago: Nelson-Hall, 1979.

Maltin, Leonard. *The Great American Broadcast.* New York: Dutton Books, 1997.

____. *2003 Movie & Video Guide.* New York: Signet (New American Library), 2002.

McCambridge, Mercedes. *The Quality of Mercy.* New York: Time Books, 1981.

McKeever, Porter. *Adlai Stevenson: His Life and Legacy.* New York: Wm. Morrow, 1989.

McNeil, Alex. *Total Television: The Comprehensive Guide to Programming from 1948 to the Present.* New York: Penguin Books, 1996.

Michael, Paul. *The American Movies Reference Book: The Sound Era.* Upper Saddle River, NJ: Prentice-Hall, 1970.

Morse, Carlton E. *The One Man's Family Album.* Woodside, CA: Seven Stones Press, 1988.

Mott, Robert L. *Radio Live! Television Live! Those Golden Days When Horses Were Coconuts.* Jefferson, NC: McFarland, 2000.

Mowrey, Peter C. *Award Winning Films: A Viewer Reference to 2700 Acclaimed Motion Pictures.* Jefferson, NC: McFarland, 1994.

Oboler, Arch. *Fourteen Radio Plays.* New York: Random House, 1940.

____. *Free World Theater.* New York: Random House, 1944.

____. *Oboler Omnibus.* New York: Duell, Sloan and Pearce, 1945.

Osgood, Dick. *W.Y.X.I.E. Wonderland.* Ohio: Bowling Green University Press, 1981.

Rhoades, Eric. *Blast from the Past: A Pictorial History of Radio's First 75 Years.* West Palm Beach, FL: Streamline Publishing, 1996.

Roberts, Garyn. *Dick Tracy and American Culture: Morality and Mythology, Text and Content.* Jefferson, NC: McFarland, 1993.

Roberts, Jerry, and Steven Gaydos (eds.). *Movie Talk from the Front Lines: Filmmakers Discuss Their Works with the Los Angeles Film Critics Association.* Jefferson, NC: McFarland, 1995.

St. John, Robert. *The Encyclopedia of Radio and Television.* Milwaukee: Cathedral Square Publishing, 1967.

Schemering, Christopher. *The Soap Opera Encyclopedia (TV).* New York: Ballantine, 1987.

Schwartz, Jon D. *Handbook of Old Time Radio: A Comprehensive Guide to Golden Age Radio Listening and Collecting.* Metuchen, NJ: Scarecrow Press, 1993.

Sennett, Ted (ed.). *Old Time Radio Book.* New York: Pyramid Publications, 1986.

Settel, Irving. *A Pictorial History of Radio.* New York: Grosset & Dunlap, 1967.

Seuss, Dr. *Thidwick, the Big-Hearted Moose.* New York: Random House, 1993.

Shapiro, Mitchell E. *Radio Network Prime Time Programming.* Jefferson, NC: McFarland, 2002.

Shulman, Arthur, and Roger Yourman. *The Golden Age of Television (How Sweet It Was).* New York: Bonanza Books, 1979.

Sies, Luther F. *Encyclopedia of American Radio.* Jefferson, NC: McFarland, 2000.

Skaeverd, Marlene. *Dietrich.* New York: Haus Publishing, 2002.

Sketvedt, Randy, and Jordan R. Young. *The Nostalgia Entertainment Sourcebook: The Complete Guide of Classic Movies, Vintage Music, Old Time Radio and Theater.* Beverly Hills, CA: Moonstone Press, 1991.

Skutch, Ira (ed.). *The Golden Years of Radio.* Lanham, MD: Scarecrow Press, 1998.

Slate, Sam J., and Joe Cook. *It Sounds Impossible.* New York: Macmillan, 1953.

Slide, Anthony. *Great Radio Personalities in Historic Photographs.* New York: Dover, 1982.

Smith, Ronald L. *Who's Who in Comedy: Comedians, Comics and Clowns from Vaudeville to Today's Stand-Ups.* New York: Facts on File, 1992.

Soares, Manuela. *The Soap Opera Book.* New York: Harmony, 1978.

Stedman, Raymond William. *The Serials: Suspense and Drama by Installment.* Norman: University of Oklahoma Press, 1971.

Sterling, Christopher H., and John M. Kittross. *Stay Tuned: A Concise History of American Broadcasting.* Belmont, CA: Wadsworth, 1978.

Stumpf, Charles K. *Ma Perkins, Little Orphan Annie and Heigh Ho, Silver.* New York: Carlton, 1971.

Sturcken, Fred. *Live Television: The Golden Age of 1946–1958.* Jefferson, NC: McFarland, 2002 (1990).

Summers, Harrison B. *A Thirty-Year History of Programs Carried on National Radio in the United States.* Columbus: Ohio State University Press, 1958.

Terrace, Vincent. *Radio Programs, 1924–1984: A Catalog of Over 1800 Shows.* Jefferson, NC: McFarland, 1999.

Treadwell, Lawrence P., Jr. *The Bulldog Drummond Encyclopedia.* Jefferson, NC: McFarland, 2001.

Tyler, Kingdon S. *Modern Radio.* New York: Harcourt, Brace, 1947.

Waller, Judith. *Radio, the Fifth Estate.* Boston: Houghton Mifflin, 1946.

Wertheim, Arthur Frank. *Radio Comedy.* New York: Oxford University Press, 1979.

Whitman, Alden. *Portrait: Adlai Stevenson — Political Diplomat, Friend.* New York: Harper Row, 1965.

Woodin, June. *Of Mikes and Men.* New York: Doubleday, 1961.

Periodicals

Radio-TV Mirror magazine
Radio Guide magazine
TV Guide magazine
Radio Stars magazine
Time magazine (June 2, 1947)
Life magazine (July 23, 1965)
Films in Review
SPERDVAC Radiogram newsletter
Hello Again newsletter
Current Biography
Radio Life magazine
Variety newspaper
Show Business newspaper
Old Time Radio Digest newsletter

Web Sites

http://www.Google.com (Personalities and shows)
http://www.Biography.com (Personalities)
http://www.imdb.com (Personalities, TV series, feature films)
http://www.ibdb.com (Broadway shows and actors)

Interviews

The author conducted personal interviews with the following personalities who had known or worked with Mercedes McCambridge over the years: Arthur Anderson, George Ansbro, John Archer, Parley Baer, Jackson Beck, Ralph Bell, Court Benson, Himan Brown, Vanessa Brown, Anne Burr, Fran Carlon, Lon Clark, Hans Conried, Norman Corwin, Joe DeSantis, Margaret Draper, Robert Dryden, Howard Duff, Sam Edwards, Win Elliot, Ann Elstner, Elspeth Eric, Ray Erlenborn, Eileen Farrell, Laurette Fillbrandt, Arlene Francis, Florence Freeman, Betty Garde, Beverly Garland, Earl George, Betty Lou Gerson, Bob Guilbert, George Hamilton, Bob Hastings, Mary Jane Higby, Pat Hosley, Raymond Edward Johnson, Joseph Kearns, Teri Keene, Abby Lewis, Peg Lynch, Gil Mack, Charlotte Manson, Fletcher Markle, Ian Martin, Grace Matthews, Burgess Meredith, Jan Miner, Bret Morrison, Carlton E. Morse, Frank Nelson, Jeanette Nolan, Arch Oboler, Virginia Payne, Alan Reed, Elliott Reid, Alice Reinheart, Rosemary Rice, Rosa Rio, Peter Roberts, Larry Robinson, William N. Robson, Ruth Roman, Adele Ronson, Vivian Smollen, William Spier, Ezra Stone, Les Tremayne, Sybil Trent, Lurene Tuttle, Vicki Vola, Balir Wallister, Gertrude Warner, Carl Weber, Betty Winkler, Miriam Wolfe.

Index